Education for Diversity
and Mutual Understanding

To Dolores and colleagues –

in appreciation for your
inspiration and encouragement
to teachers around the world!

Norman C. Richardson

September 2011

RETHINKING EDUCATION
VOLUME 1

Series Editors:

Dr Marie Martin

Dr Gerry Gaden

Dr Judith Harford

PETER LANG

Oxford · Bern · Berlin · Bruxelles · Frankfurt am Main · New York · Wien

Norman Richardson and Tony Gallagher (eds)

Education for Diversity and Mutual Understanding

The Experience of Northern Ireland

PETER LANG

Oxford · Bern · Berlin · Bruxelles · Frankfurt am Main · New York · Wien

Bibliographic information published by Die Deutsche Nationalbibliothek.
Die Deutsche Nationalbibliothek lists this publication in the Deutsche National-
bibliografie; detailed bibliographic data is available on the Internet at
http://dnb.d-nb.de.

A catalogue record for this book is available from the British Library.

Library of Congress Cataloging-in-Publication Data:

Education for diversity and mutual understanding : the experience of
Northern Ireland / Norman Richardson and Tony Gallagher (eds.).
        p. cm. -- (Rethinking education)
    Includes bibliographical references and index.
    ISBN 978-3-03911-985-1 (alk. paper)
    1. Multicultural education--Northern Ireland. 2.
Multiculturalism--Study and teaching--Northern Ireland. I. Richardson,
Norman, 1947- II. Gallagher, Tony.
    LC1099.5.G7E394 2010+
    370.11709416--dc22

                                    2010038318

Community Relations Council

This book has received financial support from the Northern Ireland Community
Relations Council which aims to promote a pluralist society characterized by equity,
respect for diversity and interdependence. Views expressed in this book do not
necessarily reflect those of the Community Relations Council.

Cover picture: Reconciliation Monument, Stormont Estate, close to Northern
Ireland's Parliament Building. Photograph: Richard Greenwood.

ISSN 1662-9949
ISBN 978-3-03911-985-1

© Peter Lang AG, International Academic Publishers, Bern 2011
Hochfeldstrasse 32, CH-3012 Bern, Switzerland
info@peterlang.com, www.peterlang.com, www.peterlang.net

Printed in Germany

World is crazier and more of it than we think,
incorrigibly plural. I peel and portion
a tangerine and spit the pips and feel
the drunkenness of things being various.

— from *Snow* by LOUIS MACNEICE
(*Collected Poems*, Faber and Faber)

None of us is born intolerant of those who differ from us. Intolerance
is taught and can be untaught – though often with great difficulty. But
in this area, as in others, prevention is far preferable to cure. We must
work to prevent intolerance from taking hold in the next generation. We
must build on the open-mindedness of young people, and ensure that
their minds remain open.

— KOFI ANNAN (2002)

Contents

8

Foreword

As I write this foreword to a book that is both interesting and necessary I am at a meeting in Turkey as an invited guest of Euroclio, the European History Teachers' Association. They are here in Turkey to work with Turkish teachers on upgrading the manner in which history is taught. Key aims of all Euroclio work are to focus on issues such as human rights, peace, multiple perspective teaching and multiculturalism. The Turkish government has recently called for more human rights education so the fit seems perfect. What I observe here reminds me again of the importance of the book Norman Richardson and Tony Gallagher have written.

On this occasion more than sixty teachers have come together to present activities they have developed after an initial training. The presentations are engaging and creative and the criticism from other teachers respectful and supportive. The presentations show that the Turkish teachers have come a long way and that they understand modern teaching methods well. There are multiple examples of project based learning, pupils as researchers, music, art, creative writing, role play, drama and psychodrama, interviewing, developing exhibitions, and photo journalism; all of this to make history teaching more interactive and motivating and to develop knowledge, understanding, attitudes and skills. I remember my own school career in the United States and the Netherlands. I did one minor research project and one presentation. The field has clearly moved on. The teachers' grasp of methodology reminds me how critical it is to work with student-centred approaches and in a constructivist way, to be creative and flexible. But it also reminds me of how even the most interactive, engaging methods can fall short.

Almost all of the activities start from a (Turkish) nationalist framework. There are multiple activities on Ataturk, none of them involving a critical approach to this key figure in Turkish history. There are multiple activities on past wars, but none on peace. There are no activities that discuss positive examples of co-existence and cooperation with Turkey's neighbours.

The voices of minority communities (there are plenty in Turkey) are rarely if ever included in the activities (though there is considerable focus on gender). In one activity students are asked to sympathize with hungry half-dead Turkish soldiers in the forest during the Ottoman period. The author mentions this is meant as an anti-war statement, but one outside expert asks if it might not be better to replace the photo (or add one) of suffering Bulgarian or Romanian soldiers to balance the overall presentation. The comment draws a blank. Applying innovative educational methodologies to nationalistic content might not have the intended effect if our aim is to bring communities together and promote respect, understanding and cooperation.

At the same meeting, a very skilled international expert makes the mistake, in my view, to start her presentation with a slide she uses with her students in Western Europe. She asks the teachers if the text matches the image – both relate to killings by Turkish armies. After the presentation, one teacher asks if this slide might promote stereotypes and prejudice in the west. She comments that in her view history teaching is not necessarily about confronting prejudices but on using sources in a variety of ways. Thank goodness, the book in front of you places challenging prejudices and stereotypes at the forefront.

Finally, there were no teachers who were Roma, only two (and mostly invisible and ignored) from the Kurdish region, from religious minorities, etc. These are opportunities missed in teacher education: opportunities to allow alternative and corrective voices.

For most of us in the education field who are not from Northern Ireland, our images of this region are those of violence and intolerance – a society torn apart by sectarian tensions. However, during my many travels to post-conflict societies, I also see developments in Northern Ireland as an inspiration. Educators and politicians in Northern Ireland are starting to succeed – yes, there is a long way to go – where some other societies continue to fail. My most recent conversations with academics from Cyprus and Bosnia and Herzegovina had them frowning when they reflected on the possibilities for sending children from different religious backgrounds to integrated schools. Two Cypriot professors even tersely commented that 'it will never happen'. They were first surprised then inspired by the advances being made in Northern Ireland.

In many ways, the recent experiences of educators in Northern Ireland in confronting stereotypes and prejudices, and developing integrated schools, can serve as a model in other ways for Europe. Many of the strategies and insights gained from developing co-existence models in Northern Ireland are relevant for a continent that is increasingly being defined by nationalism and intolerance towards immigrants, Muslims, refugees, Roma (gypsies) and other minority groups. Last year I visited a school in Slovakia with a population of pupils that was 50 per cent Roma. The director proudly proclaimed that in the past he had been forced to integrate the classes but in 2010 he would finally have the opportunity to segregate the classes, sending all Roma to one classroom and all non-Roma to another classroom.

So I welcome this book and the insights it provides, not just for those interested in education in Northern Ireland, but for all of Europe.

BARRY VAN DRIEL
International Association for Intercultural Education

Acknowledgements

The editors would like to express their sincere appreciation and thanks to the following: the staff of the Northern Ireland Community Relations Council for their generous support and encouragement in the production of this book; the authors of Chapters 6, 7, 8, 9 and 12, whose details appear in the Notes on Contributors at the end of the book; David Higham Associates Limited for their kind permission to use the extract from *Snow* by Louis MacNeice, from *Collected Poems*, published by Faber and Faber; the Northern Ireland Department of Finance and Personnel, as managers of the Stormont Estate, for their permission to use a photograph of the Reconciliation monument for the cover of this book; Richard Greenwood of Stranmillis University College, for his cover photography; the editorial staff of Peter Lang Ltd for their support and encouragement throughout the publication process.

NORMAN RICHARDSON AND TONY GALLAGHER

Introduction

Mankind owes to the child the best that it has to give...
— Declaration of the Rights of the Child, issued by
the League of Nations, 1924

The education of the child shall be directed to:
... the preparation of the child for responsible life in a free society, in the
spirit of understanding, peace, tolerance, equality of sexes, and friendship among all peoples...
— United Nations Convention on the Rights of the Child,
1989 – extract from Article 29

The ideals of education for diversity and mutual understanding have been
evident in the educational experience of Northern Ireland since at least the
1970s. Even prior to then, the concept was aired from time to time as an
objective in the desire for education to broaden horizons and cross barriers
in a divided and often violent society. In the 1980s the terminology of 'Education for Mutual Understanding' took on a more defined and approved
status as a term to draw together concepts such as schools' community relations, peace education and social and cultural studies, strongly influenced
by multicultural and intercultural programmes from other parts of the
world and encouraged by broader concerns about issues of equality and
human rights. From the introduction of the Northern Ireland Curriculum
at the start of the 1990s, Education for Mutual Understanding – EMU –
became an official and mandatory educational theme. Its close association
with cultural diversity (especially through the related educational theme
of Cultural Heritage) was also well established during these years. Often
during this period, however, such work was perceived as being primarily

about cross-community contact between Catholics and Protestants, despite its much broader ideological and statutory basis and the efforts of those most closely involved with its promotion. Now, in the first decades of the twenty-first century, respect for diversity and the development of mutual understanding feature significantly and officially within statements of the key purposes of education in many countries, not least as important dimensions of specific areas of the Revised Northern Ireland Curriculum, notably *Personal Development and Mutual Understanding* (primary) and *Local and Global Citizenship* (post-primary).

This book has taken shape during much of the period indicated above, culminating in 2008–9. Earlier drafts of chapters have given way to new ones in response to recent developments in curriculum thought and planning. This reflects changing perceptions of educational programmes for diversity and mutual understanding but also their growth in significance in a plural society, locally and globally. Such work can clearly never be static and will always be taking new shape.

These papers are compiled from a conviction that the notion of 'diversity and mutual understanding', whatever terminology may be used now or in the future, is a sound and important educational concept. Like any other educational process it should be rigorous, involving the development of good thinking skills, and enable teachers and learners alike to appreciate the relationship between knowledge and understanding. Work on these themes will often be challenging and sometimes uncomfortable, inevitably touching on sensitive and controversial issues. In the discussion about how to promote change in a conflicted and disputed society the notion of mutual understanding is clearly in the 'hearts and minds' camp, although naïve over-optimism about the capacity of education to *change* attitudes should be treated with caution. The philosophy of education represented here, however, is not about simply preserving the status quo. An educational approach which seeks to promote awareness of diversity, respect, human rights and mutual understanding must go beyond the accumulation of knowledge into processes of emotional development, personal growth and social challenge. It could be argued that this is an essential part of a good, balanced education in any society.

In Northern Ireland, scepticism in some quarters about the effectiveness of the statutory Educational Theme of Education for Mutual Understanding (EMU) during the 1990s sometimes led teachers and others to be extremely dismissive of this whole area. Some might perceive the introduction of new areas of learning within the Revised Northern Ireland Curriculum as an indication of the failure of previous approaches and the need to start from a clean sheet. The approach taken by the writers and editors of these chapters, however, is that these newly introduced curriculum areas are built on the foundations laid in previous decades and one of the purposes of this book is to indicate what can be learnt from earlier models, positively and negatively, in order to ensure greater effectiveness in the future. Those teachers and others from a range of agencies and organisations who have worked hard to develop a broadly based and balanced approach to diversity and mutual understanding under the Educational Themes approach may take encouragement from the fact that their experience has contributed to the strengthening of these concepts within a new context.

Others have suggested that given the changed circumstances of Northern Ireland – the diminution of violence and the establishment of partnership government – such work has 'had its day'. As the preparation of this book draws to a close, however, many people in Northern Ireland have been dismayed by recent outbreaks of sectarian conflict and racist antagonism. Mutual understanding and respect for diversity can never be taken for granted in any society; they need to be part of the continuing process of building a fair and inclusive society, whether the issues are about sectarianism, racism or any other failures in human relationships.

This is not intended to be a 'cover-to-cover' book and the editors hope that readers will make use of different chapters according to their needs. Part 1 surveys the development of the ideas which have shaped education for diversity and mutual understanding, taking note of the community relations context in Northern Ireland and of the local and global rationale for such work, including consideration of some of the objections which have been put forward. This part may be of particular interest to those wanting to explore issues of principle and policy, and to students charged with writing academic assignments and dissertations. Part 2 will be of particular interest to teachers and others who have to implement the ideas in classrooms and other group situations with children and young people. It offers background and practical guidance on some of the key approaches and strategies employed in teaching and learning for diversity and mutual understanding, such as dealing with conflict, tackling controversial issues, confidence building and circle-based work. Finally Part 3 provides an intro-duction to the development of Citizenship Education in Northern Ireland and an evaluation of such work up to the present time.

The editors would like to thank all those who have contributed to this collection in terms of their writing and also their experience. Represented on these pages are many hours of discussions with teachers and others engaged in the task of teaching for diversity and mutual understanding. Over many years there has been much sharing with, and learning from, the staff of various statutory organisations and NGOs involved in this work. The teachers who took part in In-Service courses on Education for Mutual Understanding and Cultural Heritage at the School of Education in Queen's University Belfast during the period 1990–7 influenced an important early stage in this process, and although few of their names are recorded here their contribution to the shape of this book has been very significant. More recent work with initial teacher education students has been similarly valuable, and it is hoped that this book will be of particular help to them in encouraging greater effectiveness in their future work as educators committed to the development of positive approaches to living with diversity and building relationships based on respect and mutual understanding.

PART I

The Background

NORMAN RICHARDSON

1   Education for Diversity and Mutual Understanding: Context and Rationale

> Preventing conflicts is the work of politics; establishing peace is the work of education.
>
> — MARIA MONTESSORI (tr. Dale, 1992, p. 24)

> Life is about encounters with others; about meeting and exchanging; about one to one as well as group communication; about recognising and respecting differences; about recognising that there are some people whom you like, and others for whom that is not an attainable goal. Meeting and exchanging and sharing will not necessarily make us like one another; but they will help towards understanding. Children, as well as adults, need to be given opportunities to live with diversity and to recognise that differences exist in the family, in the school, in the Northern Ireland community and in Europe as a whole.
>
> — IVAN WALLACE, former DENI Senior Chief Inspector
> (Wallace, 1990, p. 46)

In the early 1990s schools in Northern Ireland began the process of implementing what was originally termed the 'Common Curriculum', following the pattern, though not the detail, of the newly introduced National Curriculum in England and Wales. One of the distinctive features of the Northern Ireland process was the formal inclusion of six statutory Educational (cross-curricular) Themes, two of which were *Education for Mutual Understanding* (EMU) and *Cultural Heritage* (CH). It was not long before some teachers in the Province made inevitable comparisons with the situation on the other side of the Irish Sea and questioned why *they* were required to teach EMU while teachers in the rest of the UK apparently

were not.[1] To some it seemed as though the introduction of these new
Themes as mandatory requirements on all schools in Northern Ireland
meant that an unfair political burden was being placed on teachers. It is
still sometimes suggested that these innovations were an example of how
education was being used by government to distract attention from their
failures in the hope that the answers to political divisions could be found
through the schools.

There is no doubt that there were, in some quarters, political motives in
the plans to place EMU and CH into the statutory curriculum, especially
when one considers the high-profile promotion of such work by Northern
Ireland Office ministers such as Nicholas Scott (Minister of Education
1981–6) and Brian Mawhinney (Minister of Education 1986–90) from the
early 1980s onwards. But this is not an entirely helpful perception, for while
these innovations did indeed receive political promotion and support, the
reasons for their establishment within the Northern Ireland Curriculum
owed more to educational factors than they did to political influence. It will
be the purpose of this chapter to outline a soundly educational rationale for
teaching diversity, mutual understanding and related concepts, in Northern
Ireland as elsewhere, and to demonstrate the professional motivation that
has led educators to support and develop such processes.

A Local and Global Context

A Society Emerging from Conflict

It would be surprising if any study of education in Northern Ireland over
recent decades did not pay some attention to the impact of sectarian civil
conflict on children and schools. These issues have, however, been well

---

1   Some Cross-Curricular Themes (not including EMU or Cultural Heritage) were also
     introduced as part of the National Curriculum in England and Wales, but, unlike
     Northern Ireland, they were not mandatory and to a considerable extent they were
     marginalised and ignored. This point is discussed later in this chapter.

documented elsewhere (for example: Darby, 1983; Dunn, 1995; Gallagher, 2004, and many others) so only the briefest reference will be offered here to some of the key features of that situation, together with some indication of resonances in other parts of the world. Nevertheless the Northern Ireland 'Troubles' form an important backdrop to many of the issues discussed in this book, and this will be evident both explicitly and implicitly in many of the subsequent chapters.

At the risk of over-simplification, the issues centre on how children deal with growing up in a society which has been, and to a considerable extent continues to be, divided in its sense of cultural/religious/political identities and allegiances, and on how teachers and schools can or should respond. Since the subsidence of overt violence after the mid-1990s Northern Ireland has often been described as 'a society emerging from conflict', and thus the experience of the generation of children growing up since then has been in many ways significantly different from that of previous generations who lived much closer to the violence of the period following the most recent outbreak of conflict in 1968–9. It will be important to remember, however, that many of the parents and teachers of this more recent genera-tion of school-age children certainly did experience those conflicted years considerably more intensely, and in some cases very directly. Studies of the psychological impact on those who have sometime been termed 'children of the Troubles' (see, for instance, Muldoon, 2004; Trew, 2004; Cairns et al., 2004; and others) have noted both the devastating impact on some and significant resilience on the part of others. Notwithstanding the significant improvements enabled by political co-operation, many of the issues and factors that contributed to the conflict and violence remain in place – keenly felt negative attitudes and suspicions towards 'the other'; separate housing and social patterns in many areas; relative economic disadvantage in certain 'flashpoint' areas; and (controversially in this context) separate systems of education experienced by about 90 per cent of the school-going population. These factors have often affected any discussion of whether it is appropriate for children to take part in programmes of education for diversity and mutual understanding at all, and while the 'official' view has been for some time that this is both desirable and important, this is certainly not universally accepted in a society that continues to be, for some of its citizens, both disputed and controversial. Those who have tackled issues relating to children and education in other divided societies – South Africa, Sri Lanka, Israel/Palestine, the southern states of the USA (see Smyth and Thomson, 2001; Gallagher, 2004) – have often recognised many similar or parallel factors, albeit sometimes at a significantly more intense level.

Key Terms and Concepts

When they were introduced, the terms Education for Mutual Understanding and Cultural Heritage were unique to Northern Ireland. No other education system appears to have used them (so far, at least) as official curriculum terminology. Yet the underlying concepts were evident in many education systems world-wide, including those in other parts of Ireland and Britain, and there seems little doubt that they will remain significant long after the terminology of the day has been superseded by something else. When educationists in the twenty-first century make a case for the development of citizenship education, or diversity education, or human rights education or other related initiatives, much of their argument bears close similarity to that used in the 1980s and early 1990s for the development of Education for Mutual Understanding.

In Northern Ireland 'EMU' came into currency only in 1983 and 'Cultural Heritage' was not introduced as an educational term until the initial proposals for the Northern Ireland Curriculum appeared in 1988, but the ideas behind them are evident from at least the early 1970s.[2] Globally these concepts go back further still, under a range of distinct but related terms, all reflecting similar educational concerns and values.

The traumatic experience of the Second World War and the events which led up to it was formative in the establishment of the United Nations (1945) and its various sub-units such as UNICEF and UNESCO, and later of other multinational organisations such as the Council of Europe (1949). The articulation of policies with the ideals of democracy, pluralism and human rights at their heart was particularly evident in the references

---

2   These developments are detailed in Chapters 3 and 4.

to education in the various statements and declarations generated by these organisations. Thus Article 26 of the UN Universal Declaration of Human Rights states that 'Education shall be directed to the full development of the human personality and to the strengthening of respect for human rights and fundamental freedoms. It shall promote understanding, tolerance and friendship among all nations, racial and religious groups...' (United Nations, 1948; Article 26)

This was supported by a 1974 UNESCO Recommendation on Education for International Understanding which included the proposal that 'Member States should promote... study of different cultures, their reciprocal influences, their perspectives and ways of life in order to encourage mutual appreciation of the differences between them' (UNESCO, 1974, para. 17).

The UN Convention on the Rights of the Child (1989, Article 29) further strengthened this in the statement that:

> the education of the child shall be directed to:...
> ... the development of respect for... his or her own cultural identity, language and values, for the national values of the country in which the child is living, ... and for civilizations different from his or her own;
> ... the preparation of the child for responsible life in a free society, in the spirit of understanding, peace, tolerance, equality of sexes, and friendship among all peoples, ethnic, national and religious groups and persons of indigenous origin.

More recently the 2001 *UN World Conference Against Racism, Racial Discrimination, Xenophobia and Related Intolerance* emphasised the importance of states implementing effective measures and policies to 'maximise the benefits of diversity within and among all nations... in particular through public information and education programmes to raise awareness and understanding of the benefits of cultural diversity' (UN World Conference, 2001: paragraph 59).

In Europe these fundamental principles have been shaped over several decades and promoted particularly by the Council of Europe into the related concepts of intercultural education and human rights education. Formal recommendations within the Council of Ministers (for example: Council of Europe, 1984; 1985) have gradually been translated into educational literature (Starkey, 1991; Perotti, 1994) and teacher training programmes; these have been taken up with commitment by some countries though less so by others. Since the fall of the Berlin Wall in 1989 such programmes have been adapted and new ones developed with particular enthusiasm by former communist countries anxious to explore and educate for democratic processes. A United Nations *International Decade for Human Rights Education* (1995–2004) led to the development of practical teaching resources for primary and secondary schools (for example, OHCHR, n.d.) and to a *World Programme for Human Rights Education* (2005, ongoing). Considerable emphasis has been attached to intercultural learning on a global scale since the suicide attacks on the United States in September 2001 and subsequent related attacks in other continents, with significant new documents being produced by UNESCO (2006) and the Council of Europe (e.g. Keast, 2007; Council of Europe, 2008). Throughout this period there has also been considerable interest from other divided or conflicted regions in Northern Ireland's particular experience of developing its own approaches to teaching diversity and mutual understanding.

Those who wrote these global documents and designed subsequent educational programmes did not shrink from the view that education can be a force for positive change in society. Such a reconstructionist position has been influential but not unchallenged over recent decades, however. Critics argue that there is little evidence that education is effective as an agent of social change, and particular criticism, practical and ethical, has been reserved for those who have sought to use education as a means of *changing* attitudes. Nevertheless, many educators have adopted a more or less reconstructionist approach, albeit with a recognition that social change emanating from education is likely to be limited and slow. The various strategies which have been developed to promote mutual understanding and cultural diversity through education are certainly expressions of a reconstructionist position, and several of those who played key roles in the process in Northern Ireland, such as Malcolm Skilbeck and John Malone (see Chapter 2), were unashamedly reconstructionist in their philosophy. Whether or not a full-blooded reconstructionism is adopted, there would seem to be a broad consensus among educators in all the countries where such work has been taken forward that it is an important function of education to *challenge* social attitudes, if not overtly to seek to change them, in order to promote and build societies based on respect for diversity and for mutuality and human rights.

The post-war period also saw a growing awareness of the potential role of education in promoting better race relations in the United States, Britain and some other countries. Initially such work took a somewhat simplistic assimilative approach, but gradually the notion of *multicultural education* as an expression of pluralism took shape in Britain in the 1970s. Subsequent criticism of multicultural education as being too politically neutral and uncommitted in the face of growing racism led to the adoption by some of the much sharper term *anti-racist education* in Britain in the 1980s. Setting aside the ethical questions which this raises for some educators, there has been a general feeling that educational ideals are best expressed in positive rather than negative terms, and certainly the possible Northern Ireland equivalent, 'anti-sectarian education', has never been promoted earnestly as a description of such work in the Province's schools. Interpretations of the Northern Ireland conflict as one of plural cultural identities became more frequent during the 1980s, and several influential writers clearly viewed EMU and Cultural Heritage as the Northern Ireland form of multicultural education (Dunn, 1989). Nevertheless there has been much criticism of the use of terms such as 'the two traditions' or 'the two communities' to describe Northern Ireland, in recognition of the significantly greater diversity of cultures present in the Province and also in acknowledgement of the considerable diversity *within* the two perceived dominant groups which are far too easily labelled as 'protestant-unionists' or 'catholic-nationalists'. More recently the discourse on multicultural education has been sharpened by those who describe a 'critical multiculturalism' which avoids the simplistic emphasis on commonalities and instead seeks to encourage respect for the practices of other cultural groups as well as one's own group but at the same time to encourage critical reflection and awareness of power imbalances and inequalities in society (see Nieto, 2000). Use of the more common European term, *intercultural education*, has been endorsed by Connolly and others in relation to concerns about racist attitudes in Northern Ireland, as indicated later in this chapter.

A closely related concept, *peace education*, was influential for a while in Northern Ireland from the late 1970s. The term *Education for Peace* was, in fact, used as early as the 1930s by no less an educational figure than Maria Montessori (as may be seen from the edited collection of her various lectures on the subject, newly translated and published in 1992). It was also promoted, in somewhat idealistic terms, by a UNESCO Report, *Learning To Be*, in 1972:

> In educational activities, anything designed to help man live at peace with himself... also helps towards harmony among the peoples. For hostility towards others, the desire to destroy, are closely linked to frustration, failure and diverse feelings of inferiority... Educational action must dissipate such self-defeating attitudes, by contributing to a full development of the individual and his personal integrity. Then... it will be able to develop in all human beings a profound aspiration for peace... (Faure, 1972, p. 153)

In its present form the term 'peace education' became familiar from the mid-1970s, especially in the United States, extending to Northern Ireland by 1978. While in some countries peace education was very much a product of Cold War realities, and was thus ostracised as such by conservative governments, in Northern Ireland it became yet another expression of multicultural and community relations education. In this context it had the advantage of reference points which indicated beyond the merely local situation and a rationale which related it to a broader range of global concerns as well as to local needs. This Northern Ireland usage was particularly attractive to voluntary bodies with a religious background (such as the Churches' Peace Education Programme and the Quaker Peace Education Project), but the terminology gradually lost currency as politically motivated misperceptions about peace education gained ground during the 1980s. Nevertheless, some of the early documents which considered the role of peace education in a Northern Ireland context were particularly helpful in that they offered a sharper analysis of the causes of conflict and indicated the importance of social justice issues and conflict mediation skills in the development of teaching approaches and materials. Elsewhere the peace education concept has regained some 'respectability' in recent years especially in the developing world where the United Nations Children's Fund (UNICEF) in particular has developed a basic model for adaptation to local needs (UNICEF, 1995b). In Sri Lanka during the 1990s, for instance, the government invited UNICEF to develop materials and processes for peace education and values education (now more formally known as the ECR programme – Education for Conflict Resolution) in order to help encourage understanding and respect between the island's main communities in response to the long-term conflict there (UNICEF, 1995a, p. 21; 1996, p. 32). In Europe too the credibility of peace education seems to have been to some extent restored, with recent documents emphasising a holistic approach to peace education based on the interrelationship of inner peace, peace with others and peace with nature (Connect, 2001).

In many countries such work has been developed through subjects such as *Civics* or *Citizenship Education*, although it is not difficult to see why there was for many years a reluctance to introduce such terms into Northern Ireland, where there is no consensus on citizenship. Indeed, civics/citizenship education was often criticised for appearing to offer little more than a state-oriented view of how to be a good, conformist member of society. With the introduction of the 1988 National Curriculum in England, *Education for Citizenship* became a non-statutory but recommended cross-curricular theme and was certainly the nearest equivalent to Northern Ireland's EMU and CH themes. However, in the early 1990s its official tone was notably different: 'Education for citizenship is essential for every pupil. It helps each of them to understand the duties, responsibilities and rights of every citizen and promotes concern for the values by which a civilised society is identified' (NCC, 1990, Foreword).

While the original English documentation on Citizenship included clear hints of many of the features of EMU/CH and the global notions of education for democracy and multiculturalism (especially in *Component 2, A Pluralist Society*), the overall impact of the official account of the theme was one of knowing how society in Britain works and how to take part in it effectively. Despite the excellent work and publications of organisations such as the Citizenship Foundation and the Council for Education in World Citizenship there seemed to be a real danger that Education for Citizenship was being treated simply as a means towards promoting social conformity. An equivalent programme developed by the Curriculum Council for Wales, *Community Understanding*, issued in June 1991, bore closer similarity to the Northern Ireland approach, and indeed acknowledged the documentation on Cultural Heritage as one of its sources (CCW, 1991, p. 2). The mid-1990s process of slimming down the National Curriculum in England and Wales, however, appeared to push Citizenship even further out of sight, to the dismay of those who had attempted to make imaginative and creative use of the theme to create space for concerns which would otherwise have been squeezed out of the curriculum.

Since 1997, however, there has been a renewed positive approach in England, and the publication of the Crick Report (DfEE/QCA, 1998) led to the introduction of a statutory programme of Citizenship Education for schools, commencing in 2002 (DfEE/QCA, 1999). This is closely related to the *Framework for Personal, Social and Health Education* which is to run throughout the four Key Stages. (QCA 2000a; QCA 2000b) Three interrelated strands were identified by the Crick Report: social and moral responsibility, community involvement, and political literacy. However, some have criticised the renewed English approach to Citizenship on the grounds that it is still predominantly informational rather than transformational.

In the Republic of Ireland the *Civic, Social and Political Education* (CSPE) programme, introduced in the mid-1990s, has become a mandatory part of the Junior Cycle core curriculum. The course focuses on awareness and skills in relation to the exploration of contemporary social and political issues, and emphasises that 'pupils will be encouraged to recognise values and develop positive attitudes in relation to themselves, other people, the environment and the wider world' (CSPE Syllabus, 1996). Four main themes are developed:

- The Individual and Citizenship
- The Community
- The State – Ireland
- Ireland and the World.

The Department of Education in the Republic initially acknowledged the influence of the Northern Ireland model (Bhreathnach, 1996). These influences then began to turn full circle as educators in Northern Ireland saw potential in the CSPE model for future developments in the Province.

A CCEA (Northern Ireland Council for Curriculum, Examinations and Assessment) pilot project was established in association with the University of Ulster in 1998 and this formed the basis for the introduction of Education for *Local and Global Citizenship* into the Northern Ireland Curriculum (as an element of *Learning for Life and Work*) at Key Stages 3 and 4, officially commencing in September 2007 after extensive piloting. The links between citizenship education and EMU, starkly obvious to some, were not always acknowledged by everyone in the system, but more recent curriculum revisions (notably the introduction of primary *Personal Development and Mutual Understanding* – see below) have made this relationship much clearer. (A fuller account of developments in Citizenship Education in Northern Ireland is given in later chapters.)

Elsewhere the concept of *values education* has become significant. This term emphasises the need to recognise certain values, shared or otherwise, and to help children to clarify their own values by means of interaction and dialogue. Such a values-clarification concept indeed played a part in the Northern Ireland *Social and Cultural Studies Project* (1974–80) (see SCSP, 1978, for example), and has been promoted as an element of various other projects. However, the values-clarification approach in particular has received sharp criticism from the political and religious right in the Republic of Ireland and in Britain, who have argued that education should teach and *promote* certain values – family life and respect for authority, for instance – rather than simply appearing to offer such values on a take-it-or-leave-it basis. Research in Northern Ireland (Montgomery and Smith, 1997) demonstrated a growing interest in the role of values education, and also indicated that 'many teachers perceived EMU as being the quintessential expression of values within the curriculum' (p. 76). The Revised Northern Ireland Curriculum has, from the commencement of its development in 1999, been presented as 'a values-based curriculum', emphasising certain 'underpinning' values, including the following:

> ... each individual's unique capacity for spiritual, moral, emotional, physical and intellectual growth; and:
> equality, justice and human rights within our society and our capacity as citizens to resolve conflict by democratic means... (CCEA, 2000, p. 12)

Although the discussion about 'values-clarification' is not addressed directly in these documents, the tone of the Revised Curriculum is not one of 'inculcating' values in a directive sense, but rather of placing values-related issues within the various 'Areas of Learning' and encouraging focused thought and reflection on them.

*

The concepts explored above may be perceived as constituting a family of global educational concerns with particular local expressions, ranging from very informal experiments to more highly developed government-supported programmes. In their various forms they have been particularly influential in regions where there is inter-racial or inter-communal conflict, although by no means exclusively so. They all serve to indicate something of the context and the conceptual origins and influences on (and in some cases influences by) the process of developing education for diversity and mutual understanding in Northern Ireland.

All these expressions of the basic idea are heavily values-laden, of course, and as such have many controversial elements. The notion of education for pluralism and democracy assumes that these are intrinsically good and worthwhile ends, but not all agree – some politicians, and even educators, would wish to argue that *order*, even if it has to be imposed in an authoritarian manner, is more important than democracy. Multiculturalism and the notion of improving community relations have sometimes been opposed from the political left as being too 'soft', while at the opposite end of the political spectrum some have rejected such concepts in favour of a pragmatic separation of the conflicting races or communities. Ethnic cleansing and apartheid may be perceived as ugly extremes, but some people are clearly wary or even fearful of the consequences of too much inter-racial or inter-community mixing among young people, especially in relation to the possibility of mixed marriages. Such points of view are not unknown in Northern Ireland, as indicated by the work on prejudice of Connolly, Keenan and others (see below).

Educational Separation and Culture in Northern Ireland

> At the most basic level Catholics and Protestants know that they are Catholics and Protestants because they have been sent to Catholic and Protestant schools.
>
> — FLANAGAN AND LAMBKIN, 1993, p. 196

Knowledge of the school which one attended remains one of the most effective means of detecting the cultural-religious background of people brought up in Northern Ireland, and is thereby used as a point of reference by many employers (especially those in the public sector) in the mandatory monitoring process to ascertain the 'perceived religious affiliation' of members of the workforce and job applicants which became required under employment legislation (e.g. the Fair Employment (NI) Act 1989; DED, 1987; DED, 1989, pp. 19–21).

Studies such as that carried out in the late 1970s by Dominic Murray (Murray, 1985, pp. 8–9; p. 91ff), have indicated how a range of cultural symbols and perceptions (often *mis*perceptions) have reinforced the separateness and the sense of 'otherness' between pupils and teachers from different schools in Northern Ireland. Critics from within and from without have pointed the finger at a system of education which separates children and young people during their most formative years. (Indeed, the term 'segregation' is often used by critics, although this term does imply an enforced separation, which is not a fair representation of the realities of the situation.) Such separation, according to Crone and Malone in the early 1980s, is inevitably going to have a 'conservatising and inhibiting' influence on the system as a whole (Crone and Malone, 1983, p. 163). Yet the system has many defenders, some motivated by religious factors and others from the perspective of community solidarity and security. The question is often raised as to whether separate school systems are a cause or merely a symptom of the suspicion and conflict in Northern Ireland, but it seems likely that cause and symptom have become inextricably linked. Thus in a society where education is one of the key markers of its division, it is not surprising that educators have sought in education itself some of the means of challenging and ameliorating those divisions.

Whatever position may be taken on the analysis of why Northern Ireland's children are so effectively separated during the years of schooling, a growing number of educators has taken the view that the situation is unsatisfactory, as indicated in the preceding chapters. In as much as these criticisms have been influential over time in urging people to consider how education should respond in such a situation, a number of specifically educational arguments may be advanced (rather than purely social ones) in support of a proactive policy for educational processes which explore and challenge community relationships and help pupils to develop mutual respect within a context of cultural diversity. That such an approach is now much more mainstreamed within government thinking is evident from statements such as those in the 2005 'A Shared Future' policy strategy, which proposes that 'All schools should ensure through their policies, structures and curriculae that pupils are consciously prepared for life in a diverse and inter-cultural society' (OFMDFM, 2005, para 2.4).[3]

It is, however, impossible to discuss educational separation in Northern Ireland without reference to the growth of planned integrated schools from the early 1980s (as indicated in Chapter 2). For some educationists and others the situation described above is evidence of the need for an end to educational separation on perceived religious lines, and the case for integration has been made vigorously. The presence even of a small but growing sector of such schools (numbering just over sixty at the time of writing, but catering for only about 6 per cent of the school-going population) is in itself a challenge to the existing system, and the discussion continues to raise strong passions on both sides, no less than the 'faith schools' debate in other parts of the UK. It is not the major purpose of this book to make a case for integrated education, but the issue cannot be ignored. (One significant difference from the faith schools issue elsewhere in the UK is the comprehensive scope of separate schooling in Northern Ireland, which continues to impact on over 90 per cent of pupils according to government

---

3   It appears, however, at the time of writing, that this strategy has been set aside by
     the dominant parties in Northern Ireland, in favour of what some fear may be a
     pale shadow of 'A Shared Future', in the form of a policy on 'Cohesion, Sharing and
     Integration' (CSI). How this might impact on the future of education for diversity
     and mutual understanding remains to be seen.

figures.) The reality of educational separation is what makes education for diversity and mutual understanding particularly significant in the Northern Ireland context. Nevertheless, even when children are enjoying the benefits of being educated together it would be naïve to assume that the process is thereby complete. This has been recognised by many who are involved in integrated schools, and has led to the promotion of strategies and materials designed to develop awareness and relationships *within* the integrated sector (see NICIE, 2002, 2008a, 2008b). However, if it is recognised that there is a need to highlight diversity and mutual understanding even in schools where pupils are being educated together on a cross-community basis, this could be seen as indicating just how much further the separate schools have to go in such a process.

Prejudice, Sectarianism and Racism

It used to be suggested that despite the very evident sectarian conflicts in Northern Ireland there was little or no racial tension because of the relatively small numbers of members of racial and ethnic minorities present in Northern Ireland. This, however, was not the experience of many members of racial and ethnic minorities, even when numbers were smaller than they have since become! One of the disturbing factors following the 1994 paramilitary ceasefires in Northern Ireland was the rise in the number of reported racist attacks, often taking place in or near Chinese or Indian take-out restaurants. A decade later, as the presence of minority ethnic groups had increased, such attacks had also increased and appeared to be closely associated with continuing paramilitary activity in certain urban areas. An article examining levels of bigotry in western countries (Borooah and Mangan, 2007) received considerable publicity when it revealed that 'the highest proportion of bigoted persons (bigotry count ratio) was in Northern Ireland and Greece' (p. 305), with various associated headlines describing Belfast as 'the race-hate capital of Europe' (as reported, for example, in *The Guardian*, 10 January 2004, and similarly in *The Belfast Telegraph*, 16 October 2006).

In the past, members of the various minority communities often felt invisible and unheard because of the much greater prominence of sectarian conflict and violence. Since the mid-1990s these communities have been able to express their concerns with increasing public awareness and impact, aided by anti-racist legislation (Race Relations [NI] Order 1997) and the provisions of the Northern Ireland Act 1998. Section 75 of the latter legislation was particularly significant in imposing a statutory duty on public authorities to ensure that all functions are carried out with due regard to the need to promote equality of opportunity and good relations between persons of various groups and minorities, including racial groups (ibid. Section 75). Legislation, however, may be effective in regulating behaviour but it cannot, of itself, affect attitudes.

American research has been available for some decades indicating the capacity of very young children to develop and express racist attitudes. More recently research carried out in Northern Ireland has affirmed this disturbing reality, in relation to both sectarian and racial attitudes. Connolly, Smith and Kelly (2002) have shown that young children in Northern Ireland are influenced from an early age by cultural and political events and symbols:

> For a very small number, this developing awareness provides the foundations upon which they have already begun to identify with a particular community and/or develop sectarian attitudes. However, for the majority, it represents the foundations upon which a significant minority tend to develop community identities and prejudiced attitudes over the following few years. (p. 50)

Three 'particularly significant sources' of such awareness and attitudes are identified as: the Family; the Local Community; and the School. While they argue that schools alone 'cannot be regarded as the whole problem nor the whole solution', the factor of educational separation means that 'schools can too easily become fertile learning grounds for young children where they soon develop awareness of themselves as part of a particular community and develop prejudiced attitudes about others' (p. 51). They conclude that: '... schools need to ensure that they develop and foster an inclusive ethos. They certainly have a responsibility to encourage meaningful cross-community contact and to create an environment within which difference and cultural diversity are valued and respected' (p. 51).

Noting the implications of these conclusions for community relations and intercultural education work with young children, Connolly et al have proposed specific initiatives commencing at age 3 and 'a wider debate about early years education and the role of cultural diversity and citizenship within this' (p. 53). Elsewhere Connolly has made a strong argument for 'a community relations curriculum' for preschool children (Connolly, 1999, p. 68ff), and this work has received particular attention by means of a Media Initiative for Young Children by Early Years (formerly NIPPA), with associated training and resources (Early Years, 2008).

Other work by Connolly and his associates suggests that racial prejudice is, in fact, even more prevalent than sectarianism:

> Overall racial prejudice appears to be around twice as significant as sectarian prejudice in the initial attitudes of the population of Northern Ireland. Around twice as many respondents stated that they would be unwilling to accept and/or mix with members of minority ethnic communities than they would with members of the other main religious traditions (i.e. Catholic and Protestant). (Connolly and Keenan, 2001)

Following the racist murder of the black teenager Stephen Lawrence in London in 1993, the Macpherson Report highlighted the problem of what it called 'institutional racism', defined as 'processes, attitudes and behaviour which amount to discrimination through unwitting prejudice, ignorance, thoughtlessness and racist stereotyping which disadvantage minority ethnic people' (Macpherson, 1999, para 6.34). Macpherson's conclusions were focused particularly on the Metropolitan Police, but the Northern Ireland Equality Commission published its own review of the implications of the Macpherson findings for various organisations and institutions in the Northern Ireland situation, including education. The document highlights differences between those who regard racism and sectarianism as 'the same issue' and therefore see the appropriate response as being in general 'diversity programmes', and those who wish to focus specifically on race without diluting it further. Nevertheless, there is a general recognition that schools have an important role in the process:

> The Department of Education and the Council for the Curriculum, Examinations and Assessment are publicly committed to eradicating racism and should continue discussions with ethnic minorities to ensure the curriculum promotes diversity in

Northern Ireland and that the examinations and assessment systems are free of cultural bias, as recommended in the Equality Commission's Good Practice Guide to Racial Equality in Education. (Equality Commission, 2002)

Negative attitudes towards racial and ethnic minorities, including Travellers, have all too frequently extended into negative behaviour in the form of racial harassment, including verbal and physical abuse, bullying and vandalism. This, in Connolly's view, highlights the need for an intercultural dimension to the curriculum, including an awareness of religious, cultural, linguistic and dietary needs (Connolly, 2001, pp. 82–3), and recently published materials supported by the CCEA and the Education and Library Boards (*Starting Out*, 1998, *Interlinks*, 2001, and *NetConnect*, 2003), along with the work of organisations such as the Northern Ireland Inter-Faith Forum (2002), have set this process in motion. New materials under development to support *Personal Development and Mutual Understanding* (primary) and *Local and Global Citizenship* (post-primary) in the Revised Northern Ireland Curriculum also address these issues directly.

There can be little doubt that the educational processes required to challenge racism are very similar to those which may be used to challenge sectarianism, and that both are crucial in the community and schools of Northern Ireland.

*

While an examination of the context and conceptual lineage of educational processes which promote mutual understanding and awareness of cultural diversity may help to clarify that these are familiar features in many education systems, this does not of itself provide a clear case for the inclusion and priority of such ideas in the way that they have been developed in Northern Ireland. To attempt to offer a clear rationale for this dimension of education, especially for those teachers whose task it is to provide learning opportunities around diversity and mutual understanding, we must look more closely at the values and aims of education appropriate to a conflicted society.

A Rationale

The School as a Community

> Life is characterised by conflict; a main aim of education is to prepare pupils for life, which must mean helping them to cope with conflict in themselves, with their peers, in the domestic setting, at work and in the community.
>
> — MAURICE HAYES, former Northern Ireland Ombudsman
> (Hayes, 1990, p. 1)

Schools are not just about academic activity. Their effectiveness is not to be judged purely on academic achievements or (even more narrowly) on league tables of examination results. Schools are complex places where a wide range of human interchange takes place. In them children (and adults) experience social situations and learn social skills. Home influences may be very dominant in the formation of young human beings (and teachers often feel that too much is being expected of their own ability to influence attitudes and behaviour), but the interface between the influence of the home and the wider society is significantly influenced by the experience of school as a community at a very formative time in children's lives.

Most schools have recognised this involuntary role in socialisation, accepting that if they do not seek to shape it as a positive experience it may well function negatively, whether because of deliberate activity (for instance, teacher sarcasm or verbal abuse) or neglect (for instance, failure to establish a system of pastoral care for pupils, or allowing bullying to fester, or 'turning a blind eye' to sectarian remarks). The 'hidden curriculum' exists whether we like it or not, as a positive or a negative influence.

The concepts of 'lifeskills education' or Personal and Social Education constitute a recognition that an important function of the school is as a place of preparation for life in society. If the school is experienced positively as a community, then there is some hope that children's good community experiences will be carried out into other aspects of life. Teachers of very young children know unhesitatingly that fundamentally they are teachers of *children*; that they are significant formative influences on young human beings. Sometimes teachers of older pupils have forgotten this and have become too preoccupied only with their role as teachers of *subjects*. Schools which recognise their important role in establishing good patterns of relationships, in dealing creatively with conflicts and in building a caring community have already taken significant steps towards establishing some of the key elements of education for the respect of diversity.

Schools in the Real World

Schools do not exist in a vacuum, and their important socialisation role does not function only in relation to the narrow confines of the school itself and the family or local community. If it is important for teachers to recognise their human role in relation to learning for life in a local community, it is no less important for them to recognise that children are growing up in a far more global context than ever before. Television and other media bring the events of the world into everyday life, and children need some points of reference to help them understand this often bewildering complex of influences – whether it be issues of world poverty, natural disasters, global terrorism or violence on local streets.

Children need to be offered pointers which help them to understand human aggression – not least their own – and to learn how to channel their energies into creative ways of dealing with conflict. They need to learn how to develop their keen sense of what is or is not fair into awareness of justice and injustice in the world around them. Teachers have to help children to relate their experiences, their awareness of what is going on and their accumulation of knowledge through the curriculum into a cohesive whole of which they can begin to make some sense and with which they can cope. It is not the teacher's place to offer closed explanations – the process of understanding is a life-long one – but it is surely important for teachers to recognise that they have a role in these formative processes.

During the early years of the 'Troubles' in the 1970s it was not unusual to hear Northern Ireland's teachers argue that in the interests of giving children security they had to shut out of the school the terrible things which were going on outside (classically recorded by Morris Fraser in his controversial book *Children in Conflict*; Fraser, 1973). While this is understandable, and may indeed be a reasonable course of action in certain circumstances, ultimately it is impossible to keep the nasty outside world at bay. If we wish to help children build a sense of security we can only really do so on a basis of what is real, rather than pretending that unpleasant things do not take place, or that they are of no concern to the school. Security of the defensive kind, symbolised by barriers and walls, has been far too common in Northern Ireland and is not unknown elsewhere. The common imagery of schools as 'oases of calm' or 'safe havens' needs to be replaced with the more potent image of *schools as bridges to understanding* and dealing with the real world (see Richardson, 2002).

This has presented many teachers, especially those whose own background has been relatively sheltered, with the challenge of a steep learning curve. It is a reality that some have had to face, for instance, in helping children to cope with bereavement, and it is no less important in relation to issues of conflict and violence. Many of the processes in such work are concerned with helping children to make sense of the real world and to develop appropriate skills and attitudes, as suggested by a former Chief Inspector of Schools, Ivan Wallace:

> In as much as children's attitudes to relationships stem from their observation and response to the prevailing atmosphere in which they live and grow up it may be that we have much to do to sort out relationships within schools before we turn our attention outwards. But we cannot, of course, wait until all internal flaws are eliminated before we move outward. ... Children live outside school as well as in it; they need to learn to cope with the real, wider world, through controlled and protected experiences which allow them to evolve strategies to deal with situations that they will undoubtedly face. (Wallace, 1990, p. 45)

Schools, Cultural Transmission and Diversity

According to the Victorian anthropologist Sir Edward Tylor, culture '... is that complex whole which includes knowledge, belief, art, law, morals, custom and any other capabilities and habits acquired by man as a member of society' (Tylor, 1871, p. 1). This fundamentally anthropological understanding of culture has been considerably influential in Ireland through the teaching and writings of E. Estyn Evans, the founder of the Queen's University Institute of Irish Studies, who took a holistic view and emphasised the significance of artefacts and 'folkways' in understanding people's ways of life and attitudes (Evans, 1973). His thinking was reflected in the definition offered by the Cultural Heritage Working Party for the N.I. Curriculum in 1989: 'In its widest sense [culture] is the artefacts, ideas, and learned behaviour which comprise people's way of life' (NICC, 1989, p. 7).

Culture, understood thus, is clearly a process which both influences and is influenced by life in society – it carries a sense of continuity for people's collective experience, but it is also constantly changing. This is of particular significance for schools, which are generally recognised as being a major factor in the process of cultural transmission, whether actively or passively. In this sense all education is cultural, and schools are influenced by a range of cultural experiences, whether local, national, international, or – of increasing importance, especially in relation to 'popular culture' – transnational. No age group, no subject and no aspect of life in a school is remote from this process. A difficulty may arise, however, in that 'in the eyes of the general public... the teacher's job is still "to teach"... and project a set of values that characterise the dominant culture' (Cohen, Manion and Morrison, 1996, p. 143).

In a society like Northern Ireland which is perceived as comprising two dominant and conflicting cultural groups (though in reality there are significantly more than the traditional two), an appreciation of the cultural role of education is important. As they grow older, children become increasingly aware of cultural diversity and interaction, whether in their own immediate local and national experience or in the wider world. At a basic level children need to have some sense of their own cultural roots if they are to appreciate (and feel secure in exploring) cultural diversity

– especially in relation to experience within divided communities such as Northern Ireland where cultural differences may be regarded as alien or threatening. Such processes, however, if they are to lead to increased inter-cultural enrichment and mutual respect, must include recognition of how one's own cultural background is perceived by others. Above all children (and indeed many adults) need to learn how to approach and interpret cultural differences, especially those which they encounter first-hand, and to learn to regard cultural diversity as a means of enrichment, not as a source of threat. As Maurice Hayes has observed: '... cultural diversity enriches and strengthens a society... a society is strong in proportion to the number of disparate elements which it can contain without actually blowing apart' (Hayes, 1990, p. 3).

During the early 1970s, a period when the education authorities and many individual schools and teachers were wary of taking any steps in the community relations direction, a significant challenge came from educa-tional reconstructionists such as John Malone and Malcolm Skilbeck. As Professor of Education at the (then) New University of Ulster, Skilbeck offered 'a stimulating philosophy that threw teachers into the front line as cultural change agents' (Robinson, 1993, pp. 10–11). In his now notorious remark suggesting that teachers in Northern Ireland were 'naive bearers of (sectarian) culture' (Skilbeck, 1976, pp. 16–17; see also Chapter 2), his point was that to assume that it was best to do nothing was in fact to opt for the status quo and condemn schools, even if inadvertently and unwittingly, to function as transmitters of cultural separateness with the accompanying baggage of overt or covert sectarianism. This was also emphasised by the former principal of one of Northern Ireland's first integrated secondary schools: 'Schools should not simply reflect the existing divisions, prejudices and injustices, for in so doing they legitimise them; instead they should take a lead in providing a working model where every structure and activity is permeated by the concepts of justice, equality, democracy and fairness' (Rowley, 1993, p. 52).

Schools in Northern Ireland bear many symbols of cultural division and community isolation (as indicated in Murray, 1985, pp. 51–66, referred to above), and this inevitably forms part of the hidden curriculum. But it is no longer possible to imagine that schools can concur uncritically with this situation. It is a fundamental function of education to help develop children's awareness and understanding of cultural differences and similarities, even (or perhaps *especially*) in those schools which remain reasonably homogeneous places for the present. Some schools in areas of Britain that have not experienced a significant presence of ethnic minority groups have argued that they have no need of multicultural elements in their curriculum; likewise some teachers in Northern Ireland have taken the view that cross-cultural exploration and understanding are irrelevant in their area because 'there is little mixing here' or because there has been little experience of sectarian conflict or ethnic diversity. Such a utilitarian view fails to take account of the kind of world in which children are growing up – a world in which mobility and communications media make plural cultural experiences and intercultural learning a far greater part of life than ever before.

Such experiences can and should be recognised and incorporated in a proactive manner into all aspects of the life of a school. Seamus Heaney angrily attacked the Northern Ireland culture of silence in his poem *Whatever You Say, Say Nothing* (Heaney, 1975), and it could certainly be argued that education no longer has room for such avoidance of important cultural and inter-cultural issues.

Relationships and Contact

Some writers have characterised mutual understanding fundamentally as 'relationships education', a point emphasised by former Education Minister Nicholas Scott who on a number of occasions in the early 1980s spoke of educational community relations initiatives as 'the fourth R' (Scott, 1985, p. 1). Many aspects of such work in schools are clearly related to issues of personal and social development and in the past were included in their Personal and Social Education (PSE) programmes. In this regard the fundamental need of children to develop a healthy positive self-image as a basis for all other relationships, at different levels, is widely recognised by teachers, as is the need of children to develop skills in communication, cooperation, negotiation and other dimensions of inter-personal encounter.

Such an approach implies a significant critique of the increased focus on 'non human' aspects of education, such as measurable outcomes and league tables. Lawrence, emphasising the importance of self-esteem, has argued eloquently that: '... education is not just about learning cognitive skills. It is also about helping children to learn about themselves, to be able to live peacefully with themselves, and with others, and to help them develop into competent, mature, self-motivated adults' (1996, p. xii). This was surely also central to the thinking of the authors of the UNESCO-sponsored Delors Report (1996) when they wrote of one of the key pillars of education as being 'learning to live together'.

An important distinctive feature of many activities associated with education for diversity and mutual understanding is the way in which the foundations of self-esteem and good inter-personal relationships may be built on to help gain experience in inter-group and inter-community relationships. This is particularly important in terms of a place like Northern Ireland where individual relationships are often cordial or even friendly, but where encounters may be more difficult, and even antagonistic, when people are perceived as representative of religious, political or cultural groups.

This inter-group dimension is a more pertinent – and perhaps more important – context in which children and young people should have opportunities to explore differences and similarities. *The Schools' Community Relations Programme* (which provides funding for inter-school cross-community contact, based on the principles of the Contact Hypothesis) has been closely associated with mutual understanding work in many schools and provides valuable opportunities for learning first-hand about shared and diverse cultural traditions. However, as various studies by Cairns and others have emphasised, it is important that these are developed especially on an *inter-group* basis (Cairns, 1994, p. 18). In describing education for diversity and mutual understanding as Relationships Education, therefore, the more difficult, and often controversial, group dimensions of relationships need to be taken into account.

Personal Intelligences and Education of the Emotions

The recognition that education for diversity cannot be dealt with in a purely informational manner has long been evident, and the point has more recently been reinforced in relation to differences in approaches to citizenship education. There has been a broad recognition that such educational strategies are first and foremost *processes* and therefore need to be treated experientially. Thus over many years curricular diversity and mutual understanding programmes, together with their accompanying inter-school cross-community activities, have frequently included activities based on principles of affirmation, communication, negotiation and co-operation, and discussion has played a similarly significant part.

This approach has been considerably sharpened in recent years by the influence of the work of the American writer Howard Gardner who has developed the theory of *Multiple Intelligences* (Gardner, 1993; 1999; Hyland, 2000). Gardner's proposal is that there are at least eight identifiable intelligences which represent the range of intelligent human functioning. These include *Interpersonal Intelligence*, which enables individuals to recognise and make distinctions about others' feelings and intentions and thereby to be able to co-operate with others; and *Intrapersonal Intelligence*, which helps people to understand their own inner feelings and to make decisions about, and take action in, their own lives.

No less influential has been the work of Daniel Goleman (1996) in the area of *Emotional Intelligence*. Goleman cites Gardner's belief that learning and intellect in the academic sense are not enough to ensure successful and fulfilling lives and suggests that emotional intelligence is crucial to that development. He argues that the emotions must be educated in relation to five domains:

- Knowing one's emotions
- Managing emotions
- Motivation
- Recognising emotions in others
- Handling relationships.

It is clear that any thoughtful educational work on self-esteem, relationships and values will need to reflect on the significance of Gardner's and Goleman's ideas. Both of these theories were taken up firmly by those responsible for the Revised Northern Ireland Curriculum process and are reflected throughout the statement of the 'Whole Curriculum Aim and Objectives' (CCEA, 2007), and particularly in the introduction to primary PDMU:

> Personal Development and Mutual Understanding focuses on encouraging each child to become personally, emotionally, socially effective... [so that] ... children can develop self confidence and self-esteem as individuals... [and] insights into their own emotions, attitudes and moral values and how they are formed... (CCEA, 2007, p. 91)

The significant influence of the strategy of *Circle Time* since the mid-1990s in schools in Northern Ireland (as in other parts of the world) is not directly linked with the work of Gardner and Goleman, but it is clearly closely associated with it in terms of the rationale for developing intrapersonal and interpersonal competencies. Through Circle Time children are enabled to develop communication skills and build relationships in an atmosphere of participation and trust (Mosley, 1996; 1999). The strategy has proved to be an ideal setting for expressing and sharing feelings and has been increasingly widely used throughout the curriculum, particularly in relation to personal and social development issues, mutual understanding, cross-community inter-school groups and other community relations activities (Edgar, 2000; see also Chapter 9) and in the development of resources for the Revised Northern Ireland Curriculum.

Broad and Global Horizons

Living as they do in a small world, children need to be able to apply their awareness and skills to a wide range of experiences. Good education helps them to have broad horizons without losing a focus on matters close to home. So many of the processes which have come to be associated with education for diversity and mutual understanding in a local context have been gleaned from broader global situations – from the family of educational concerns indicated earlier in this chapter. Education for mutual understanding and *EIU* (Education for International Understanding) may indicate different scales, but they are essentially the same thing and fundamentally complementary.

Sometimes the global dimensions of mutual understanding have been neglected in Northern Ireland because of the insularity which can be all too evident in a small and relatively remote community. But sometimes the global dimensions have been allowed to replace consideration of more emotive local issues, often to the great relief of teachers who are reluctant to delve into local controversy. It is, of course, easy to be liberal and righteous at a distance. Children and young people need opportunities to examine *both* the local and the global issues of human encounter and conflict. With a proper balance there is some possibility of each dimension informing and offering valuable insights into the other. The Revised Northern Ireland Curriculum has established these balanced emphases more firmly in using the terminology of *Mutual Understanding in the Local and Wider Community* (one of the two main strands of PDMU at Key Stages 1 and 2) and *Local and Global Citizenship* (within the Learning for Life and Work programme at Key Stages 3 and 4). If they are co-ordinated with sensitivity and imagination, subjects like History, Geography, Science, Literature, Religious Education, Music, Art, etc., can similarly serve the local and global themes of diversity and mutual understanding very well indeed.

Education as Change

At its heart the case for the inclusion of education for diversity and mutual understanding (or whatever of the inter-related terms that may be chosen to describe it) is fundamentally an argument for good education. Education without these areas of concern would be incomplete. The very concept of education (*educere*: to lead out) is about movement, change and exploration. Education has surely failed if it lacks a sense of challenge, if it simply reinforces prejudice or produces closed minds.

Perhaps this was the underlying thought of the teacher who, at an early in-service course focusing on mutual understanding in the early 1990s, observed that the process 'is like infilling the Grand Canyon with a spoon; but we shall never treat children the same again' (Robinson, 1993, p. 9).

From Concept to Practice

Definitions

Over the years since the introduction of curricular EMU and Cultural Heritage there have been various attempts to define and clarify what was perceived by many teachers to be a 'new' area of their provision. Early key documents in this field (for example, NICED, 1988) held back from proposing a formal definition, preferring to highlight the key features of the idea. Brief definitions were eventually produced in 1989 by the Working Groups which were set up to report on the shape of the proposed Educational Themes for the Northern Ireland Common Curriculum:

> *Education for Mutual Understanding* is about self-respect, and respect for others, and the improvement of relationships between people of differing cultural traditions.

The attempt to define Cultural Heritage, however, was more vague and did not do justice to the concept of cultural diversity:

> Culture... in its widest sense... is the artefacts, ideas and learned behaviour which comprise people's way of life, and *Cultural Heritage* consists of those elements of culture which are inherited. (NICC, 1989b, pp. 15 and 17)

Over time the intended close links between EMU and CH did become more apparent (DENI, 1992, pp. 5–11), and the definitions focused increasingly on diversity and how to live with it, as expressed in the CCEA's 'EMU Review Working Group' definitions published in 1997:

Education for Mutual Understanding... means learning to live with and appreciate human differences of all kinds, ... in a spirit of acceptance and respect. It is also about preparing pupils to deal constructively with conflict.

Cultural Heritage... is concerned with affirming the richness of diversity and the potential to live within a pluralist society in a spirit of mutual acceptance and respect. It involves helping pupils to appreciate the shared and distinct characteristics of cultural traditions within Northern Ireland and further afield... This may mean having to reflect on how aspects of our own culture may be perceived differently by others. (CCEA, 1997, p. 5f)

As the educational themes of EMU and CH have been transformed into the new model of *Local and Global Citizenship* and *Personal Development and Mutual Understanding* (PDMU), the definitions have clearly changed to reflect a greater emphasis on diversity, intercultural awareness, interdependence and human rights. It has been suggested that educational work in this field, wherever it takes place, normally includes the following components:

- the promotion of healthy self-esteem / self-respect
- the development of positive relationships (inter-personal; inter-group; international)
- the exploration of human diversity (cultural; religious; racial; ethnic; national, etc.) on a local and global scale
- understanding dependence and interdependence
- learning how to deal with conflict and prejudice
- understanding violence and finding alternatives
- awareness of human rights and social responsibilities
- the development of a sense of fairness, justice and equality
- experience of inter-group / inter-community / intercultural / international encounter.

(See Richardson, 2002)

Some of these key elements relate specifically to factual information (for instance knowledge of one's own and other people's cultures) while others are substantially experiential, attitudinal, and skills-related (for instance, relationships and dealing with conflict). If the principal distinction between diversity and mutual understanding is that the former is mainly related to *content* while the latter is mainly related to *process* and *experience*, it is clear, nevertheless, that content and process must of necessity function together in education.

Implementation

The Educational Themes approach often led to uncertainty and vagueness as to how the themes could be implemented, especially at the post-primary level. The argument in favour of educational themes was that some issues were too important simply to be restricted to one particular area of the formal curriculum. It also represented a particular vision of education which is concerned to help children and young people understand how knowledge, skills and attitudes to life are integrally related. This was particularly important in the context of a statutory curriculum which could be perceived as compartmentalised and product-based with a heavy emphasis on statutory programmes of study, assessment and league tables. It was a statement that some important issues, values and processes need to be addressed on a whole-school basis, taking into account the totality of relationships in and around a school. The terminology of educational or cross-curricular themes has been dropped in the Revised Northern Ireland Curriculum, but the holistic vision has not been lost and the integration of these concepts seems to be more clearly established by means of the emphasis placed throughout on underpinning values, on *Connected Learning* and on *Thinking Skills and Personal Capabilities* (Northern Ireland Curriculum, 2007).

Whole-school commitment will be crucial for the implementation of an intercultural diversity and mutual understanding model built around PDMU and Citizenship. In relation to these specific areas, an effective approach will have several dimensions:

Within the formal Areas of Learning:
a range of relevant curriculum content, both subject-specific and inter-disciplinary.

By means of the teaching and learning styles employed:
pedagogical processes associated with co-operative and collaborative
work, skills in group work and discussion, and the development of
positive attitudes. (In this regard the teacher's prior task is that of a
teacher of children, rather than that of subject specialist.)

Through the pastoral structures of the school:
the development of a caring school, emphasising mutual respect and
good relationships at all levels, with well developed whole-staff policies on positive behaviour.

In the school's community and cross-community contacts:
relationships enriched at an inter-school, inter-community, intercultural level, providing opportunities to relate theory to practice.
(Dabbling with occasional or token contacts is unlikely to have much
impact, but where schools are able to develop in-depth contact programmes integrally related to the broad curriculum this can open up
a whole new dimension of experiential learning to develop mutual
respect.)

In the whole-school ethos:
the ethos of a school is the sum of the parts – shaped by everything else
in the school, and, in turn, shaping the school as a whole. A poor or
negative whole-school ethos can easily contradict good work done by
individual teachers or in particular subjects. Statements about respect
for diversity, mutual understanding and democratic participation are
meaningless if they are not supported positively by the ethos of the
school.

This approach increasingly reflects the wider issues around intercultural
education, particularly as articulated by international bodies such as
UNESCO, the Council of Europe and the Organisation for Security and
Co-operation in Europe (OSCE). One of the key principles advocated by
UNESCO (2006) is that intercultural education 'provides all learners with
cultural knowledge, attitudes and skills that enable them to contribute to
respect, understanding and solidarity among individuals, ethnic, social,

cultural and religious groups and nations' (Guidelines for Intercultural Education, Principle III).

Perhaps the best summary of the nature and purposes of this work as a whole is found in the Council of Europe's terminology of 'intercultural competences':

> The competences necessary for intercultural dialogue are not automatically acquired; they need to be learned, practised and maintained throughout life. Public authorities, education professionals, civil society organizations, religious communities, the media and all other providers of education... can play a crucial role here in the pursuit of the aims and core values... in furthering intercultural dialogue. (Council of Europe, 2008:4.3)

Summary

The educational ideas which have been expressed in Northern Ireland for many years under the terminology of community relations, mutual understanding, cultural heritage, citizenship, etc., relate closely to similar ideas and practices which may be found in many education systems around the world. It has been proposed that these are key elements of sound educational practice. They are of particular relevance to Northern Ireland because they seek to offer insights on plural cultural traditions, on rights and responsibilities and on developing values and skills appropriate to the building of positive relationships and creative approaches to conflict at all levels, but these are exactly the factors that make them so relevant to many other countries and regions. To attempt to avoid dealing with these issues in schools in a divided society may be to reinforce the potentially sectarian status quo of educational separateness. Essentially such work centres on helping people to live with their differences in a spirit of respect – the development of 'intercultural competences'. Whatever terminology is used to describe this work, these are important concerns which need to be applied broadly on a whole-school basis, with particular emphasis on the ethos of the school.

References

Bhreathnach, N. (1996) *Speech by the Minister for Education at the Launch of the Civic, Social and Political Education Programme for Second-Level Schools* (15.02.96), Dublin: An Roinn Oideachais/Department of Education.

Borooah, V. and Mangan, J. (2007) 'Love Thy Neighbour: How Much Bigotry is there in Western Countries?' in *Kyklos: International Review for Social Sciences*, 60(3), 295–317.

Cairns, E. (1989) *A Welling Up of Deep Unconscious Forces: Psychology and the Northern Ireland Conflict*, Coleraine: Centre for the Study of Conflict, University of Ulster.

Cairns, E., Campbell, A. and Mallet, J. (2004) 'Northern Ireland: The psychological impact of the Troubles', in *Journal of Aggression, Maltreatment and Trauma*, 1(2), 175–84.

CCEA (1997) *Mutual Understanding and Cultural Heritage: Cross-Curricular Guidance Materials*, Belfast: Council for Curriculum, Examinations and Assessment.

CCEA (2000) *Proposals for changes to the Northern Ireland Curriculum Framework (Northern Ireland Curriculum Review, Phase 1 Consultation)*, Belfast: Council for Curriculum, Examinations and Assessment.

CCEA (2007) *The Northern Ireland Curriculum: Primary*, Belfast: Council for Curriculum, Examinations and Assessment.

CCW (1991) *Advisory Paper 11: Community Understanding*, Cardiff: Curriculum Council for Wales.

Cohen, L., Manion, L., and Morrison, K. (1996) *A Guide to Teaching Practice*, London: Routledge.

Connect Initiative (2001) *Peace Education in Out Of School Care: Examples of Good Practice in Three Countries*, Fundació Catalana de l'Esplai / Playboard / Scottish Out Of School Play Network and other co-publishers.

Connolly, P. (1999) *Community Relations Work with Preschool Children*, Belfast: Community Relations Council.

Connolly, P. (2001) 'Key Issues and Challenges facing Northern Ireland', in *Racial Equality in Education: Conference Report*, Belfast: Equality Commission and Department of Education (published February 2002).

Connolly, P. and Keenan, M. (2001) *The Hidden Truth: Racist Harassment in Northern Ireland*, Belfast: Northern Ireland Statistics and Research Agency.

Connolly, P., Smith, A. and Kelly, B. (2002) *Too Young to Notice? The Cultural and Political Awareness of 3–6 Year Olds in Northern Ireland*, Belfast: Community Relations Council.

Council of Europe (1984) *Recommendation No. R/84/18 on the Training of Teachers in Education for Intercultural Understanding*, as adopted by the Committee of Ministers on 25th September 1984.

Council of Europe (1985) *Recommendation No. R[85]7: Suggestions for Teaching and Learning About Human Rights in Schools*, as adopted by the Committee of Ministers on 14 May 1985 at the 385th Meeting of the Ministers' Deputies, Strasbourg: Council of Europe.

Council of Europe (2008) *White Paper on Intercultural Dialogue – Living together as equals in dignity*, Strasbourg: Council of Europe Ministers of Foreign Affairs.

Crone, R., and Malone, J. (1983) *The Human Curriculum: The Experience of the Northern Ireland Schools Support Service 1978–1982*, Belfast: Farset Co-operative Press.

CSPE Syllabus (1996) The Junior Certificate: Civic, Social and Political Education Syllabus, Dublin: An Roinn Oideachais/Department of Education.

Darby, J. (1983) *Northern Ireland – The Background to the Conflict*, Belfast: Appletree Press.

DED (1987) *Religious Equality of Opportunity in Employment: Classification of Schools for Monitoring Purposes*, Belfast: Department of Economic Development.

DED (1989) *Fair Employment in Northern Ireland: Code of Practice*, Belfast: Department of Economic Development.

Delors Report (1996) *Learning: the Treasure Within – Report to UNESCO of the International Commission on Education for the Twenty-first Century*, Paris: UNESCO Publishing.

DENI (1992) *Educational (Cross-Curricular) Themes: Objectives*, Belfast: Department of Education for Northern Ireland/HMSO.

DfEE/QCA (1998) *Education for Citizenship and the Teaching of Democracy in Schools – Final Report of the Advisory Group on Education for Citizenship*, chaired by Prof. Bernard Crick, London: Qualifications and Curriculum Authority.

DfEE/QCA (1999) *Citizenship – The National Curriculum for England*, London: The Stationery Office / Department for Education and Employment.

Dunn, S. (1989) 'Multicultural Education in the North of Ireland', in *The Irish Review No.6, Spring*, 32–8.

Dunn, S. (1995) *Facets of the Conflict in Northern Ireland*, Basingstoke: Macmillan / St. Martin's Press.

Early Years (2008) *Media Initiative for Young Children* <http://www.early-years.org/> (accessed 5 July 2010)

Edgar, K. (2000) *Circle Time: The Theory and Practice in Northern Ireland*, unpublished M.Ed. dissertation, Belfast: Queen's University Belfast.

Equality Commission (2002) *A Wake-up Call on Race: Implications of the Macpherson Report for Institutional Racism in Northern Ireland*, Belfast: Equality Commission for Northern Ireland.

Evans, E.E. (1973; new edition 1992) *The Personality of Ireland: Habitat, Heritage and History*, Belfast: Lilliput Press.

Faure, E. (ed.) et al (1972) *Learning to Be: The World of Education Today and Tomorrow, Report of the International Commission on the Development of Education*, London: UNESCO/Harrap.

Flannagan, C.E.T. and Lambkin, B.K. (1993) 'Religious Identity and Integrated Education', in Moffat, C. (ed.), *Education Together for a Change*, Belfast: Fortnight Educational Trust.

Fraser, M. (1973) *Children in Conflict*, London: Secker and Warburg.

Gallagher, T. (2004) *Education in Divided Societies*, Basingstoke: Palgrave Macmillan.

Gardner, H. (1993) *Frames of Mind – The Theory of Multiple Intelligences*, London: Fontana Press.

Gardner, H. (1999) *Intelligence Reframed. Multiple intelligences for the 21st century*, New York: Basic Books.

Goleman, D. (1996) *Emotional Intelligence*, London: Bloomsbury Publishing.

Hayes, M. (1990) Opening Address, in Watson, L. and Bowring-Carr, F. (eds), *Education for Mutual Understanding: A Collection of Papers presented at the final DENI Summer School Conference*, Bangor: Department of Education for Northern Ireland.

Heaney, S. (1975) 'Whatever You Say, Say Nothing', in *North*, London: Faber and Faber.

Hyland, A. (ed.) (2000) *Multiple Intelligences Curriculum and Assessment Project – Final Report*, Cork: University College Education Department.

Keast, J. (ed.) (2007) *Religious Diversity and Intercultural Education: A reference book for schools*, Strasbourg: Council of Europe.

Lawrence, D. (1996) *Enhancing Self-Esteem in the Classroom* (2nd edn), London: Paul Chapman Publishing.

Macpherson Report (1999) *The Stephen Lawrence Inquiry: Report of an Inquiry by Sir William Macpherson of Cluny*, London: The Stationery Office.

Montessori, M. (1992) *Education and Peace* (new translation by Helen R. Lane), Oxford: Clio Press.

Mosley, J. (1996) *Quality Circle Time in the Primary Classroom*, Wisbech: LDA.

Mosley, J. (1998) *More Quality Circle Time*, Wisbech: LDA.

Muldoon, O. (ed.) (2004) *The Cost of Conflict – Children and the Northern Ireland Troubles*, Oxford: Blackwell.

Murray, D. (1985) *Worlds Apart: Segregated Schools in Northern Ireland*, Belfast: Appletree Press.

NCC (1990) *Curriculum Guidance 8: Education for Citizenship*, York: National Curriculum Council.

NICC (1989a) *Cultural Heritage: A Cross Curricular Theme – Consultation Paper*, Belfast: N.I. Curriculum Council.

NICC (1989b) *Cross-Curricular Themes: Consultation Report*, Belfast: Northern Ireland Curriculum Council.

NICED (1988) *Education for Mutual Understanding: A Guide*, Belfast: N.I. Council for Educational Development.

NICIE (2002) *Integrating Through Understanding*, Belfast: Northern Ireland Council for Integrated Education.

NICIE (2008a) *Elephant, Bee or Other: Including Everyone in our Schools (Recommendations from the IntegratING Education Project)*, Belfast: Northern Ireland Council for Integrated Education.

NICIE (2008b) *ABC: Promoting an Anti-Bias Approach to Education in Northern Ireland* (revised edition), Belfast: Northern Ireland Council for Integrated Education.

Nieto, S. (2000) *Affirming diversity: A sociopolitical context of multicultural education* (3rd edn), White Plains, NY: Longman.

Northern Ireland Act 1998, Office of Public Sector Information <www.opsi.gov.uk/Acts/acts1998/ukpga_19980047_en_1> (accessed 19 August 2009).

Northern Ireland Curriculum (2007) *N.I. Curriculum* website <http://www.nicurriculum.org.uk/index.asp> (accessed 15 July 2010).

OFMDFM (2005) *A Shared Future: Policy and Strategic Framework for Good Relations in Northern Ireland*, Belfast: Office of the First Minister and Deputy First Minister.

OHCHR (n.d.) *ABC, Teaching Human Rights*, Office of the High Commissioner for Human Rights, European Wergeland Centre website <http://www.theewc.org/library/category/view/abc.teaching.human.rights.practical.activities.for.primary.and.secondary.schools/> (accessed 15 July 2010)

Perotti, A. (1994) *The Case for Intercultural Education*, Strasbourg: Council of Europe Press.

QCA (2000a) *Citizenship at Key Stages 3 and 4: Initial guidance for Schools*, London: Qualifications and Curriculum Authority.

QCA (2000b) *Personal, Social and Health Education and Citizenship at Key Stages 1 and 2: Initial guidance for Schools*, London: Qualifications and Curriculum Authority.

Richardson, N. (2002) *Schools As Bridges – Education for Living with Diversity*, unpublished paper presented at the Ninth Annual International Conference on Education, Spirituality and the Whole Child – Education for Peace, June 2002.

Robinson, A. (1993) Education for Mutual Understanding, in Caul, L., *A Common Curriculum: The Case of Northern Ireland*, Belfast: Learning Resources Unit, Stranmillis College.

Rowley, T. (1993) 'Contextual Education: The Hazelwood Model', in Moffat, C. (ed.), *Education Together for a Change*, Belfast: Fortnight Educational Trust.

Scott, Nicholas (1985) *Relationships – the Fourth R of Education: Education Minister Urges Action on Prejudice*, Belfast: Northern Ireland Information Service, 21 February 1985 (Press release taken from an address at the Centre for the Study of Conflict, University of Ulster at Coleraine).

SCSP (1978) Statement of the Objectives of the Schools Cultural Studies Project in *Network No.6, March*, Coleraine: Schools Cultural Studies Project.

Skilbeck, M. (1976) 'Education and Cultural Change', in *Compass: Journal of the Irish Association for Curriculum Development*, 5(2), 3–23.

Smyth, M., and Thomson, K. (eds) (2001) *Working with Children and Young People in Violently Divided Societies – Papers from South Africa and Northern Ireland*, Belfast, Community Conflict Impact on Children / INCORE.

Starkey, H. (ed.) (1991) *The Challenge of Human Rights Education*, London: Cassell Educational; Strasbourg: Council of Europe.

Trew, K. (2004) 'Children and socio-cultural divisions in Northern Ireland', in *Journal of Social Issues* 60, 507–22.

Tylor, E.B. (1871) *Primitive Culture, Vol. 1*, London: John Murray.

UNESCO (1974) *Recommendation concerning Education for International Understanding, Co-operation and Peace and Education relating to Human Rights and Fundamental Freedoms*, Paris: UNESCO.

UNESCO (2006) *Guidelines on Intercultural Education*, Paris: UNESCO Education Sector.

UNICEF (1995a) *Children Working for Peace*, Oxford: Oxford Development Education Centre, United Nations Children's Fund.

UNICEF (1995b) *Education for Peace and Tolerance Fundraising Kit*, Geneva: United Nations Children's Fund.

UNICEF (1996) *The State of the World's Children*, Oxford and New York: Oxford University Press, United Nations Children's Fund.

United Nations General Assembly (1948) *Universal Declaration of Human Rights – Article 26:* <http://www.un.org/en/documents/udhr/> (accessed 18 August 2009).

United Nations World Conference (2001) *World Conference against Racism, Racial Discrimination, Xenophobia and Related Intolerance* (Durban) <http://portal. unesco.org/culture/en/file_download.php/428cbb4e50dbd13f09a17de998aa0 1e9Durban_Declaration_2001.pdf> (accessed 15 July 2010).

Wallace, I. (1990) 'Education for Mutual Understanding' in Watson, L. and Bow-ring-Carr, F. (eds), *Education for Mutual Understanding: A Collection of Papers presented at the final DENI Summer School Conference*, Bangor: Department of Education for Northern Ireland.

TONY GALLAGHER

2   The Community Relations Context

Introduction

The aims of this chapter are to examine the evolution of community relations policy in Northern Ireland and to locate educational initiatives within
this broader policy context. The discussion is organised in the following
manner. Following this short introduction we examine the first wave of
reform measures in Northern Ireland at the end of the 1960s, as this provided a backdrop to the development of a specific community relations
strategy. The chapter will argue that the priority attached by government to
community relations policy varied from this point onwards. In the period
from 1969 to 1974 it will be suggested that the policy was given a fairly high
priority, but that this changed from 1974 up to the mid-1980s. The chapter
will go on to argue that a renewed commitment to community relations
was given by government from the mid-1980s onwards and some reasons
for this will be discussed. The third main period of policy development
occurred during the Peace Process of the late 1990s and early 2000s, but
it will be suggested that progress has stalled since the restoration of the
Northern Ireland Assembly and shared Executive during 2002–2004 and,
more especially, since 2007.

The next main part of the discussion will shift the focus towards educational initiatives. We will outline briefly the way in which issues related to
community relations have been addressed within education. We will then
go on to examine the range of specific strategies that have been adopted
within the educational system in order to contribute to an improvement
in community relations and offer some assessment of their effectiveness.

First Wave of Reform

Before the outbreak of violence in Northern Ireland at the end of the 1960s, a convention had developed within the Westminster parliament such that issues related to Northern Ireland were not discussed, barring a few exceptions. Northern Ireland issues were seen to be the prerogative of the Northern Ireland parliament at Stormont. The net effect of this Westminster convention was that many British MPs, and most of their constituents, were unaware of the vagaries and particularities of Northern Irish politics. This was to change when the violence began and British troops were sent onto the streets of Northern Ireland to stabilise a rapidly deteriorating situation (Gallagher, 1995a; Darby, 1997).

Once British troops got involved in maintaining civil order, it was inevitable that the British government would have to become politically involved in a manner which had hitherto been avoided. One consequence of this was pressure on the Northern Ireland government to introduce a series of legislative reforms to mitigate some of the more intolerable aspects of religious and political discrimination. The measures introduced in this period were wide ranging. They included changes in the system for allocating public housing and the development of procedures through which individuals could seek redress for alleged maladministration by public bodies. Political reforms included changes in the voting system to introduce universal adult suffrage and new arrangements for the determination of electoral boundaries. There was legislation also to make employment discrimination on the basis of religion or political opinion illegal and to establish various bodies to oversee fair employment practices in the public and private sectors. The underlying theme of much of the measures in the 'first wave of reform' can be seen exemplified in Harold Wilson's Downing Street Declaration of August 1969: '... every citizen of Northern Ireland is entitled to the same equality of treatment and freedom from discrimination that obtains in the rest of the United Kingdom'.

Establishing Community Relations Policy

If equality of treatment provided the main rhetorical basis for the early legislative reforms, the idea of promoting reconciliation played a more overt role in the first explicit version of community relations policy. In this period the policy was to be carried forward by two new bodies. A Community Relations Commission was established to promote the policy among the public, while a Ministry of Community Relations was established within the Northern Ireland government.

The Community Relations Commission was required to support work which aimed to improve community relations. This included a duty to provide advice on community relations issues to government, to support research on community relations issues, and to provide ideas and expertise on educational and other programmes (Darby, 1973). At an early stage the Commission decided to adopt a community development strategy. In large part this strategy was based on a pragmatic acceptance that the widespread rioting of the period had resulted in increased residential segregation in many parts of Northern Ireland, but especially in Belfast. While the long-term goal of community relations might be to bring people in the segregated areas together, more immediate and limited short-term goals were required. The Commission came to the view that contact between the segregated communities was going to be difficult not least because people lacked confidence in themselves and others. Under the community development strategy the Commission would employ Field Officers who would try to encourage the development of voluntary organisations within the segregated communities. Once such a community infrastructure was in place, it was argued, people in segregated communities would feel more confident and willing to reach across the divide. Elected politicians were not, however, enamoured of this strategy, at least in part because some of them felt that strong voluntary networks might operate as an alternative to the leadership they were providing.

The main functions of the Ministry of Community Relations were to oversee the policy generally and to act as the main link between government and the Community Relations Commission. In addition, the Ministry was given responsibility for the administration of the Social Needs Fund, which was intended to be a mechanism for diverting some government funding towards areas of greatest social need. In practice the Ministry did not develop a strong profile. Only a small number of civil servants were ever employed in the Ministry, and individual Ministers came and went with a startling, not to say disappointing, frequency (Hayes, 1972). Indeed, it is the demise of community relations policy that takes us to the next part of our discussion.

The Decline of Community Relations Policy

In 1972 the local Northern Ireland parliament at Stormont was abolished, to be replaced by an elected Assembly which was charged with the goal of seeking political accommodation. Towards the end of 1973 the British and Irish governments persuaded some of the local politicians in Northern Ireland to agree to share power in a new Executive body. The power-sharing Executive involved representatives from the Ulster Unionist Party (UUP), the Social, Democratic and Labour Party (SDLP) and the Alliance Party (AP), although it became increasingly clear that the UUP was deeply divided over the arrangement.

For the present purposes the main significance of the power-sharing Executive was in the way it dealt with the community relations issue (Frazer and Fitzduff, 1991). The essence of the situation was that the SDLP Minister of Community Relations seemed to take the view that the power-sharing arrangement had 'solved' the community relations problem. Since there was no longer a community relations problem, there was little need for a body to tackle the problem. On the basis of this unerring logic the decision was taken to abolish the Community Relations Commission. Not surprisingly, many within the community relations field felt that the decision was based more on the politicians' suspicion of the community development strategy. In the event the power-sharing Executive itself did not last too long. In May 1974 the self-styled Ulster Workers' Council brought Northern Ireland to a standstill through strike action, the Unionist representatives in the power-sharing Executive resigned, the Executive collapsed and the Assembly went into abeyance.

In the political vacuum created by this situation the Ministry of Community Relations was quietly abolished and responsibility for the policy shifted into the Department of Education in Northern Ireland (DENI). Even DENI officials will accept that in the immediate following period little was done to promote the policy. At the broader government level it would seem that attention shifted away from the possibility of reconciliation and political accommodation. A retrospective judgement on the period would suggest, in fact, that government sought a military solution through the defeat of the IRA. The view may have been held that the achievement of this goal would make political accommodation more likely and, in any case, by that time a new generation of politicians may have come on the scene.

The Field Officers who had been employed by the Community Relations Commission to promote the community development strategy moved into the District Councils where they were employed as community service officers. Ostensibly their role was to be the same. In practice it is probably not too cynical to suggest that their role shifted from one of organising people to one of overseeing resources.

All this highlights the declining significance of community relations policy in this period. The expertise and energy that had been gathered together in a relatively short period was dissipated. Less money was spent on community relations measures, and less time and words were devoted to community relations concerns. While the period can be seen, then, as the nadir of community relations policy, the spirit and idea of reconciliation was kept alive by at least two distinct interest groups.

The first of these was provided by a variety of reconciliation groups. There were very many of these groups although they were often small in number and, in this period, even more limited in their apparent impact. Many of these groups were linked to inter-church or ecumenical organisations and were committed to working together across the community divide to demonstrate that reconciliation in Northern Ireland was possible.

The second interest that helped to maintain the idea of reconciliation was provided by groups of parents who were interested in promoting integrated education (Moffat, 1993). These parents had tried to persuade government and other educational authorities to take proactive measures to create religiously integrated schools. Their lack of success prompted one group to establish their own school, Lagan College, which was quickly followed by others. The reconciliation groups and the integrated schools movement both played a key role in that they demonstrated what could be achieved, given sufficient will. In doing this they helped to keep alive the idea that alternatives to the brutalising Manicheism of a conflicted society were possible.

The Restoration of Community Relations Policy

From the mid-1980s onwards it was possible to discern a new direction, marked by the renewed priority given to community relations policy. At this time government announced a new set of policy objectives on community relations, established a new infrastructure to carry that policy forward and demonstrated the significance of the rhetoric through a number of pieces of legislation. Here we will examine each of these aspects.

The new government policy on community relations involved three distinctive objectives. The first objective was that government was committed to encouraging greater contact between the Protestant and Catholic communities. The second was that government was committed to the promotion of greater tolerance of cultural diversity. The third and final objective was that government was committed to the achievement of equality of opportunity in Northern Ireland.

The achievement of these goals was to be enhanced by the creation of two new bodies, one to work within the government system and across the various departments, the other to focus on the wider community. In 1987 the Central Community Relations Unit (CCRU) was established within the Central Secretariat of the Northern Ireland Civil Service. The role of

CCRU was to promote community relations issues within government, to challenge government departments to consider and develop the community relations aspects of their work and to report directly on progress to the Head of the Civil Service. In its early years CCRU was responsible also for the allocation of funds to voluntary bodies working in the community relations field, but this function was to be largely handed over to the other part of the new community relations infrastructure. In 1990 the Community Relations Council (CRC) was established to promote community relations issues among the public in Northern Ireland. In some respects it is possible to see the CRC as a restoration of the Community Relations Commission, although on a stronger resource base and, perhaps more important, in a more supportive political environment. The CRC is responsible for allocating funds for work on community relations and, through the Cultural Traditions Group, for the promotion of cultural diversity and tolerance. In addition, the CRC provides expertise and advice.

As indicated above, two particular pieces of legislation, both coming into law in 1989, helped to demonstrate the way in which the new community relations policy informed government practice. One of these was the 1989 Education Reform Order, which we will consider in more detail below. For the present the key aspect of the Order was that it provided a legislative basis for various reconciliation strategies in education that had hitherto been largely voluntary. The second was the 1989 Fair Employment Act, which provided perhaps the strongest legislative measures against discrimination in employment in any European jurisdiction. Under the Act employers are required to monitor the religious composition of their workforces, report these data to the Fair Employment Commission which publishes annual reports on labour market patterns, and initiate affirmative action measures when imbalances in the workforce are detected. These provisions provided some evidence of the commitment to equity (see also Gallagher et al., 1994). The outworking of the Act, and policy on employment equality more generally, was reviewed by the Standing Advisory Commission on Human Rights (SACHR). The government's response to the review became part of the new context created by the 1998 Good Friday Agreement and involved a recasting of the equality infrastructure. Thus, for example, a new Equality Commission was established, as was a strengthened Human Rights Commission.

Why did this new commitment to community relations policy arise at this time? It seems likely that a combination of circumstances and pressures influenced the new direction. Following the hunger-strikes by Republican prisoners in the early 1980s, Sinn Fein rose to electoral prominence. This significant change in the political context seems to have prompted a reappraisal of policy by the government. Other external pressure was provided by the MacBride Campaign in the United States which raised important questions on the weaknesses of the 1976 Fair Employment Act and, thus, government's commitment to fairness and equity. Within Northern Ireland two reports by SACHR, one on the need for a clearer community relations strategy and the other a critical assessment of the 1976 Fair Employment Act, made an important contribution to the evolving discussion. Some individual Ministers in Northern Ireland were keen to promote particular measures within government policy. Perhaps the most notable in this respect was Dr Brian Mawhinney who held strong views on the need for and appropriateness of specific reconciliation measures in education policy. This interest at a political level may also have been matched by interest among key officials in the Northern Ireland Civil Service.

While all of these factors influenced the development of the new policy environment, the present view would be that the 1985 Anglo-Irish Agreement was perhaps the most significant part of the jigsaw. The 1985 Agreement was important because it committed the British and Irish governments to a collaborative approach to Northern Ireland. In this way the London-Dublin axis provided a stable framework within which Northern Ireland politicians could explore grounds for agreement. Importantly, the framework would remain stable even in the absence of local agreement. While this had undoubted symbolic significance, it would seem also that one of the practical consequences of the Agreement was to extend the range of options available to those framing policy. It seems possible, if not likely, that this influenced the emergent priority on community relations in Northern Ireland (Gallagher, 1995b).

This framework remained in place up to and through the ceasefires, in 1994, and the Good Friday/Belfast Agreement, in 1998. However, the new circumstances prompted another review of policy out of which emerged the Shared Future proposals. This was based on the contention that, despite the end of political violence, Northern Ireland remained a deeply divided society in which patterns of segregation were becoming even more pronounced. The Shared Future policy suggested that government should work proactively to reverse this process of creeping segregation and encourage greater interconnections and integration throughout society. Although the Good Friday/Belfast Agreement had included arrangements for a new Assembly and a system of shared governance in an Executive, it was not until 2000 that agreement was reached to operate the Assembly and it went into suspension in 2002. Thus, during most of the period when community relations policy was under review this was being overseen by Direct Rule Ministers. This was still the case when the formal policy was adopted and published in 2005,[1] but it soon got embroiled in the emerging political talks that were working towards a restoration of the Assembly which was actually achieved in 2007. However, by this time the balance of political support had shifted from the UUP and SDLP to the DUP and Sinn Fein respectively. The UUP and SDLP had been little more than reluctant enthusiasts for the Shared Future approach. Indeed, at various points of the consultation process there seemed to be a view among some politicians that the agreement had ended the community relations problem and that the CRC's role could quite easily be accommodated within the District Councils – 'déjà vu all over again', as Yogi Berra once said! After the 2007 Assembly elections the DUP and Sinn Fein were the main parties in government and neither had any evident enthusiasm for the Shared Future policy. Ostensibly this was on the basis that the policy was a product of 'direct rule'; more prosaically it might be wondered if parties whose appeal is largely rooted in essentially theocratic or ethnic principles would have any temperamental interest in an approach rooted in principles of sharing. Officially the Shared Future policy has been set aside and work is continuing on a new policy framework, tentatively entitled Cohesion, Sharing and Integration (or CSI), although when, or even if, this policy will be published remains unclear.

---

1   See <http://www.asharedfutureni.gov.uk> (accessed 26 February 2009).

Community Relations and Education

Having examined the evolution of community relations policy generally, we now turn to the more specific area of education. A key feature of the education system in Northern Ireland lies in the predominance of religious segregation. Currently schools in Northern Ireland are about evenly divided between Protestant and Catholic schools. The religious nomenclature of the schools reflects a de facto rather than a de jure position and is based on the high degree of religious homogeneity of the pupils and teachers within the separate school systems. Data from the Department of Education in Table 1 show that between 2 and 8 per cent of Catholic pupils attend non-Catholic schools of various types, with the proportion being notably higher for Catholics attending non-Catholic grammar schools. As noted above, since 1980 a number of integrated schools, catering for both Protestant and Catholic pupils, have opened. They currently enrol about 6 per cent of the total pupil enrolment in Northern Ireland.

School type	Management type	% Catholic pupils
Primary	Protestant (Controlled)	5
	Catholic	98
	Integrated	38
Secondary	Protestant (Controlled)	2
	Catholic	99
	Integrated	40
Grammar	Protestant (Controlled or Voluntary)	8
	Catholic	98
	Integrated	n/a

Table 1 Proportion of Catholic Pupils by School Type and Management Type,
2007–2008
Source: Calculated from Department of Education data.

Schools and Social Division

In the early years of the conflict a number of commentators attached some responsibility for social breakdown to religiously segregated schooling and argued for the development of integrated schools (Heskin, 1980; Fraser, 1973). It has to be said that some of these early views, which were often strongly held, tended to be based, at least partly, on a simplistic translation of research evidence and practice in the United States of America rather than a more detailed assessment of the nature of social factors in Northern Ireland. In the USA the key arguments for desegregation were centred round the idea of equality. In Northern Ireland, by contrast, the primary arguments for integration were social.

Since these early debates, views on the role of segregated schools in Northern have been based on two main hypotheses. The 'cultural hypothesis' suggested that segregated schools enhanced community divisions by introducing pupils to differing, and potentially opposing, cultural environments. This view emphasised differences in the curriculum of the separate school systems (Magee, 1970; Smith, 2005; Arlow, 2004). The 'social hypothesis' suggested that, regardless of what was taught in schools, segregated schooling initiated pupils into conflict by emphasising and validating group differences and hostilities, encouraging mutual ignorance and, perhaps more important, mutual suspicion. This view emphasised the impact of segregation *per se* (Murray, 1983; Murray, 1985). A third view suggested that religious segregation of schools was much less relevant to understanding the conflict than pervasive inequality and social injustice (Gallagher et al, 1993).

Throughout most of this period it is possible to discern three broad intervention strategies that have been followed, although a fourth approach has emerged in recent years. The first involved curricular initiatives within the existing segregated schools. This was the approach adopted by some of the earliest intervention programmes, including the Schools Community Relations Project (1970) and the Schools Cultural Studies Project (1974), and was encouraged by the DENI in 1982 (O'Connor, 1980). In

the following year the Education for Mutual Understanding (EMU) programme was initiated. This programme encouraged schools, on a voluntary
basis, to introduce themes related to community relations into their curriculum (McKernan, 1982; Taylor, 1992; Smith and Robinson, 1992). More
recently the theme of citizenship has been introduced into the curriculum
(Arlow, 2004; Smith, 2003).

The second broad strategy also worked within the context of segregated schools and sought to encourage contact programmes between
pupils in Protestant and Catholic schools. In the early years these contact
programmes faced problems because of their *ad hoc* and often transient
character (Darby et al., 1977; Dunn et al., 1984). In an attempt to overcome
some of these problems, the Inter School Links project was established
in 1986. The project established a contact programme between a number
of Protestant and Catholic schools in a medium-sized town in Northern
Ireland. The aim was to do this in a way that both integrated the contact
work into the normal day-to-day activity of the schools and made it independent of any specific individuals (Dunn and Smith, 1989; Smith and
Dunn, 1990).

The third strategy sought to develop integrated schools to serve both
Protestant and Catholic pupils. An Act of Parliament in 1978 provided
a basis for existing Protestant schools under state management to change
status to integrated schools. In part because of the failure of schools to
follow this option, a group of parents opened Lagan College in 1981, the
first planned integrated school in Northern Ireland. Following the success
of Lagan College other groups of parents came together to open planned
integrated schools with the medium term goal of having at least one primary
and post-primary school in each of Northern Ireland's twenty-six District
Council areas. These new schools are referred to as planned integrated
schools as they consciously attempt to maintain a religious balance among
their pupil enrolments and teacher workforce, and seek to reflect both
cultural traditions in their curriculum (Moffatt, 1993; Smith, 2001).

There was a great deal of overlap between these strategies. In particular
there were close links between work on EMU and the contact schemes. It
was clear too that official support for some of these initiatives was strengthened in the following ways: guidance material on EMU was produced and

circulated to schools, the Cross Community Contact Scheme was initiated by the DENI in 1987 to provide funds for schools that wished to engage in contact programmes, some of the Education and Library Boards appointed EMU Field Officers to support the work of teachers, and a variety of new agencies were opened, funded by government and charitable trusts, to provide support and advice to teachers.

The community relations dimension to education was strengthened still further by the Education Reform Order (1989), the Northern Ireland version of the 1988 Education Reform Act (ERA) for England and Wales. In broad terms the ERO was closely modelled on the provisions of ERA in that it introduced a common curriculum for all schools, devolved greater managerial and financial powers to schools, and accorded a higher degree of school choice to parents. However, in contrast to the situation in England and Wales where the issues of racial equality and multiculturalism appeared to be little more than an afterthought in the statutory curriculum, the Northern Ireland reform measures were strongly influenced by community relations concerns. For the first time government took on the formal responsibility of supporting new initiatives towards the development of planned integrated schools. While the main realisation of this commitment was through public funding for the Northern Ireland Council for Integrated Education (NICIE), a transformation procedure was also created whereby the parents of pupils in existing Protestant or Catholic schools could vote to change the school to integrated status.

Alongside these measures on integrated schools, and in recognition of the likelihood that most pupils would continue to be educated in de facto segregated schools, the ERO required that EMU and Cultural Heritage would become compulsory cross-curricular themes in the Northern Ireland common curriculum. In other words, all schools in Northern Ireland would be required to reflect community relations themes in their curriculum. Under the themes of EMU and Cultural Heritage, schools would be encouraged, but not required, to engage in contact programmes. In other words, the measures contained in the ERO did not opt for any one of the strategies that had been developed within education over the previous years, but attempted to provide support for all the main strategic approaches.

The period of the mainly statutory curriculum is now coming to an end. In response to teacher criticisms that the statutory curriculum had got too overloaded the new Northern Ireland Revised Curriculum (NIRC) allows for a much greater degree of flexibility for pupils post-14 years. As noted above the NIRC has also introduced a new programme called Local and Global Citizenship which addresses issues related to democracy, equality, rights and justice within Northern Ireland, European and global contexts (Arlow, 2004; see also Chapter 12). Further, in response to an entirely separate review of the selective system of secondary and grammar schools (Gallagher and Smith, 2001; Gallagher, 2004) and the effect of falling school enrolments, official policy has moved towards the support of collaboration between schools, with an allied recommendation that there should be the active encouragement of collaboration across the denominational sectors (Bain Report, 2006). This is the fourth option currently being pursued through the Sharing Education Programme (SEP)[2], an initiative supported by Atlantic Philanthropies and the International Fund for Ireland which is trying to establish effective models for cross-denominational shared teaching and related activities between schools. An important difference between this initiative and previous efforts to encourage schools to work together is that it aims to promote systemic collaboration on core curriculum subjects.

Evaluating Government Initiatives

So what has been the impact of these measures? By the time of the cease-fires and the beginning of the peace process in the mid-1990s the government had been spending almost £9 million per annum on community relations, with a little over a third of this total spent by the Department of Education. Within the education budget a little over a third was spent

2   See <http://www.schoolsworkingtogether.co.uk> (accessed 28 February 2009).

on contact programmes for pupils in Protestant and Catholic schools. A further quarter was spent in grant-aid to reconciliation bodies, many of which provided curriculum support for schools, and a similar amount was spent on cultural traditions programmes.

Some consequences of this legislative and financial support are clear. The rate of increase in the opening of new integrated schools increased following the 1989 Education Reform Order and, over time, the proportion of post-primary schools has steadily increased, at least until the impact of falling rolls made it virtually impossible to open new schools. The money available to reconciliation bodies and the contact programmes led to the growth of a host of organisations providing support for EMU work in schools, including statutory and voluntary organisations which offered training, materials, including videos, games, books, pamphlets and worksheets, on EMU-related themes. As a result of this, over time, a considerable body of expertise developed from which teachers and schools could draw. It would be true to say that some of these resources and support would have been available even without an overarching government policy on community relations initiatives in schools. It is equally true to say, however, that the sheer amount of support available has been enhanced by the policy climate and the underpinning support of public money. This official underpinning of community relations work in education was enhanced still further with the decision to implement the Local and Global Citizenship programme. The programme itself developed out of a pilot project which tested materials and pedagogies (UNESCO Centre, 2009) and the roll-out was accompanied by a major training programme aimed at resourcing at least four teachers in every post primary school to deliver the programme.

Overall, however, the impact of some of the curricular interventions has been mixed. Three main reports have provided a picture of work in schools up to the 1990s: Smith and Robinson (1992) suggested that the EMU work lacked clear definition, thus leaving open the danger that the 'cutting edge' of the initiative could be lost if people focused on its less controversial and 'safe' aspects. There is reason to suppose this might occur: there is plenty of evidence that a 'social grammar' exists in Northern Ireland such that people tend to avoid talking about the issues of religion and politics in (religiously) mixed company (Harris, 1972; Burton, 1978; Gallagher, 1994). While broaching these issues can be considered 'impolite', this unwritten social rule means that people can engage in cross-community contact while remaining largely ignorant of the views of members of the 'other' community on the fundamental social divisions that exist within the society.

Smith and Robinson (1992) went on to suggest that there was a lack of coordination between the various statutory bodies with a responsibility for EMU, concerns about an over-emphasis on contact, as opposed to curricular, work within EMU, and that schools tended to accord the policy a relatively low priority. Anecdotal evidence gained from talking with teachers in Northern Ireland would confirm the perception that EMU is seen by many as synonymous with 'contact', a point further reinforced by classroom based research in schools (Leitch and Kilpatrick, 1999) and by the financial priority given to contact, as seen above.

The difficulty with this over-emphasis on contact work is that a significant proportion of these programmes appear to be limited value and, all too often, fail to address issues of division and conflict. In the worst cases they merely reproduce the degree of 'polite' contact that exists in the wider society which, as has been suggested above, is suffused with a social grammar of avoidance. More generally, an emphasis on contact programmes can lead to a diminution of curricular work within schools and encourage a perception that community relations is the responsibility of only those limited numbers of teachers involved in contact programmes: Smith and Robinson (1996) estimated that while two-fifths of primary schools and three-fifths of post-primary schools were involved in contact work, this comprised only about a fifth and a tenth of pupils respectively. More recent data from the Department of Education suggests that in 2000–1 21 per cent of primary school pupils, but only 3 per cent of post-primary pupils were involved in funded contact programmes (O'Connor et al. 2002). This report went on to argue that a refocusing of EMU work was needed to emphasise its whole-school dimensions, to highlight the implications for teaching and learning, to encourage teachers to address more controversial issues and to reduce the focus on contact work.

The O'Connor et al (2002) report was a Department of Education funded evaluation of the Schools Community Relations programme, which provided funds for schools to engage in contact work. O'Connor et al. identified some strengths in the work, including the commitment of ELB officers and NGOs, and the undoubted commitment of some teachers to work in this area. In addition, they identified the strength of long-term link programmes and the fact that there were examples of good practice. However, they also found that this work was often accorded a low strategic priority, that it lacked a coherent definition of community relations and a strategy for evaluation, and that some school links programmes lacked purpose. The report had been established to offer recommendations on future practice. These covered a wide variety of issues, but at their heart were the ideas of extending funding support beyond simply contact work and encouraging a clearer examination of the purpose and strategic direction of any initiative. Although, at the time of writing, a Department of Education review of community relations policy was underway, in part as a belated response to the O'Connor et al. (2002) report, in many senses the curricular emphasis had shifted towards work on citizenship.

Research on the integrated schools has focused on a number of different aspects. Morgan et al (1992) and McEwen et al. (1993) found that parents had a variety of motivations in sending their children to integrated schools, and sometimes they were preferred as a better alternative to secondary schools if a place could not be achieved in a grammar school. Despite this, claims that the integrated schools have a largely middle-class intake are unfounded: in 2008–9, for example, the average grammar school had 6 per cent of pupils entitled to free school meals, as compared with an average of 26 per cent in secondary schools and 20 per cent in integrated schools. A study into pupils in Lagan College, the longest established integrated school, found that friendship networks did cut across religious boundaries, so the school did seem to be providing a genuinely integrated environment (Irwin, 1993; see also McGlynn et al., 2004), a finding which was confirmed in an ethnographic study of another integrated school (McMullan, 2003). Gallagher et al. (1995) found that the second oldest integrated school (Hazelwood College) had developed innovative approaches to the curriculum and teaching, and staff were using the

opportunity provided by an integrated setting to address issues related to
social division and conflict. In addition, there is clear evidence that many
within the integrated schools movement were innovative in the development of new curricula and pedagogies to address issues related to a divided
and conflicted society (Moffett, 1993).

However, there is some emergent research which is suggesting that this
aspect of the schools is being constrained, in part due to the pressure of
success, the consequent turnover of staff and the limited specific training
that is available for teachers wishing to work in integrated settings. Other
pressure arises from the enhanced accountability systems, the pressure of
benchmarking and other performance-driven initiatives that draw time
and energy from other activities, while other research suggests that the
integrated schools sector may be characterised by weak systemic links,
and a consequent limited consistency in their internal organisation and
practice (Milliken and Gallagher, 1998). The emergent problems are being
addressed by the integrated schools movement, but they serve as a reminder
that simply changing the structure of the schools does not, in itself, solve
all the problems of a divided society – a more proactive approach is not
only needed, but arguably the problems of a divided society will only be
addressed if they are constantly and explicitly being addressed.

The most significant issue facing the integrated sector, however, lies
in the prospects for growth. Despite consistent majorities in social surveys
saying that they would prefer integrated schools, as we saw above the proportion of pupils currently in integrated schools comprises about 6 per
cent of the total pupil population. Most of the existing integrated schools
developed as entirely new schools, usually initiated by groups of parents. The
government's preferred route of expansion is through the transformation of
existing schools as a consequence of parental ballots. This is so both because
this is a less expensive route to change, but also because there is already a
significant surplus of places in the system and a significant demographic
downturn. However, this raises a number of problems. The first is that a
transformation school has not just to develop a new ethos and character
as an integrated school, but it has to do so by casting off an existing ethos
and character. In order to ensure that any process of transformation represents a genuine process of change, the legislation governing the process

requires that a school has a minimum 10 per cent minority enrolment in its entry cohort at the point of transformation, and raises its overall minority enrolment significantly within ten years. A number of integrated schools have closed, mainly as a consequence of low pupil enrolments, and while none have been closed on the grounds that they have failed to achieve a balanced enrolment of Protestant and Catholic pupils, it is undoubtedly the case that some schools are in this imbalanced position.

A further issue is that, to date, all of the transformed schools began life as Protestant, or controlled, schools. There is the potential for this to create a political problem if a perception grows within the Protestant community that it is 'their' schools that are being 'taken over' through this process of change. This seemed even more likely during a period when many Protestants felt alienated by political developments, although even with their role in government the DUP remain generally antipathetic to integrated schools. Part of the reason for a shift towards an approach based on the encouragement of collaboration between schools was to avoid some of these problems by leaving a pattern of differential owner-ship while attempting to make the institutional boundaries between pupils and teachers more porous.

The peace process provides the most significant backdrop to current educational developments. This process began in the early 1990s with secret, and later open, negotiations between Republican paramilitaries and the British and Irish governments, leading eventually to ceasefires in 1994. For a variety of political reasons, significant progress was delayed until after the 1997 elections in Britain and Ireland, but progress then did lead to the establishment of working, if fragile, political institutions in Northern Ireland. These institutions seemed almost always to be on the verge of collapse, although at moments of crisis the politicians appeared to find some way to maintain progress. That said, following a period of increasing political tension and sparked by a number of security-related incidents, the Assembly went into suspension in October 2002 and did not re-emerge until 2007. As noted above, the political balance within the Assembly has shifted with major gains by the two more extreme par-ties in elections in 2003 and 2007. Unlikely as it once seemed, the current Executive is anchored on a coalition between the DUP and Sinn Fein, and although there are significant tensions between them, the Executive and Assembly continue to function. The present view would be that the community relations work of the 1980s onwards helped create an environment within which talks became possible and agreement was achievable, although validating causality is virtually impossible.

The decade and more of the peace process has been longer, more difficult and more fragile than anyone imagined. And while it has largely (although not completely) ended political violence, the underlying conflict remains. It has, nevertheless, achieved significant success. The unlikely coalition between the DUP and Sinn Fein is perhaps the most visible mark of this success: this form of coalition was, literally, unimaginable even a few years ago. But there have been marked changes in other ways as well. An affirmative action programme in recruitment for the reformed police service (PSNI) has led to a significant increase in the proportion of Catholic officers; the British army is nowhere to be seen; and the IRA has decommissioned its weapons. Table 2 shows that there has been a marked reduction even in low level violent incidents, while Table 3 shows an increasingly positive public perception of the state of relations between the two communities.

Year	Shooting incidents	Bombs used
1987	674	384
1997	225	93
2007–8	42	24

Table 2 Number of Reported Shooting Incidents and Bombs Used
Source: PSNI statistics.

Year	... are better now than 5 years ago	... will be better in 5 years' time
1989	22	26
1991	29	34
1993	25	29
1994	26	32
1995	56	63
1996	45	43
1998	50	62
1999	50	55
2000	42	40
2001	28	33
2002	30	39
2003	44	48
2004	56	56
2005	52	50
2006	56	55
2007	65	64

Table 3 Percentage Saying that Relations between Protestants and Catholics...
Source: Northern Ireland Life and Times Survey.

Conclusions

In this chapter we have focused on three main areas. Firstly, we examined the evolution of community relations policy from its inception at the outbreak of violence in Northern Ireland. In this part of the discussion we examined the way in which the priority attached to community relations issues has changed over time. A relatively high priority was attached to community relations policy from the mid-1980s onwards and it has been argued that this contributed to the environment which helped the peace process to emerge. We looked at the review of policy which took place during the period of the peace process and highlighted some unresolved political tensions on future directions.

In the second part of the chapter we examined community relations themes within education policy. This included attempts to understand the role of a largely segregated education system in a divided society, and an outline of the various strategies that have been developed within education to promote reconciliation. It was possible to identify four main strategic approaches including curriculum initiatives, contact programmes, the development of integrated schools and, most recently, efforts to encourage school collaboration.

The third part of the chapter tried to offer an account of the evidence we have on the consequences of all the policies and initiatives. This is an account of a glass that may be half-full, or half-empty. There have been undoubted advances in educational work on community relations as a consequence of the stronger policy environment, but it is equally true that, in many respects, the advances have been limited and, to some extent, disappointing. One societal gain in the latter half of the 1990s was the negotiations which led to paramilitary ceasefires and a level of political agreement. However, the fact that the Assembly initially only operated between 2000 and 2002 was a reminder that political discourses had not yet broken free of the traditional zero-sum debates over territory and identity. The restoration of the Assembly in 2007 has been associated with improved public perceptions of the state of community relations. However, the lukewarm, at best, attitude of the two main political parties towards a proactive approach to a shared future does raise questions of the future shape of our society: will it be one which actively addresses reconciliation and seeks to promote a sense of a common good; or will it be a future marked by deeper institutional divisions in which politics is primarily about elites, representing different communities and managing these divisions? As the new political architecture of Northern Ireland settles into place, these are the options we are facing.

References

Arlow, M. (2004) 'Citizenship education in a divided society: the case of Northern Ireland', in Tawil, S. and Harley, A. (eds), *Education, Conflict and Social Cohesion*, Geneva: International Bureau of Education.

Bain Report (2006) *Schools for the future: funding, strategy, sharing. Report of the Independent Strategic Review of Education*. Bangor: Department of Education.

Burton, F. (1978) *The politics of legitimacy: Struggles in a Belfast community*. London: Routledge and Kegan Paul.

Darby, J. (1973) 'Divisiveness in Education', *The Northern Teacher*, 11(1), 3–12.

Darby, J. (1997) *Scorpions in a bottle: Conflicting cultures in Northern Ireland*, London: Minority Rights Group.

Darby, J., Murray, D., Batts, D., Dunn, S., Farren, S., and Harris, J. (1977). *Education and Community in Northern Ireland: Schools Apart?* Coleraine: New University of Ulster.

Dunn, S., Darby, J., and Mullan, K. (1984) *Schools Together?* Coleraine: New University of Ulster.

Dunn, S., and Smith, A. (1989) *Inter School Links*. Coleraine: University of Ulster.

Fraser, R.M. (1973) *Children in Conflict*. London: Secker and Wartburg.

Frazer, H., and Fitzduff, M. (1992) *Improving community relations*. Belfast: NI Community Relations Council.

Gallagher, A. (1994) 'Dealing with conflict: schools in Northern Ireland', *Multicultural Teaching*, 13(1), 10–13.

Gallagher, A.M. (1995a) 'The approach of government: community relations and equity', in Dunn, S. (ed.), *Facets of the Conflict in Northern Ireland*, London/New York: Macmillan/St Martin's Press.

Gallagher, A.M. (1995b) 'Equity, contact and pluralism: Attitudes to community relations', in Breen, R., Devine, P., and Robinson, G. (eds), *Social Attitudes in Northern Ireland*, Belfast: Appletree Press.

Gallagher, A.M., Cormack, R.J., and Osborne, R.D. (1994) 'Religion, equity and education in Northern Ireland', *British Educational Research Journal*, 20(5), 507–18.

Gallagher, A.M., Osborne, R.D., and Cormack, R.J. (1993) 'Community Relations, Equality and Education', in Osborne, R.D., Cormack, R.J., and Gallagher, A.M. (eds), *After the Reforms: Education and Policy in Northern Ireland*, Aldershot, Avebury.

Gallagher, A.M., Osborne, R.D., Cormack, R.J., McKay, I. and Peover, S. (1995) 'Hazelwood Integrated College', in National Commission for Education (ed.), *Success Against the Odds: Effective schools in disadvantaged areas*. London: Routledge.

Gallagher, T. (2004) 'The effects of selective education in Northern Ireland', in DFES (ed.), *DFES Research Conference 2003 – Learning by comparison: International experiences in education and training*, London: DFES.

Gallagher, T., and Smith, A. (2001) 'The effects of selective education in Northern Ireland', *Education Review*, 15(1), 74–81.

Harris, R. (1972) *Prejudice and tolerance in Ulster*. Manchester: Manchester University Press.

Hayes, M. (1972) *The Role of the Community Relations Commission in Northern Ireland*. London: Runnymeade Trust.

Heskin, K. (1980) *Northern Ireland: A Psychological Analysis*. Dublin: Gill and Macmillan.

Irwin, C. (1993) 'Making integrated education work for pupils', in Moffatt, C. (ed.), *Education Together for a Change*. Belfast: Fortnight Educational Trust.

Leitch, R., and Kilpatrick, R. (1999) *Inside the Gates: Schools and the Troubles*. Belfast: Save the Children Fund.

Magee, J. (1970) 'The Teaching of Irish History in Irish Schools', *The Northern Teacher*, 10(1), 15–21.

McEwen, A., Agnew, U., Salters, J., and Salters, M. (1993) *Integrated education: The views of parents*. Belfast, Queen's University.

McGlynn, C., Niens, U., Cairns, E., and Hewstone, M. (2004) 'Moving out of conflict: The contribution of integrated schools in Northern Ireland to identity, attitudes, forgiveness and reconciliation', *Journal of Peace Education*, 1, 147–63.

McKernan, J. (1982) 'Constraints on the handling of Controversial Issues in Northern Ireland Post-Primary Schools', *British Educational Research Journal*, 8(1), 57–71.

McMullan, C. (2003) *A bridge or an island? An ethnographic study of an integrated school in Northern Ireland* (unpublished PhD thesis), Queen's University Belfast.

Milliken, J., and Gallagher, T. (1998) 'Three Rs – religion, ritual and rivalry: Strategic planning for integrated education in Northern Ireland', *Educational Management and Administration*, 26(4), 443–56.

Moffat, C. (ed.) (1993) *Education Together for a Change*, Belfast: Fortnight Educational Trust.

Morgan, V., Dunn, S., Cairns, E., and Fraser, G. (1992) *Breaking the mould: The roles of parents and teachers in integrated schools in Northern Ireland*. Coleraine, University of Ulster.

Murray, D. (1983) 'Rituals and symbols as contributors to the culture of Northern Ireland primary schools', *Irish Educational Studies*, 3(2), 238–55.

Murray, D. (1985). *Worlds Apart: Segregated schools in Northern Ireland.* Belfast: Appletree Press.

O'Connor, S. (1980) Reports – 'Chocolate Cream Soldiers: Evaluating an Experiment in Non-Sectarian Education in Northern Ireland', *Curriculum Studies*, 12(3), 263–70.

O'Connor, U., Hartop, B., and McCully, A. (2002) *A review of the schools community relations programme 2002.* Bangor: Department of Education.

Smith A. (2001) 'Religious Segregation and the Emergence of Integrated Schools in Northern Ireland', *Oxford Review of Education*, 1 December, 27(4), 559–75.

Smith, A. (2003) 'Citizenship Education in Northern Ireland: beyond national identity?' *Cambridge Journal of Education*, 33(1), 15–31.

Smith, A., and Dunn, S. (1990) *Extending Inter School Links.* Coleraine: University of Ulster.

Smith, A., and Robinson, A. (1992) *Education for Mutual Understanding: Perceptions and Policy.* Coleraine: University of Ulster.

Smith, A., and Robinson, A. (1996) *Education for Mutual Understanding: The initial statutory years.* Coleraine: University of Ulster.

Smith, M. (2005) *Reckoning with the Past: Teaching history in Northern Ireland,* Lanham, MD: Lexington Books.

Taylor, A. (1992) 'The Bond and Break Between Us', *English Education*, 26(3), 24–30.

UNESCO Centre (2009) *Evaluation of the pilot introduction of education for local and global citizenship into the revised Northern Ireland Curriculum.* Coleraine: University of Ulster.

NORMAN RICHARDSON

3 Formation: The Roots of Education for Diversity and Mutual Understanding

> ... What is required is a wholesale reassessment of aims and objectives and relative priorities – not within the schools alone but within the whole education system – in the light of the needs of this community and the children who are growing up in it.
>
> — JOHN MALONE, 1972

It could be argued that a study of the origins of education for diversity and mutual understanding in Northern Ireland is of purely academic and historical interest when set against the challenges of implementing its ideals within education today. An alternative view, however, is that to understand the roots and growth of such an important concept is to gain deeper insights into its present form and practice so as to be able to shape future practice more effectively. The roots of what came to be known as 'EMU' do go deep – much more so than has sometimes been perceived within the educational community – and an awareness of the nature of those roots is crucial for those who wish to emphasise the significance of education's contribution to the shaping of a democratic and inclusive society, in Northern Ireland and in the wider world.

Over a period of almost four decades these concepts have nudged at the education system in Northern Ireland under different names and forms, just as they have done in many other parts of the world. For most of the 1970s the terminology was that of *community relations education*. As the 1980s brought greater cohesion to the concept a new name was sought and found in Education for Mutual Understanding, with the possibly less helpful acronym of EMU. The establishment of EMU and its partner Cultural Heritage (CH) in the statutory Northern Ireland Curriculum of the early 1990s brought greater public awareness of the idea, though perhaps not sufficient clarity as to the purposes and processes of mutual understanding. As the 1990s drew to a close disappointment with the apparent lack of impact of EMU and CH gave rise to a call for a harder edge and sharper focus to such work. At the time of writing these concerns have been re-shaped into two new areas within the Revised Northern Ireland Curriculum, commencing in 2007 – Personal Development and Mutual Understanding for primary schools and Local and Global Citizenship (one element of 'Learning for Life and Work') in the post-primary sector.

Several dominant inter-related themes and factors can be perceived in the process which has led to the establishment of education for diversity and mutual understanding within and beyond the statutory curriculum in Northern Ireland. These are the following:

- the regular and growing critique of separate education systems for children from Catholic and Protestant backgrounds in Northern Ireland, especially within the context of continuing civil unrest and violence;
- the pressure for integrated education and related educational initiatives;
- the influence of experimental curriculum development programmes and related academic research in relation to the humanities and social education;
- the work of voluntary 'peace and reconciliation' organisations committed to the improvement of inter-community relationships;
- a recognition (based on experience in other countries) of the importance of finding creative ways of exploring controversial social, political and religious issues through the school curriculum (as in community relations work in general);
- a horizon-widening internationalist approach to education expressed in concepts such as Education for International Understanding, Development/Global Education and European Awareness;
- awareness of experience in multicultural and inter-cultural education, human rights education, anti-racism and peace education in a number of other countries, particularly Britain and the United States (and, more recently, in Europe);

- the particular influence of American programmes in the field of conflict management, co-operative skills, mediation, etc.;
- the increasing involvement of government in community relations and equity issues, and a growing public awareness of the importance of such initiatives.

While the thrust of this chapter (and the following one) is based on a more or less chronological account of these developments, it will be helpful to keep these themes in mind as a backdrop as the narrative progresses. (The political and policy context of this process is dealt with in Chapter 2.)

Naming the Concept

The scepticism towards EMU which was sometimes evident within educational circles or the general public at certain times may well have been linked to the belief that it was a government-imposed attempt to get schools to achieve a 'solution' to Northern Ireland's conflicts which had so far eluded them. This was reinforced at the introduction of the 1989 Education Reform (Northern Ireland) Order by the high profile approach adopted by Dr. Brian Mawhinney, Minister of Education in the Northern Ireland Office (for the unusually long period of January 1986 to December 1990). Mawhinney, a controversial figure with a Northern Irish family background, was at the time moving steadily upwards in the echelons of the Conservative Party and Government, and seemed to be generally happy to claim the credit for the introduction of EMU. But while his contribution was significant – not least as a politician with 'clout' setting EMU into a statutory educational framework – it is important to emphasise that by the time of its statutory introduction 'the EMU idea' had been in development for almost two decades. Indeed, it has been suggested that if it had been nothing more than a government imposition there would have been severe difficulties in persuading teachers to take it on. Its strength was precisely in its long gestation period; or (to amend the metaphor), its educational roots were clearly deep enough by 1989 to support EMU as a newly flowering statutory educational theme.

Brian Mawhinney did not invent EMU – certainly not the concept and not even the name. The actual term 'Education for Mutual Understanding' was agreed in a formal sense by the first meeting, in June 1983, of a committee established by NICED (the Northern Ireland Council for Educational Development, a precursor of the NI Council for Curriculum, Examinations and Assessment – CCEA). Set up as a 'Specialist Steering Group on Community Relations' the new term was adopted enthusiastically as a perceivably more neutral and less controversial term than some of the possible alternatives such as 'Peace Education' or even 'Community Relations Education'. The mutual understanding terminology occurs in earlier documentation, however, in materials published by the Schools' Cultural Studies Project and UNESCO (see below). But the underlying concept, with or without the name, is apparent as a recurring theme in educational theory and history in Northern Ireland as teachers, politicians, church leaders and others have acknowledged at different times and places that education at its best does have the capacity to contribute to the improvement of relationships between divided communities.

The purpose of these chapters is to provide an alternative perspective to the view that EMU was an ephemeral whim of remote politicians or academics, and to suggest that it has grown up over a lengthy period from a range of experiences and ideas. The chronology outlined here will be most useful when read alongside Chapter 1, which reflects thematically on the development of the concept and offers a rationale.

Separate Education Systems

At the outbreak of 'The Troubles' in 1969 many observers, from within and from outside Northern Ireland, commented sharply and negatively on what they perceived as the divisive (and, some would add, sectarian) effects of the Province's education system – or, more accurately, its separate education *systems*, functioning in parallel for each of the two dominant religio-cultural communities. McEwan (1990, p. 133) has described them as 'two almost mutually exclusive school systems [which] were the outward manifestations of a deeper divergence of identities between Protestants and Catholics'. It is hardly surprising that Northern Ireland's schools should reflect the divided and controversial nature of the society. But education was sucked into the controversy even more by the assertion that it is, in itself, a part of the problem (which at least some would dispute) and thereby that it must be part of the answer (which perhaps fewer would dispute).

However, awareness of the potentially malign effects of educational separation (or, if a more controversial term is preferred, *segregation*) was not new. It had informed the desire of the authorities in the early 19th century to set up a national system of education which would cater for all, just as it featured a century later in the attempts of the new Northern Ireland government to establish non-denominational schools in the 1923 Education Act. Both attempts ultimately failed, largely due to the lack of enthusiasm or even outright opposition of the churches and the tacit acceptance of church views on the part of the general public and the educational authorities. While on the one hand the Roman Catholic hierarchy has promoted educational separateness by insisting on schools with a 'Catholic ethos' for Catholic children, it is clear that on the other hand the activities of some of the Protestant Church leaderships at the time of the 1925 and 1930 Education Acts and since have, in Rex Cathcart's judgement, been responsible for '*perverting* [present writer's emphasis] the non-denominational character of the state schools' (Cathcart, 1990, p. 4).

Yet the spirit of challenge to the norm of educational separation and the likely negative attitudes which might grow from it was evident even in the nineteenth century. The much quoted Catholic Bishop James Doyle of Kildare and Leighlin gave clear support to the original shared concept of the National Schools (and unsuspectingly to the late twentieth century advocates of integrated education) when he wrote:

> I do not know any measures which would prepare the way for a better feeling in Ireland than uniting children at an early age, and bringing them up in the same school, leading them to commune with one another and to form those little intimacies and friendships which often subsist through life. (Doyle, 1830, qtd. in Moody and Beckett, 1959, 426–7)

Doyle's relatively liberal spirit, however, was soon to be swept aside by the ultramontanist movement, and statements like this are hard to find from such sources thereafter.

Recognising the important role of education in developing attitudes of tolerance and respect the Commissioners of the National Schools issued a *General Lesson*[1] to all their schools from 1835 onwards:

> Christians should endeavour, as the Apostle Paul commands them, to live at peace with all men (Romans, c. 12, v.18), even with those of a different religious persuasion.
> Our Saviour, Christ, commanded his Disciples to love one another. He taught them to love even their enemies...
> Many men hold erroneous doctrines; but we ought not to hate or persecute them...
> If any persons treat us unkindly, we must not do the same to them...
> Quarrelling with our neighbours and abusing them, is not the way to convince them that we are in the right, and they in the wrong...
> We ought, by behaving gently and kindly to every one, to show ourselves followers of Christ, who, when he was reviled, reviled not again...
> (General Lesson)

While to modern ears the tone of the General Lesson may appear patronising (and this accounts for some of the reactions when Education Minister Mawhinney 'rediscovered' a copy of the Lesson in the Ulster Folk and Transport Museum in 1988 and had it sent to every school in Northern Ireland) it should be read in its nineteenth-century context and recognised for what it is – an early genuine attempt to promote mutual understanding through the curriculum.

The failure of these attempts to establish a system of education in which the various religious or cultural needs of children would be met while yet ensuring educational and social sharing has been much commented on, especially during the period of civil unrest and violence which followed after 1969. The cases for and against an integrated or shared system of education are well rehearsed and continue to raise strong passions on both

1   *General Lesson*: issued by the Commissioners for the National Schools in Ireland from 1835 onwards; copy displayed in the Ulster Folk and Transport Museum.

sides. Those who defend the status quo from either side of 'the community divide' have often argued that people feel comfortable and safe with educational separation and that integration of schools cannot take place without integration in the wider society. The suggestion that separate schools are a direct cause of a divided society is dismissed by some as over-simplistic in that such divisions are only the symptoms of a much greater problem. Sometimes a form of the cultural pluralist position has been taken up as an argument in favour of separate provision for distinct ethnic and religious groups, based on the ideal of a liberal society. The official position of the Catholic Church in Ireland, and indeed of many individual Catholics, remains strongly supportive of the retention of Catholic schools; the position of some Protestant church leaders has sometimes indicated a sense of regret for having handed over the former Protestant-managed schools to state control following the 1930 Education Act. Many others, however, from various religious-cultural backgrounds, have argued that at the very least educational separation heightens the effects of social, cultural and political divisions and provides an ever firmer base for polarisation of the communities (for instance, Fraser, 1973; Cathcart, 1979; Murray, 1983; Irwin, 1991; Moffat, 1993; O'Connor, 2002). This position has perhaps been most effectively summed up by Seamus Dunn:

> The result is that Catholic and Protestant children do not meet or know each other as a group in any sustained or rooted way, and so have no personal experience against which to test the stereotypes and the half-truths about differences and beliefs. The separation begins as religious, but inevitably becomes both cultural and national. It is also both cause and effect... (Dunn, 1989, p. 33)

The phenomenon of educational separation on religious or cultural or ethnic grounds (often a combination of all of these) is certainly not unique to Northern Ireland, and similar issues are evident in other regions where there has been inter-community division and conflict (see, for instance, Gallagher, 2004).

Attempts to overcome the impact of educational separation in Northern Ireland have developed in two often distinct but by no means mutually exclusive directions during the last decades of the twentieth century. Some have taken the radical route of attempting to change the system by promoting integrated education, and since 1981 this has been a process rewarded by many achievements and successes. Others, however, accepting (reluctantly or otherwise) the likely continuation of largely separate systems for the foreseeable future and conscious of the considerable numbers of children continuing to attend separate institutions (still significantly around 90 per cent in the early years of the twenty-first century according to Department of Education statistics) have recognised that there is much to be done to improve the present system and to create curricular, inter-school and collaborative opportunities for building awareness and respect, whatever views may be held about ultimate changes. This, generally speaking, has been the route of education for diversity and mutual understanding (under its various names and forms over the years), and is, of course, the primary focus of this study.

Experiment and Frustration (1970–1982)

While it is undoubtedly the case that some teachers and others concerned with education have long sought ways of countering or minimising the effects of educational separation, it is only in very recent years that this has begun to relate to any co-ordinated effort or to involve significant numbers of schools. Those who pursued such work in the context of the politically chaotic and violent decade of the 1970s – mainly under the auspices of higher education institutions, individual schools and voluntary bodies – experienced many frustrations and disappointments in the process of attempting to make effective inroads into educational and community insularity.

Latterly recognised as something of a guru or prophetic figure in the process of the development of what became EMU, John Malone was a highly respected secondary school head teacher who, in January 1970 was seconded with the support of the then Ministry of Education and the Secondary Heads Association to establish and develop a *Schools Project in Community Relations*. Based at Queen's University, Malone's remit was to investigate the contribution schools might make to improve community relations, and to this end he explored several areas with the help of a number of field officers, some of them based in schools as members of staff.

The project included experiments in cross-community contact (in Malone's term, 'meeting') using venues such as the Ulster Folk Museum and Benburb Priory, and the adaptation of materials developed by the Schools Council in Britain. Extensive use was made of the Oxford-based *Moral Education Project* which aimed to help the 13–16 age group to adopt 'a considerate style of life'. Malone and his colleagues developed a local version of this programme, and it was piloted under the name 'We Live In Northern Ireland', with firm plans for publication by Longmans in 1972. Topics were to be used in graded sequence, beginning with simple inter-personal relationships, then group relationships and conflicts, discussion of 'in-groups' and 'out-groups', religious divisions, including those in Northern Ireland, and finally national and international problems (QUB, c. 1971, p. 7). In April 1972 the Schools Council, in consultation with the N.I. Ministry of Education, suddenly decided not to proceed with publication on the grounds that the materials were too 'politically sensitive'. A well-piloted adaptation of the York-based *General Studies Project* met a similar fate. In an interview between Malone and the then Minister for Education (under the new Direct Rule arrangements), Paul Channon, Malone was deeply hurt at the Minister's 'arrogant and abrasive' attitude (in the words of one of his colleagues who was present). His written report does not completely disguise his bitterness at this, nor does it hide his considerable continuous frustration at the attitude which he found within the N.I. Curriculum Committee: 'the Project in Community Relations always appeared to be an embarrassment to it' (Malone, 1972, p. 37). This is confirmed by Maurice Hayes, a senior civil servant who was responsible at this time for the Northern Ireland Community Relations Commission, for which Malone was the educational adviser:

> [Malone] raised hackles in the educational establishment... by his insistence that community relations work had to go far beyond the curriculum, and had to involve school structures and government and the manner in which the school engaged with the individual pupil. ... his pioneering work was disgracefully ignored by the sceptical and non-practising pundits in the Ministry of Education. (Hayes, 1995, p. 90)

It is not difficult to see why Malone's work is, with hindsight, perceived as 'an early vision' (Kilmurray, 1984, p. 3), and he continued to animate and motivate a group of educators who were concerned about the role of education in a divided society. Malone's 1972 Report is full of insights which appear to have been 'rediscovered' several times over the intervening years, not always with awareness of Malone's own findings. Of particular interest is his prophetic observation that 'the danger which faces a project in community relations is that teachers and pupils will see it primarily as certain selected teachers doing a certain type of thing.' But what is really necessary, he suggests, is 'the creation of an extra dimension of awareness within every teacher's work', and: '... What is required is a wholesale reassessment of aims and objectives and relative priorities – not within the schools alone but within the whole education system – in the light of the needs of this community and the children who are growing up in it.' (Malone, 1972, p. 4)

Among his other advice was that 'it is important that joint activities should not be seen as extra or special' (ibid., p. 10), and he warned that single one-off meetings were of little use. Schools need to examine the whole range of what they offer to pupils, he argued, giving special attention to staff-pupil relations, overall policy planning and the concept of the school as a democratic institution.

Malone, who died in 1982 (ironically only a few months before the Department of Education took initiatives along the lines that he had advocated ten years earlier) was deeply committed to the concepts of 'education in values' and education for renewal and social reconstruction, and he recognised that schools would have to find ways of tackling contentious issues as part of such processes. Nevertheless a recurring theme in his writing is the warning that schools alone cannot change Northern Irish society, and that the task will be a long-term one. It would take another quarter century before these insights of John Malone were to appear to impact significantly on official thinking about education and society.

If the prevailing attitude at the time, for officialdom as for many teachers, was one of wariness about venturing into such issues for fear of making matters worse and dragging schools into political controversy, there were others in the system as well as Malone who were prepared to challenge this. In a paper entitled 'Education and Cultural Change' (presented at a conference in 1973 but not published until 1976), Malcolm Skilbeck, then Professor of Education at what was at the time the New University of Ulster, focused attention not just on the divisions of the system, but rather more sharply and provocatively on the role of the Province's teachers. Arguing that in a divided schools system 'the divisions and the differences of values and belief are very clearly exhibited in various aspects of the lives of the pupils, teachers and parents', Skilbeck described the culture which they perpetuate as being 'militant... highly ideological... expansionist, aggressive and sectarian'. It is also 'encapsulated and fixed', 'thin and translucent', lacking in variety, complexity, diversity and openness and 'highly reproductive'. Teachers, he argued, participate in this process to the extent that they are 'naive bearers of (sectarian) culture' (the word in brackets being used, according to contemporary accounts, when the paper was delivered orally), and that they are insufficiently reflective and reflexive about it. (Skilbeck, 1976)

Skilbeck's case was that to opt for education only as 'an oasis of calm', as in the past many teachers have done, is not a neutral position; it is, in the analysis of many who have worked in this area of concern, to side with the continuation of a status quo which is ultimately harmful to children and society in general. Like Malone, Skilbeck was committed to the concept of the school as a democratic institution, and thereby to the view that education should not, whether by sins of omission or commission, perpetuate sectarian, exclusive and antagonistic attitudes. This is the base-line argument of those who have espoused a reconstructionist position in Northern Ireland, however 'minimalist' (to use Skilbeck's term).

Undoubtedly the most significant programme of work of the 1970s – spanning the period between Malone's pioneering and the initial government interventions of the early 1980s – was the Coleraine-based *Schools Cultural Studies Project* (SCSP) which was originally conceived in 1973 by Skilbeck. The project proper took place from 1974 to 1980 and its influence continued well into the late 1980s by the independent organisation to which it had given rise, the Association of Teachers of Cultural and Social Studies (ATCSS). From 1976 the Project was directed by Alan Robinson of the University of Ulster, who remained at the forefront of community relations education in Northern Ireland for many years.

Based on Skilbeck's reconstructionist approach, and considerably influenced by the Schools' Council *Humanities Curriculum Project* in Britain (Stenhouse, 1970), the Project's basic aims were to:

1. develop creative experimental approaches in schooling and curriculum;
2. develop pupils' skills in clarifying their personal values;
3. cultivate increased modes of sensitivity and tolerance; and
4. encourage personal awareness and mutual understanding in social relationships among school pupils in Northern Ireland. (SCSP, 1978)

A carefully graded mixed ability programme of materials for secondary schools was produced, starting with consideration of personal awareness and identity, moving through the family, communities, issues of territory and terrorism and, in Year 5 (15- to 16-year-olds), concluding with consideration of Northern Ireland as a divided society. The principal strategy to be employed was discussion, and, as the years went by, joint work between schools was encouraged and incorporated as much as possible. In the later years of the project local trails were developed exploring the features of the conflicting communities as a basis for inter-school discussion. Despite the limited number of schools involved, the cumulative influence of the SCSP over more than a decade was substantial.

One 'spin-off' of the Project was the development of a Primary Schools Educational Trails Project, commencing in 1977, involving a score of schools in the Londonderry area. These schools adopted the strategies of fieldwork and joint-work, based around local trails, although joint inter-school work developed only slowly with teachers advising against 'forcing' and 'rushing'.

In an independent evaluation published in 1980 it was suggested that the great success of the Project was to have introduced an effective strategy for dealing with controversial issues in the curriculum (Jenkins, 1980, p. 23), and Clem McCartney, writing some years later, was also positive in his assessment of SCSP because 'it showed publicly that controversial issues can be successfully handled in the school situation provided the teachers have the necessary skill and there is proper preparation' (McCartney, 1986, p. 106).

Alan McCully, who served for a time as an SCSP seconded field officer, later emphasised the importance of joint work in the project, suggesting that: 'the longer SCSP progressed the greater was the absurdity of discussing highly controversial issues in the segregated environment of the Northern Ireland classroom. The confidence to bring the pupils together grew from the enriching experience of the two sets of teachers working together' (McCully, 1985, p. 63).

By any account the Schools Cultural Studies Project is a giant among the educational community relations initiatives of the 1970s and 1980s, and its experience played an important role in the development of later strategies.

Other significant diversity education work during this period preceding the formal promotion of EMU by the educational authorities focused on specific curriculum subjects, notably Religious Education and History. Particularly important in this regard is the *Religion in Ireland Project* and other related projects headed by John Greer and colleagues, also based at the then New University of Ulster. Religious Education (RE) had normally been perceived as induction into one or other religious tradition, and Greer and his colleagues were only too aware of how 'Religious Education may easily become part of the process of initiation into the tribalism in Northern Ireland' (Greer and McElhinney, 1985a, p. 11). Furthermore there was a widely accepted convention whereby RE was treated as a *shibboleth* with which educational authorities and institutions should not tamper. In this unpromising climate Greer proposed an alternative model of RE, based on a reconstructionist approach, which was about understanding and respect built on awareness of *both* the Protestant and Catholic traditions. Greer's working thesis was that RE must make substantial use of discussion techniques to approach controversial issues in the classroom and that teachers need to be properly trained and equipped in appropriate pedagogical skills. He and his colleagues developed a series of materials designed to help young people to 'grasp the nettle' in relation to divisive religious and community issues which had been chosen on the basis of Greer's own ongoing research. Materials were developed by project teachers, piloted by them and eventually published (though after a long delay) in 1985 (Greer and McElhinney, 1985b). Teaching strategies were encouraged which would start with the pupils' own experiences, feelings, and the feelings of others. Visits to a range of church buildings and/or acts of worship were also proposed, and guidance offered on how to carry these out.

In reviewing the impact of the project, Eugene McElhinney recognised that teachers had some difficulty with the open discussion aspects of the programme, and also that there was wariness and reluctance about visiting churches 'across the community'. This led to a final phase of the project which was designed to improve and develop pedagogical skills in these areas. In their own assessments Greer and McElhinney noted 'only limited success', concluding that 'schools do not have the primary role in promoting change in society'.

> While we have no definite 'hard' evidence of the project changing intolerant attitudes, we do have evidence from teachers and pupils of greater interest in and understanding of the 'other community'; (McElhinney, 1983, p. 450)

> Schools in general and religious education in particular have a limited though none the less important role in creating better community relations. (Greer and McElhinney, 1984, pp. 341–2)

This forward looking project undoubtedly had a profound impact on a number of RE teachers who found inspiration for developing further aspects of shared and inclusive approaches. As one observer remarked: 'What has been so encouraging a feature of the Project is the way in which teachers from both Roman Catholic and Protestant traditions have grown in mutual trust and in the ability to help each other' (McElhinney et al., 1988, p. 94).

However, the innate religious conservatism and over-caution of many in the teaching profession, Catholic and Protestant alike, meant that these approaches did not impact the system as a whole. (Particular disappointment was expressed, for instance, that the 1992 *Core Syllabus for Religious Education*, despite being developed on a notional cross-community basis, seemed to have learned nothing from the experience of projects like *Religion in Ireland*, and to have backed off from its potential for promoting mutual understanding.)

Important developments were also taking place in relation to teaching History. Long recognised as a potential briar patch in the curriculum, official education policy in Northern Ireland worked against the teaching of Irish History in all kinds of schools. Even in the 1930s a Schools Inspector had observed that this neglect was 'a steep place going down into a sea of ignorance' (PRONI, 1938)! In effect many History teachers in schools serving the Protestant community were on the whole quite happy to avoid Ireland, while Catholic schools either omitted it too, in line with Ministry of Education guidelines or to meet the requirements of exam syllabuses, or else taught it somewhat covertly with a strongly nationalistic interpretation of events. There is evidence that this had been a concern of some educationists for a long time, but the 1960s and 1970s saw new initiatives, fronted by Rex Cathcart of Queen's University and Jack Magee of St. Mary's College and aided by adventurous BBC publications and policy developments in the newly established Northern Ireland Schools' Examination Council. This was reinforced at the level of curriculum development in the establishment by the Queen's University Teachers' Centre (in association with the Wiles Trust and DENI) in 1976 of the Wiles History Week for teachers. At the Wiles Week Open Lecture in 1978, Cathcart articulated the innovations: 'The thrust of our Irish History teaching today is... the promotion of the understanding of difference, the creation of a willing and enthusiastic acceptance of pluralism' (Cathcart, 1979, p. 13).

This approach to history teaching was strengthened by activities such as the annual 'Studying Our Past' History Competition/Project (operated by the Churches Central Committee on Community Work in association with the Belfast Telegraph) which, for a number of years, enabled some schools (mainly primary) to explore difficult historical and social issues through joint work. This steady, long-term developmental process in relation to History teaching came to fruition after 1989 when the History programme of study in the Northern Ireland Curriculum embodied these ideals within a statutory framework for all schools.

By the late 1970s the concept of peace education was attracting interest amongst some educators in Northern Ireland. One of the earliest innovatory contributions was made by an American academic, Dr Joe Fahey, Director of the Peace Studies Institute at Manhattan College, New York, who in 1977 was Visiting Research Fellow in the Department of Further Professional Studies in Education at Queen's University, Belfast. Fahey's approach was to encourage schools, universities and teacher-training institutions to introduce specific curricula and training in peace education, which he described as 'an academic response to the problems of human violence and injustice' (Fahey, 1978, p. 3). Such programmes, he argued, must include one or more of the themes of Conflict Resolution, Non-violence, War and Peace, Social Justice and World Order, although he recognised that at the primary school level the focus would be more on 'practical training in conflict resolution, on values formation and appreciation of other cultural outlooks' (ibid., p. 6). In Northern Ireland, Fahey suggested, Peace Studies was relevant to the immediate troubled situation but also to the longer term healing process of bringing reconciliation after the violence had ended. Among various practical proposals he promoted the establishment of a Northern Ireland peace education centre (which was eventually taken up by the Joint Peace Education Programme of the Irish Council of Churches and the Irish Commission for Justice and Peace in 1984).

A small-scale primary schools peace education initiative was set up by Daniel McQuade of St Joseph's College of Education (later merged into St. Mary's College), who, feeling that some of the global approaches to peace education which were being promoted at that time were too heavily cognitive and remote from the needs of society in troubled Belfast, took on board an American Quaker project, 'The Children's Creative Response to Conflict Program' (Pruzman et al., 1974). In 1978–9 this was piloted by McQuade's students in schools in troubled areas of East, West and North Belfast, and in-service courses on peace education were organised to make the work and its findings known. The programme was built on the themes of inter-personal relations and conflict-handling and an initial report recorded some satisfaction with the processes. Tentative plans were laid for further development, including its use 'on an interdenominational basis whenever possible' (McQuade, 1979). Many of the strands of this work were taken up later in the 1980s by the Londonderry-based Quaker Peace Education Project.

One project influenced in its early stages by Fahey's ideas was the *Joint Peace Education Programme* (later re-named *The Churches' Peace Education Programme*) of the Irish Council of Churches (which at that time represented eight Protestant denominations) together with the Irish

Commission for Justice and Peace (an Irish Catholic Episcopal Commission). Established in 1978, this was the direct outcome of an inter-Church report on violence, in which it was recommended that 'the teaching of religion in schools of both traditions must have explicitly and deliberately an ecumenical dimension' and that there should be 'a joint Committee to consider closer contact and co-operation between Roman Catholic and other schools' (Churches Joint Group, 1976, pp. 87 and 92).

The programme's work began very tentatively in adapting for use in Northern Ireland materials originally prepared in the Republic, but in 1979 a new programme of primary school peace education materials was planned, eventually to be published under the title 'Free to Be' in 1983 (ICC/ICJP, 1983). The areas of study included self-esteem, relationships with others, the environment, differences and similarities and the impact of symbols. This later extended into providing materials for the study of different churches, aimed at a younger age group than that targeted by Greer and colleagues, and the 'Looking at Churches and Worship in Ireland' programme (ICC/ICJP, 1985) was no less influential than the 'Religion in Ireland' materials (see above), remaining in print for many years.[2] Nevertheless those involved in developing this programme came increasingly to the conclusion that more urgent than the provision of good materials was the development of teacher awareness and skills in approaching these potentially controversial areas. The work of the programme's staff in developing in-service courses led them to argue for an altogether more systematic approach, as indeed Malone had done some years before.

A valuable point of contact for some schools in the mid- to late 1970s was through various programmes of extra-curricular meetings and discussions. This was perhaps most common between 6th Form groups from the Catholic and Protestant Voluntary Grammar Schools. While it bore little

---

2   Later developments through the 1980s and 1990s involved the Churches' Peace Education Programme in developing post-primary materials on conflict, violence and human rights, and further primary materials, including updates of the 'Free to Be' and 'Looking at Churches and Worship' materials. More influential was the production of early-years materials under the title of 'Little Pathways' (Hall, 1999–2003). The programme continued until 2005; for an over-view see Hall, 2005.

formal relationship to the curriculum it was nevertheless often encouraged by teachers, and it provided opportunities for joint discussion of religious, social and political issues in a context of trust-building. Such work often took place on a one-off or occasional basis, but at a more structured level the Inter-School Sixth Form Conference programme of the Christian Education Movement (CEM) Northern Ireland Council made some formal headway into schools through Religious Education Departments. The number and range of schools involved with CEM expanded considerably from the early 1980s onwards, although the programme was sometimes criticised for being superficial, based only on single, low-impact events. Another such initiative was Schools of Northern Ireland Together (SONIT), developed by the then Chaplain of Methodist College Belfast, the Rev. Henry Keys, in 1977 following a conference organised by senior pupils. This led, some years later, to the establishment of a more broadly based Greater-Belfast Sixth Form Group called *Peace and Reconciliation Inter-Schools Movement* (PRISM), also based in Methodist College on the initiative of Keys, with a similar programme of issues, discussions and joint actions. PRISM continued to facilitate such work into the mid-1990s.

Locally based educational research has played an increasingly valuable proactive role in the development of community relations education processes. From 1977, the interdisciplinary Centre for the Study of Conflict, based at the University of Ulster in Coleraine, initiated several important research projects in the related fields of segregated schools, integrated education, school links and EMU. In 1984, for instance, in its recommendations within the 'Schools Together?' report (Dunn et al, 1984) which had not found much evidence of inter-school co-operation, it suggested that the time seemed good for initiatives towards greater co-operation, and proposed a practical research project which it then undertook – the Inter-School Links Project, based initially in Strabane (see Dunn and Smith, 1989; Smith and Dunn, 1990). The Centre's approach effectively provided an objective, critical and creative overview while avoiding remote academic indifference, and it thereby became an active participant in the developmental process.

Throughout this period *The Corrymeela Community*, an ecumenical Christian organisation established in the years before the outbreak of the

Troubles, served many groups taking their initial steps in educational cross-community work. It provided excellent residential facilities for schools working together, as well as a supportive cross-community ethos, and also organised several conferences for teachers and teachers-in-training. The atmosphere of Corrymeela's residential centre on the North Antrim coast encouraged the tackling of hard issues in a spirit of trust and security, and many teachers gained inspiration there for further work back in school. Amongst its educational aims at this time Corrymeela aspired to 'support and encourage those who wish something new in terms of honesty, openness and trust in spite of the hurt, fear and bitterness that this Province is going through' (quoted in Kilmurray, 1984, p. 73). Corrymeela did not develop its own specific schools programme, or employ a full-time staff member in this field, until 1984, however, following which a more dynamic model of inter-group contact was progressively applied to the residential cross-community experience of children and young people (see below). This work has continued to develop over the decades since its initiation. (For a contemporary assessment of Corrymeela's impact see McCreary, 2007.)

Another important element in the process emanated from the advocacy of education for international understanding, which in the 1970s was particularly associated with the work of the Northern Ireland UNESCO Committee (funded by the Department of Education – DENI), the United Nations Association and the *Council for Education in World Citizenship* (CEWC). For a small but persistent group of schools this provided opportunities for entry into local issues and joint work. Teachers engaged in this series of projects were encouraged by a UNESCO document, forwarded by the Department of Education (DENI) in 1976 as a circular to all schools, which made recommendations concerning education for international understanding, co-operation and peace (UNESCO, 1974). Unfortunately DENI did not exploit the potential of this document for the local scene, and, outside the small number of already interested schools, the initiative had little impact.

Several of these early strands in the genesis of EMU were brought together in 1978 by Billy Mitchell (the principal, significantly, of an 'integrated' Further Education College) as part of a Northern Ireland UNESCO Committee Project which included a conference and a related book, both entitled *Education for Peace*. The Conference brought together teachers, youth leaders and representatives of Higher Education, Further Education, the Education and Library Boards and United Nations organisations. Recommendations from the conference and in the book encouraged schools to take seriously the relationship between local divisions and global issues and to infuse a commitment to peace education into the whole curriculum, taking care that such work was supported by the ethos of the school: 'The teacher's attitude to the students, his example of consideration and respect, can make an even greater contribution to education for peace than the lessons he teaches or the projects he organises' (Mitchell, 1978, p. 13).

Mitchell's vision, like that of John Malone some years before, pointed forward to the possibility of a more cohesive approach to educational community relations work: 'Good basic social education, followed by wisely planned contacts between young people from the two communities, can lead to better *mutual understanding*, and to that mutual consideration which is the sound foundation of a healthy society' (ibid., p. 44; author's italics).

The Watershed: Intervention and Policy (1982–1989)

In 1982 a number of groups and individuals from the programmes and projects described above, together with representatives of the Department of Education, joined forces to plan an educational conference on Peace and Development Education as part of that year's DENI Summer School programme at Stranmillis College. Only days before the conference took place DENI issued its *Circular 82/21*, marking a watershed in the Northern Ireland process of promoting education for diversity and mutual understanding. In this highly significant document (which, contrary to normal practice, was intended for individual teachers, not just schools) the improvement of community relations was described as the responsibility of all in the education system:

> Our educational system has clearly a vital role to play in the task of fostering improved relationships between the two communities in Northern Ireland. Every teacher, every school manager, Board member and trustee, and every educational administrator within the system has a responsibility for helping children to learn to understand and respect each other, and their differing customs and traditions, and of preparing them to live together in harmony in adult life. (DENI, 1982)

This newly found readiness to promote educational community relations by the Northern Ireland Department of Education seems to have been personally encouraged by the Direct Rule Education Minister Nicholas Scott and was supported by several key inspectors and civil servants. However, in the previous few months there had been considerable educational agitation over the Chilver Report (the Northern Ireland Higher Education Review Group), which had been published in March 1982 (HMSO, 1982). The Chilver committee's controversial proposals for the reorganisation (and in effect for the merger) of teacher training institutions had been met by significant and highly organised opposition on the part of the Catholic Church hierarchy and by ambivalence at best on the part of many in the protestant/unionist community; government had quickly backed off from the implementation of the proposals. There seems little doubt that along with a genuine commitment to the community relations process in education there was also a concern in some political quarters to offset some of the flack from the Chilver confrontation. (For an assessment of the responses to the Chilver Report see McMinn and Phoenix, 2005.)

A consultation process followed the Peace and Development Education conference, resulting in proposals being presented to the Northern Ireland Council for Educational Development (NICED) urging the establishment of a committee to co-ordinate such work in future, with support from the DENI Inspectorate and financial assistance. They were modest and perhaps cautious proposals, but they led, in 1983, to the establishment by NICED of the EMU Steering Committee, including representatives of several of the projects described above. The choice of name 'Education for Mutual Understanding' (as indicated at the beginning of this chapter) was certainly influenced by the presence of Billy Mitchell and others who had been involved in the 1978 *Education for Peace* conference and book.

One of the strengths of the EMU process following 1982–3 was that it had gained from a lengthy period of experimentation and bore the fruit of its own grass roots experience amongst members of the teaching profession prior to 1982, providing a sound basis for further development. In particular this experience helped to deliver EMU from the potential blandness of an over-cautious government initiative (although this was not entirely avoided). The experience of those who were committed to a process which involved strategies for joint work and teaching controversial issues gave the process a certain authenticity and strength.

The significance of this change of approach by government, whereby they became in effect both interventionist and reconstructionist, cannot be overstated, and since 1982 the promotion of community relations has been continuously stressed as a priority in education policy in the Province. From this time the Department of Education adopted an increasingly proactive position, after some years of only passive reaction since taking on responsibility for community relations in 1975. In an address in November 1982 to teachers meeting under the auspices of the East Belfast Community Council (which was soon to spawn the support agency *Community Relations in Schools* – CRIS), Education Minister Nicholas Scott outlined four basic principles which would be essential if real progress was to be made in educational community relations. These included the recognition of such work as a basic aim of education (relationships education as 'a fourth *R*', as he put it); the importance of involving parents; the need for structures to co-ordinate efforts; and, significantly, that the task must be presented as a challenge to young people: 'There must be a willingness to face the real issues which divide the community; to learn precisely where the other side stands on these issues; and to learn to accept and respect the other person's viewpoint' (Scott, 1982).

From time to time discussions ensued on the appropriateness of 'Education for Mutual Understanding' to describe these processes. Its potential for blandness sometimes served to irritate those who argued for a sharper edge to such work. Is 'understanding' an adequate objective? The process of understanding, it was argued, may simply lead people to appreciate more clearly why they dislike 'the other side'! It is worth noting that in Mitchell's 1978 book, cited above, 'Mutual Understanding' is indicated only as an intermediate stage in a process which should culminate in 'Mutual Respect and Friendship'. McCartney, in a 1986 survey for the Standing Advisory Conference on Human Rights, observed that very few of the organisations promoting EMU at that time made reference to the more divisive issues, such as social justice, in their statements of aims (McCartney, 1986). Seamus Dunn of the Centre for the Study of Conflict, in characterising EMU as the Northern Ireland version of multicultural education, also warned against blandness: '[EMU] must not simply be a search for some spurious underlying unity or lowest common denominator... Nor can it attempt to exclude controversy and aim for some form of "neutrality" which protects both sets of local sensitivities while informing neither' (Dunn, 1989, p. 36).

In the years following this commitment of government support for what became EMU a new atmosphere was created which opened up opportunities for the greater involvement of voluntary agencies (NGOs in current terminology). Several of these were organisations or programmes which had been taking shape during the 1970s (for instance the Corrymeela Schools Programme, the Co-operation North School Links Programme and the Churches' Joint Peace Education Programme) and which now benefited from the availability of funding to extend their programmes and appoint staff, often seconding experienced teachers to such posts. One of the particular strengths of some of the voluntary agencies, often working together, was in their capacity to combine opportunities for inter-school contact between pupils and teachers with relevant curriculum innovations.

Practical developments 'on the ground' were also being strengthened by the continuing involvement of academic institutions in providing a critique of and a rationale for the approaches which were being applied in the schools. The Coleraine-based Centre for the Study of Conflict remained closely involved in the processes, promoting research and stimulating active participation on the part of schools and others. One of the most influential books of the period was a study by Ed Cairns (of the Psychology Department at the University of Ulster) of cross-community contact initiatives in Northern Ireland, in which he applied the Social Identity Theory of Henri Tajfel and argued that programmes designed to improve understanding through contact must function at an *inter-group*

level rather than just at an individual or inter-personal level (Cairns, 1987).
Little by little these studies impacted many of the voluntary organisations
operating at this time and had a formative influence on their developing
programmes. While some groups continued to hold back from controversial
discussions, others took a more proactive and sharper approach. Carmel
Heaney, as Corrymeela Schools Worker from 1984 to 1989, described how
groups visiting Corrymeela from different schools were prepared for their
time together by being invited to bring along and discuss their own, often
divisive, cultural symbols:

> The pupils are told that they will be meeting 'the other sort' and are invited to bring
> with them symbols, images that suggest a pride in their own heritage and cultural
> tradition. ... After a meal and a walk, the group get together through ice-breaker games.
> The young people then work together in pairs and regroup in a large circle to name
> and articulate their questions and concerns. This is often the first time the hidden
> agenda of sectarianism is voiced... When the realities of the divisions are named, a
> more real understanding of each other's perceptions grows. (Heaney, 1989, p. 15).

Other projects were newly established within an atmosphere of openness
to such developments. One of the best known of these was the *Quaker
Peace Education Project*, directed by Jerry Tyrrell, based at the University of
Ulster's Magee College in Derry and linked to the work of the Centre for
the Study of Conflict and, originally, the Western Education and Library
Board. Initially funded on an international initiative of the Religious
Society of Friends (Quakers), the project emphasised the importance of
affirmation, communication and co-operation, and developed training and
skills in conflict management, prejudice reduction and mediation (see
Chapter 7). The skills and facilities offered by QPEP were regularly used
by other voluntary and statutory agencies in EMU training programmes,
although teachers were often found to be uneasy about the clash between
their relatively formal training and the necessity of informality and even
unorthodoxy in applying such techniques. (The project eventually transformed in the 1990s into *the EMU-Promoting School Project*, with similar
aims and programmes.)

Operating at a rather different level, the *European Studies Project*
(Ireland and Great Britain) was established in 1986 by DENI in order to

develop joint work between post-primary schools in Northern Ireland, the Republic of Ireland and England and also with other schools in continental Europe. Amongst its stated aims the Project sought 'to help pupils to understand relationships within these islands in the context of Europe... to equip students with a variety of skills, particularly those of communication and co-operation...' and 'to make students aware of being members of a wider international community' (European Studies, 1991). Studies of similarities and differences and of controversial issues, local, regional and European, provided a focus for much of the work and units were developed and piloted in Geography, History, Modern Languages and various dimensions of Personal and Social Education. Considerable use was made of information technology and, in particular, of electronic mail facilities, and also of inter-school contact. Active learning and associated participatory pedagogical techniques were encouraged, in classroom work at all stages and in the Sixth Form residential courses. Opportunities were opened up by the project for exploration of local contentious issues in a way which avoided insularity, and of broader issues in a manner which did not neglect the local context. Ill-conceived notions of using 'distancing procedures' as an excuse for skirting local problems were not evident in this work, and the project achieved the long-term involvement of schools. (The project later became a formally established Programme, in support of citizenship education, committed to the furtherance of 'tolerance, mutual understanding and appreciation of the cultures of others'.)[3]

During the highly formative period between 1983 and 1988 the NICED EMU Steering Committee met regularly and set out to develop a programme of work which would serve as a model of good practice for schools. Over its lifetime membership included representatives from schools, the Schools Inspectorate, the Higher Education institutions, the Education and Library Boards and the voluntary sector, enabling valuable contacts to be established. Two field officers were appointed to work directly with teachers at the secondary and primary levels, and their activities included the piloting of inter-school contact programmes, experiments with the use

3   See <http://www.european-studies.org> (accessed 25 June 2010).

of email to maintain contact between schools, association with the development of curriculum materials and involvement with in-service training. While the committee's work was painfully slow in its early stages (leading some members to believe that this was a deliberate policy) the pioneering work of the field officers helped to give the process confidence and momentum, and in its last eighteen months the committee focused on considering models for future structures and developing guidance materials for schools (influenced by the success of the *Primary Guidelines* and *Eleven-to-Sixteen* curriculum development processes which NICED had established during this period). *Education for Mutual Understanding: A Guide* (NICED, 1988) was eventually published and distributed to all schools in November 1988, but at the point of its public launch the Education Minister, Brian Mawhinney, unexpectedly stood down the NICED committee, promising new structures to run alongside his plans for EMU within the imminent education reform process. In fact the committee was never replaced, and many activists in the field believed this to be to the detriment of the future development of EMU as an educational theme. Perhaps the most important feature of the five years of the committee's existence was the drawing together of expertise and the growth in confidence that such work was indeed educationally sound and credible and able to influence and encourage the educational system as a whole to take it seriously.

In 1987, partly as a result of effective piloting carried out by the NICED EMU field officers, a DENI Circular announced the establishment of a new scheme to encourage greater joint work and co-operation between schools (DENI, 1987). The *Cross-Community Contact Scheme* (re-named ten years later as the *Schools' Community Relations Programme*) offered funding for schools prepared to take up joint work under certain specified conditions. While some schools had maintained such links over a long period with no public funding the scheme gave new impetus to the idea and established a clear link with the curricular development of EMU. Although take-up was modest in the first year, within two years the funds available were being increased and there was a steady growth in involvement with the scheme over the next five years. Department of Education figures suggest that while in the first year of the scheme (1987–8) there was take-up by only 13 per cent of primary and 24 per cent of post-primary schools; by 1994–5 this had risen to 42 per cent of primary and 59 per cent of post-primary schools (rising still further during the later 1990s in the case of primary schools, but indicating decline in the early 2000s).[4] However, these statistics give only a limited quantitative picture of a much more complex pattern of schools' involvement in the scheme, which will be discussed in the following chapter.

There can be little doubt that the contact scheme has produced significant examples of good practice in EMU but also some disturbing examples of cynical abuse. Some schools have been enormously enriched by the broadened horizons of working with the teachers and pupils of another school 'across the community' and have experienced improved relationships beyond the confines of the schools themselves. Others have undoubtedly made superficial use of a funding opportunity without adequate reference to the purposes of the funding (and despite the stringent application and evaluation processes which were always required by DENI and, more recently, the Education and Library Boards). An early study by the Inspectorate of fifty-one primary and thirty-eight post-primary schools involved in the scheme may with hindsight appear rather superficial in its conclusion that:

> The findings of this survey reveal an encouraging picture of the range and quality of cross-community contact among young people in schools throughout Northern Ireland... The joint work seen during the survey was of high quality... Two consistent and positive findings are that teachers have a firm belief in the benefits of joint work, and that pupils display obvious enjoyment in one another's company and enthusiasm for working together. (DENI, 1991, p. 25)

However, in some estimations one of the greatest difficulties with the whole process of developing education for diversity and mutual understanding was the persistent but inaccurate belief that to be engaged in a contact

---

4   The percentage of *schools* involved in the SCRP gives a somewhat misleading picture, especially in the case of post-primary schools. When the percentages of *pupils* are noted the figures are much smaller: for example, around twenty percent of primary pupils were involved fairly consistently during the late 1990s, but only three to four percent of post-primary pupils (O'Connor et al, 2002, p. 49)!

programme was equivalent to 'doing EMU' instead of seeing it as one possible strategy among others. The establishment of a scheme to fund contact from 1987 may inadvertently have done a disservice to the development, from 1989, of EMU as an educational theme *within* the curriculum.

In their review of developments up to the end of the 1980s, particularly in relation to the establishment of improved cross-community links and relationships between schools, Smith and Dunn offered a cautiously optimistic assessment of the situation:

> The momentum for change which developed from pioneering work in the late Sixties and Seventies, has continued into the Eighties, and seen changes within the structure of education which recognise that cultural development through the curriculum is an important issue... The transition which has yet to take place is widespread acceptance of the steps which schools need to take so that their practice is more than cosmetic. (Smith and Dunn, 1990, p. 58)

References

Cairns, E. (1987) *Caught in Crossfire: Children and the Northern Ireland Conflict*, Belfast: Appletree Press.

Cathcart, R. (1979) *Teaching Irish History: Wiles Week Open Lecture 1978*, Belfast: Queen's University Teachers' Centre.

Cathcart, R. (1990) 'The Politics of "No Change"', in Caul., L., (ed.), *Schools Under Scrutiny: The Case of Northern Ireland*, London: Macmillan Education.

Churches Joint Group (1976) *Violence in Ireland: A Report to the Churches*, Belfast and Dublin: Christian Journals Ltd./Veritas Publications.

DENI (1982) *The Improvement of Community Relations: The Contribution of Schools – Circular No. 1982/21*, 1 June, Belfast: Sport and Community Division, Department of Education for Northern Ireland.

DENI (1987) *Circular 1987/47: Cross-Community Contact Programme* (issued 13/10/87), Bangor: Department of Education for Northern Ireland.

DENI (1991) *Education for Mutual Understanding: The Cross-Community Contact Scheme – Report of a Survey by the Education and Training Inspectorate, 1989–90*, Bangor: Department of Education for Northern Ireland.

Dunn, S. (1989) 'Multicultural Education in the North of Ireland', in *The Irish Review No.6*, Spring, Cork University Press.

Dunn, S., Darby, J., and Mullan, K. (1984) *Schools Together?* Coleraine: University of Ulster Centre for the Study of Conflict.

European Studies (1991) extract from *European Studies Project Report, July 1991*, Belfast and Dublin.

Fahey, J.J. (1978) 'Peace Education: Its Relevance to Northern Ireland', *The Northern Teacher, Winter 1977–8*, 12(5), Belfast, INTO/UTU.

Fraser, M. (1973) *Children in Conflict*, Martin Secker and Warburg.

Gallagher, T. (2004) *Education in Divided Societies (Ethnic and Intercommunity Conflict)*, Basingstoke: Palgrave-Macmillan.

Greer, J.E., and McElhinney, E.P. (1984) 'The Project on Religion in Ireland: An Experiment in Reconstruction' in *Lumen Vitae*, 39(3), Brussels, International Centre for Studies in Religious Education.

Greer, J.E., and McElhinney, E.P. (1985a) *Irish Christianity: A Guide for Teachers*, Dublin: Gill and Macmillan.

Greer, J.E., and McElhinney, E.P. (1985b) *Irish Christianity: Five Units for Secondary Pupils*, Dublin: Gill and Macmillan.

Hall, E. (1999–2003) *Little Pathways* [four packs for the 4–7 age group], Belfast and Dublin: Churches' Peace Education Programme.

Hall, E. (2005) *A Celebration of the Churches' Peace Education Programme 1978–2005*, Belfast: Churches' Peace Education Programme.

Hayes, M. (1995) *Minority Verdict – Experiences of a Catholic Public Servant*, Belfast: Blackstaff Press.

Heaney, C. (1989) 'The Break and Bond Between Us', in *PACE Journal*, 21(1), Spring, Belfast: Protestant and Catholic Encounter.

HMSO (1982) *The Future of Higher Education in Northern Ireland. Report of the Higher Education Review Group for Northern Ireland* (Chilver Report), Belfast: Her Majesty's Stationery Office.

ICC/ICJP (1983) *Free To Be – Primary Schools Peace Education Programme*, Belfast and Dublin, Irish Council of Churches / Irish Commission for Justice and Peace.

ICC/ICJP (1985) *Looking at Churches and Worship in Ireland*, Belfast and Dublin: Irish Council of Churches, Irish Commission for Justice and Peace, Stranmillis College (rev. edn, 1993).

Irwin, C. (1991) *Education and the Development of Social Integration in Divided Societies*, Belfast: Dept. of Social Anthropology, Queen's University.

Jenkins, D., et al. (1980) *Chocolate, Cream, Soldiers*, Coleraine, New University of Ulster.

Kilmurray, A. (ed.) (1984) *Teaching Community Relations*, Belfast: Community Information Service.

Malone, J. (1972) *Schools' Project in Community Relations* (Personal Report: June 1972), Belfast: Queen's University.

McCartney, C. (1986) *Human Rights Education: Appendix D of the 1986 Report of the Standing Advisory Commission on Human Rights*, Belfast, HMSO.

McCreary, A. (2007) *In War and Peace: the Story of Corrymeela*, Belfast: Brehon Press.

McCully, A. (1985) 'The Relevance of the Teaching of Cultural and Social Studies to the Handling of Controversial Issues in the History Classroom', in Austin, R. (ed.), *Essays on History Teaching in Northern Ireland*, Coleraine: Faculty of Education Resource Centre, University of Ulster.

McElhinney, E.P., Harris, J.E., and Greer, J.E., (1988) *Classroom Discussion: New Approaches to Teaching in Religious Education*, Coleraine: University of Ulster.

McEwan, A. (1990) 'Education for Mutual Understanding', in Caul., L., (ed.), *Schools Under Scrutiny: The Case of Northern Ireland*, London: Macmillan Education

McMinn, R., and Phoenix, E. (2005) 'The Chilver Report: Unity and diversity', in *Irish Educational Studies*, 24(1), 3–17.

McQuade, D. (1979) *Conflict Resolution in the Classroom – Some reflections on a small-scale project in progress in Northern Ireland*, Belfast: St Joseph's College [private circulation].

Mitchell, W. (1978) *Education for Peace*, Belfast and Dublin, Christian Journals Ltd.

Moffat, C. (ed.) (1993) *Education Together for a Change – Integrated Education and Community Relations in Northern Ireland*, Belfast: Fortnight Educational Trust.

Moody, T.W. and Beckett, J.C. *Queen's Belfast, 1845–1949: The History of a University* (vol. 1, lvi), London, Faber, 1959.

Murray, D. (1983) 'Schools and Conflict', in Darby, J. (ed.) *Northern Ireland: The Background to the Conflict*, Belfast: Appletree Press, Syracuse University Press.

NICED (1988) *Education for Mutual Understanding – A Guide*, Belfast: Northern Ireland Council for Educational Development.

O'Connor, F. (2002) *A Shared Childhood – The story of integrated schools in Northern Ireland*, Belfast: Blackstaff Press.

O'Connor, U., Hartop, B., and McCully, A. (2002) *A Review of the Schools Community Relations Programme 2002: A Consultation Document*, Bangor: Department of Education.

PRONI (1938) Letter from Schools Inspector – Held in the Public Record Office for Northern Ireland.

Pruzman, P. et al (1974/1988) *The Friendly Classroom for a Small Planet – A Handbook on Creative Approaches to Living and Problem Solving for Children*, Philadelphia, Children's Creative Response to Conflict Program/New Society Publishers.

QUB, (c. 1971) *We Live in Northern Ireland – Draft Teachers' Guide: Moral Education (Northern Ireland) Project*, Belfast, Queen's University.

Scott, N. (1982) *Extracts from Message on Community Relations by Nicholas Scott MP*, 23 November, Belfast, NI Information Service, Stormont.

SCSP (1978) 'Objectives of the SCSP', in *Network No.6*, March, Coleraine: Schools Cultural Studies Project.

Skilbeck, M. (1976) 'Education and Cultural Change', *in Compass: Journal of the Irish Association for Curriculum Development*, 5(2).

Smith, A., and Dunn, S. (1990) *Extending Inter-School Links*, Coleraine: University of Ulster Centre for the Study of Conflict.

Stenhouse, L. (1970) *The Humanities Curriculum Project: An Introduction*, London: Heinemann.

UNESCO (1974) *Recommendation Concerning Education for International Understanding, Co-operation and Peace and Education Relating to Human Rights and Fundamental Freedoms*, Paris: United Nations Educational, Social and Cultural Organisation.

NORMAN RICHARDSON

4 Transformation: Diversity and Mutual Understanding in the Statutory Curriculum

> Through the twin cross-curricular themes of Education for Mutual Understanding and Cultural Heritage... strides were made inside and outside the classroom to bring children from opposing communities together with a view to increasing understanding of difference and reducing fear and prejudice. ... While there has been little methodological evaluation of the lasting impact of such initiatives, there is some evidence that addressing the real issues for children and young people did not go far enough. ... what we actually will require to do will be to ensure that there are sufficient educational practitioners with demonstrable emotional competence... who can facilitate children and young people at the hard edges of their personal, social and civic understanding.
>
> — LEITCH, 2001, pp. 74–5

Towards A Statutory Framework (1988–1999)

Documentation issued in March 1988 made proposals for education reform in Northern Ireland, prominent among which was a promise on the part of government to facilitate the development of integrated education and '... to continue to support programmes and activities which bring together children from the two traditions in the interests of fostering greater tolerance and mutual understanding' (DENI, 1988a, p. 6). Further documentation later that year was more specific. The proposed new statutory curriculum was to include Education for Mutual Understanding (EMU) and Cultural Heritage (CH) as two of the six new Cross-Curricular Themes (a term which was later helpfully amended to Educational Themes, although the 'cross-curricular' tag continued to be widely used) (DENI, 1988b, p. 6). There was some surprise that Cultural Heritage was to be separated out as a distinct but nonetheless closely related theme to EMU. (The claim that Education Minister Brian Mawhinney had invented the concept of EMU is without foundation, as EMU was being promoted before his period in office, although he *was*, in fact, responsible for establishing the idea of Cultural Heritage as a separate theme.) The documentation was in fact ambiguous about the nature of EMU, appearing in places to imply that it was primarily about cross-community contact. This ambiguity was retained in the later Education Reform Order itself, especially in Clause 125.2(h) in which it is required that part of the school's annual report should 'describe what steps have been taken by the Board of Governors to develop and strengthen the school's links with the community and, in particular, to promote the attainment of the objectives of the educational theme called Education for Mutual Understanding' (HMSO, 1989, p. 132).

Working Groups established early in 1989 were charged with providing 'a clear statement of the essential content of the themes, and the knowledge, skills and understanding which pupils can be expected to have acquired at the appropriate stages in their school career' and to 'suggest how best the various parts of each theme can be incorporated within the main curriculum subjects' (Mawhinney, 1989). The historian, Jonathan Bardon, was appointed, significantly, as common chairperson to the otherwise separate groups examining EMU and Cultural Heritage, and the two groups were encouraged to work together as much as possible. The groups, however, had just three months to do their work and report in order that their findings could be taken into account by working groups set up to make proposals for the various subjects within the new curriculum, and there was therefore little opportunity for liaison between the EMU and CH teams. A major – and very contentious – issue for the EMU group was the extent to which cross-community contact should be made a compulsory element of the theme, and this was eventually resolved by recommending that it remain voluntary yet strongly encouraged. Despite the severe externally imposed schedule and limitations on liaison the documents produced by the working groups (NICC, 1989a; NICC, 1989b) were of a high quality and broadly welcomed and they provided a sound basis for the early development of EMU and CH as statutory themes. They were far superior in both scope and scholarship to the Northern Ireland Curriculum Council (NICC) Consultation Report on the themes which was issued later in 1989 (NICC, 1989c) and which unfortunately reached a wider audience than the original reports.

Article 8 of the ensuing Education Reform (NI) Order (ERO), which was passed in December 1989, mandated 'the attainment of the objectives of the... educational themes', requiring that this should be done 'wholly or mainly through the teaching of the contributory subjects [of the new curriculum] and religious education' (HMSO, 1989, p. 15).

EMU and Cultural Heritage following Education Reform

Research has suggested that of all the newly introduced educational themes EMU remained the most prominent in teachers' minds (Montgomery and Smith, 1997, p. 72). In the late 1980s growing numbers of schools had been responding corporately to these 'new' challenges by appointing EMU co-ordinators. The introduction of the ERO legislation speeded up this process and led in some cases to separate co-ordinators being appointed for Cultural Heritage as well, although many schools did see the logic of making a joint appointment (and some merged the two separate posts later). While in some schools such positions were rewarded with a responsibility payment to the teacher concerned, many schools made this a voluntary role. More often than not the EMU and CH co-ordinators were younger teachers with minimal status in the profession and this, especially in larger post-primary schools, tended to undervalue the importance of their task. Additional difficulties arose from the tendency of some schools, especially at the post-primary level, to associate particular themes with certain curriculum subjects, thus it was quite common to find EMU co-ordination linked with Religious Education, and Cultural Heritage with History or Geography. Further evidence that some schools already seemed to be missing the point of the Educational Themes concept is clear from the fact that in many cases the EMU co-ordinators were perceived to be wholly concerned with the organisation of inter-school contact programmes.

Most teachers and others, nevertheless, seemed to accept the view that in Northern Ireland the two themes, EMU and CH, were closely intertwined in as much as consideration of how cultures were similar or different could not be divorced from issues of relationships between members of those culturally defined groups, or, indeed, that processes and skills in improving relationships needed to be understood in a particular context. This was certainly the approach of the two Working Groups in 1989. In some quarters, however, there was a tendency to associate Cultural Heritage with specific traditions, particularly by some who believed in the importance of promoting the Irish language and Gaelic culture (or, rather later, with Ulster Scots). Inevitably this meant that some teachers in controlled schools became wary of what they perceived to be the 'Gaelic agenda' of the Cultural Heritage theme, especially where it was treated quite separately from EMU. Others queried the wisdom of separating the two themes and argued for their unification.

Under the new legislation the six Themes were not due formally to come into statute until September 1992. Further documentation issued at that point (DENI, 1992) attempted to clarify the close relationship between EMU and Cultural Heritage by 'conjoining' some of the objectives of each, but this only served to provide something of a tangle of statements which was not helped by the lack of adequate official guidance materials. As a result the Curriculum Council set up a new working group in 1994 to provide fuller guidance including case studies of effective practice. The basic assumption of this experienced group's approach was that EMU and CH were fundamentally to be treated as a single theme and on this premise they went on to provide more sharply defined statements together with four briefer and clearer 'shared objectives' focusing on the following:

- fostering self-esteem and building relationships;
- understanding and responding creatively to conflict;
- appreciating interdependence; and
- developing an understanding of cultural diversity.

(CCEA, 1997, p. 6; see also Chapter 1)

This later working group also attempted to clarify the nature of the themes in relation to their somewhat uncertain description as either 'cross-curricular' or 'educational', favouring the broader implications of the latter term and encouraging a whole-school approach. The concept was described as the development of an 'EMU-promoting school', as illustrated by case studies of good practice (CCEA, 1997, p. 11ff). The publication of this material, however, was delayed for three years due to a range of factors including the curriculum 'slimming down' process of the mid-1990s, and its published form did not entirely reflect the original intentions of the working group. In effect this meant that at a time when guidance and training was most needed it was not uniformly available, despite the noble efforts of some key individuals and organisations. Generally speaking many teachers continued to feel unsupported and inadequately prepared, in terms of documentation and the availability of training, to deal with the professional and personal issues brought forward by the formal introduction of EMU and Cultural Heritage, and this undoubtedly contributed to the uneven approach evident between different schools.

Support and Responsibility

In the five regional Education and Library Boards, with their enhanced responsibilities for curriculum advice and training, several new positions relating to EMU and CH were created. Only two of the five Boards (the Western and South-Eastern) had employed staff at any level with full-time responsibility for EMU prior to 1989, but now each Board made an appointment, some at field-officer level (normally by teacher secondment) and some at Assistant Adviser level. For a time it seemed as though these appointments would create greater potential for Province-wide promotion of the sound educational practices of EMU and CH, but the Boards' priorities gradually shifted and in some areas the designated role of an advisory officer with specific responsibility for EMU/CH became undermined amidst a welter of 'other responsibilities'. An Inter-Board Panel (later *Forum*) for EMU/CH was established early in the 1990s and grew in strength and effectiveness over a period of years, bringing together some of the most experienced EMU practitioners from across the Province and often including a broader constituency (that is, from other organisations) in its meetings. Such a forum is only as strong as the individual commitment of each contributing Board can make it, however, and while some of the Education and Library Boards proved themselves to be consistently highly committed over many years, others 'hung loose' to the detriment of the system as a whole and, in particular, at the expense of teachers in their own Board area who lost out on opportunities for professional guidance and training.

Within the voluntary sector, boosted by the availability of funding for professional appointments from the early 1980s onwards, there was also a build-up of 'EMU-expertise', although this was often dissipated by the short-term nature of such appointments. The range of non-statutory support bodies had grown during the late 1980s (see Chapter 2) and was, during the initial period of 'statutory EMU' in the early 1990s, making a significant contribution to training programmes and to supporting schools in their organisation of curriculum work, resource materials and, in particular, contact. Many teachers expressed their appreciation for the work of these organisations, although the criticism has been made that too many teachers came to rely upon such support and thereby failed to move on towards taking ownership of their work for themselves. The over-emphasis on contact as a means of 'doing EMU' may also in part have stemmed from the availability of organisations to support or to host contact in ways which could not be so easily applied to 'classroom EMU/CH'. Some support organisations appeared to recognise this more than others, and made significant efforts within their programmes to emphasise that it was not their task to 'do EMU' on behalf of their school clients.

Co-ordination between the various voluntary and statutory support agencies and the projects based in higher education institutions has never been organised on a regular basis, despite several attempts to establish an over-arching structure for support and cohesion. The standing-down of the NICED EMU Steering Group in 1988 (see Chapter 3) created a gap which was never quite filled. Alongside the NICED committee the *FOCUS Group* (Forum on Community Understanding and Schools) had since 1984 provided a particular opportunity for informal contact and networking between EMU-support personnel on the ground and those engaged by statutory bodies, and during the 1980s was frequently consulted (sometimes by the Department of Education or the NICED Committee itself) on the detail of innovations such as the 1987 Cross-Community Contact Scheme. Its initial membership consisted of five teachers seconded to work with various embryonic EMU programmes (following the 1982 DENI Circular 82/21), but this gradually expanded to include a much wider range of groups contributing in a range of ways to education for diversity and mutual understanding – residential centres, academic institutions, groups focusing on conflict management skills, inter-Church projects, environmentally-related organisations, heritage and museum programmes and others. During the 1990s the group had on average about thirty-five organisations on its mailing list and at the time of writing (twenty-five years after the group's establishment) it continues to meet in full forum about three or four times a year. (A *Who's Who in Education for Diversity?* directory, published every eighteen months or two years by the FOCUS Group from 1990 to 2002 [FOCUS, 2000], indicated the wide range of organisations in its membership that were involved in providing support for schools in their EMU and Cultural Heritage work.) From the outset the FOCUS Group also included representatives of statutory bodies in its membership and thus went some way towards filling the gap left by the demise of the NICED committee. The Group nevertheless continued to argue for the establishment of a new and broader professional structure to draw together all the relevant interests and to co-ordinate future developments in a spirit of partnership. Others, however, suggested a broadening of the group to take into account more recent developments in areas such as human rights and citizenship education, and this approach was gradually adopted.

Research

Research on the various aspects of EMU and CH was not extensive, perhaps surprisingly in view of the considerable attention which has been focused on Northern Ireland by academics of all kinds during the years of the Troubles. One reason for the lack of detailed research may be that for many observers the most interesting question was, naturally, 'Does EMU work?' which normally implied 'Have children's attitudes changed in terms of trust and respect for "the other community"?' While this is, of course, an important issue it is extremely difficult to assess. The measurement of attitude change is problematical, and often regarded as flawed, and many teachers have simply had to resort to anecdotal accounts of children getting along well at a given point in time (while others have sometimes countered with equally anecdotal stories of superficial occasions of inter-school contact or accounts of how children did not get along). Furthermore, such 'evidences' have tended to focus on contact and to neglect curriculum-based work. Some have thus eschewed all attempts to 'prove' or question the effectiveness of educational programmes of this kind, pointing out that such work is very long-term and that crude measures cannot hope to indicate long-term benefits.

Nevertheless, there have been several research programmes which have at the very least provided some insights into the progression of this work since the Education Reform Order, providing indicators for future developments. Undoubtedly the most consistent contributor to this research in the 1990s was Alan Smith of the University of Ulster at Coleraine, initially as a member of the Centre for the Study of Conflict team and later as director of the UNESCO Centre within the School of Education. In the late 1980s the focus was on inter-school contact programmes and some of the implications arising from this (Dunn and Smith, 1989; Smith and Dunn, 1990). In 1990 the focus switched to an 'EMU Evaluation Project', although the title proved misleading in that the evaluation appropriately and realistically focused on implementation and structural issues rather than on attitudinal or behavioural outcomes (Smith and Robinson, 1992 and 1996). While the research noted several positive benefits that the introduction of EMU had brought to the education system as a whole, not least the development of a 'broader and more sophisticated' conceptual framework (1996, p. 8), it highlighted a concern that many teachers had found difficulty with providing appropriate *progression* and *coherence* in relation to this work in schools. The authors encouraged the promotion of a whole-school approach and, at the same time, urged schools to develop a more specific agenda for EMU in relation to civics, human rights and education for political participation. Further work undertaken by Montgomery and Smith (1997) affirmed many of these earlier findings but nevertheless indicated that EMU, some years into its statutory existence, was viewed by many teachers as having an important role to play:

> Most teachers expressed some degree of commitment to promoting and developing EMU in their subject area and school. Some indicated examples of where they felt teachers had failed to harness [its] full potential... EMU... was perceived by many teachers as a frame of reference for the values which currently underpin the curriculum. (ibid., p. 78f)

This would seem to bear out experience on the ground that, despite many difficulties, by the late 1990s EMU had contributed to positive change generally within the teaching profession and that within a growing number of schools it had become increasingly accepted as a valid and important dimension of education in Northern Ireland. Nevertheless other research (Leitch and Kilpatrick, 1999; Harland et al., 1999 and 2002) continued to indicate serious deficits with the ways in which EMU was being delivered by many teachers and received, if at all, by many pupils. Commenting on the experience and 'internalisation' of EMU among a sample of Key Stage 3 pupils, Harland et al. commented that much work on EMU at the post-primary level seemed to occur in Personal and Social Education classes:

> By year 10... pupils were beginning to describe the work they had done on respect for others as *'common sense'* and to acknowledge that they already knew about this. There may, therefore, be a need to change the emphasis of EMU in Year 10 and beyond, away from work generally on respect for others, to some conceptually and behaviourally more challenging work, perhaps taking in conflict resolution, arbitration, identity formation, and relevant aspects of sociology and psychology. (Harland et al., 2002, p. 263)

Critique of EMU of a rather more subtle kind has sometimes emanated from the integrated schools movement, despite the fact that it might have been assumed that the two initiatives had similar aims. In an article focusing on religious identity in the integrated sector, Flanagan and Lambkin (who were both, at different stages, principals of the very first 'planned integrated' school, Lagan College) directed their criticism at a 'too easy' approach to EMU which they described as 'preserving separation by conceding a degree of integration' (Flanagan and Lambkin, 1993, p. 197). The danger of this superficial approach, they argued, is that children retain separate identities rather than gaining a shared identity: 'EMU and Cultural Heritage in the curriculum offer what appears to be an acceptable way out: ... Catholics and Protestants become more friendly but retain their separate schools and with them their separate identities. They become friendly through sharing some educational experiences, but not too friendly' (ibid., p. 197).

Others, not only from within the integrated sector, have observed that the enthusiastic support by Catholic school authorities is based on a belief that if they encourage relations that do not go 'too far', the future of separate Catholic schooling will be secure. At the same time some criticisms of integrated education have focused on the reluctance of some integrated school teachers to raise some of the difficult issues around community conflict within the sector. The integrated movement as a whole has recognised this and in recent years has sharpened up its own work in relation to challenging its own teachers and pupils to learn how to deal positively with diversity and conflict. Even more recently – from 2005 to 2007 – an initiative of the Northern Ireland Council for Integrated Education attempted to take the principles of integration out to 'non-integrated' schools through its 'Integrating Education' project.

Four further reports are worthy of brief note here. Following the inclusion in the 1998 Belfast ('Good Friday') Agreement of a statement that 'an essential aspect of the reconciliation process is the promotion of *a culture of tolerance* at every level of society'[1] (p. 18; author's italics), the Depart-

---

1   Many observers pointed out the inadequacy of the term 'culture of tolerance', suggesting that 'a culture of respect' would have been far more suitable. The spirit of what

ment of Education set up two working parties to consider the role of education. One examined the theme of 'integrating education' – promoting pluralism, partnership and openness in schools of all kinds (DENI, 1998) – while the second focused on 'the strategic promotion of Education for Mutual Understanding'. It advised that all statutory bodies with a responsibility for education in Northern Ireland had 'a responsibility to promote mutual understanding and respect for diversity as a seminal purpose of the education service'. (DENI, 1999, p. 25) While acknowledging that much valuable work had been carried out over many years the report highlighted the weaknesses in the implementation of EMU, especially in relation to exploring controversial issues in the classroom. Serious weaknesses were noted in the availability of appropriate training at all levels. The working group encouraged an emphasis on the promotion of core values in the education system such as pluralism, social justice, democracy and human rights and responsibilities, and promoted an approach to EMU based on whole-school ethos. More formally timetabled work was recommended in Personal and Social Education and in Civic, Social and Political Education. The group also recommended a broadening of the perceived scope of EMU to take account of race and wider diversity issues. In its conclusion the report advised that: 'For change to be meaningful... community relations objectives must move from the periphery to the core of the education service' (DENI, 1999, p. 25).

In 1999 a brief report on the Educational Themes in primary schools by the Education and Training Inspectorate of the Department of Education indicated that provision for EMU was 'judged to be satisfactory or better in almost eighty percent of schools', also noting that a similar judgement could be made of seventy percent of schools in respect of Cultural Heritage. The main features of good practice in EMU were focused mostly on cross-community links, although the importance was noted of 'a culture of openness, acceptance, inclusiveness and mutual respect' within schools. The

---

had been intended by this apparently very late insertion of the term by a member of the Women's Coalition political party was, however, valued and provided a useful basis for further development.

report noted, however, that co-ordination of all the Educational Themes in schools was limited, that integration into the curricular programmes was 'fragmented and patchy' and that in-service training (INSET) was largely unavailable (ETI/DE, 1999, pp. 6–7; 13).

A subsequent Inspectorate survey of provision for EMU in post-primary schools, carried out during the following school year (1999–2000), was much more detailed and extensive, and its conclusions pulled no punches. It noted that while there was evidence of very good curriculum practice in about twenty percent of the schools surveyed, the teaching in some schools was very poor and even counter-productive. Particular weaknesses were identified in relation to the difficulties many schools had with the area of understanding and responding to conflict, and with handling sensitive controversial issues in the classroom. As in the 'Culture of Tolerance' report, indicated above, it was noted that some schools did not explore cultural diversity beyond the culture of their own community and that there was limited awareness of cultural diversity beyond that of the Catholic-Protestant divide (ETI/DE, 2000). Perhaps the most disappointing feature of this constructive but forthright Inspectorate report was the fact that it had not been undertaken several years earlier. Some observers suggested that if it had been available earlier it would have been a valuable tool in encouraging better practice in curricular EMU. As it was, the report was published at a time when the educational system was already on the verge of moving on from EMU as an educational theme to a new model based on Personal Development and Education for Citizenship.

Prompted by the Department of Education's *Education for Diversity* recommendations (above) a survey of the Schools' Community Relations Programme (SCRP – formerly the Cross Community Contact Scheme), was carried out during 2001 (O'Connor, Hartop and McCully, 2002; followed by a supplementary report by the same authors in 2003). Although the authors indicated that the SCRP was 'an important mechanism for active community relations engagement' (ibid., 2003, 8.1.2), these reports suggested that there was little evidence of integration between EMU policy and the SCRP in many schools and noted a lack of teacher awareness with regard to the distinction between EMU and the SCRP. Criticisms were also made of some of the structures surrounding the programme and of some of the groups who were receiving core funding to provide support and facilities. The authors indicated their support for the long-term continuation of the scheme while encouraging a significant re-think on some details, including extending the remit to include a wider range of issues according to local needs – for example, cross-border, ethnic minorities, racism, the travelling community and the disabled. The 2002 report identified a need for more rigorous evaluation and for improved structural co-ordination, within the Education and Library Boards and within the Department of Education. It argued for 'a more clearly defined community relations dimension with monitoring and accountability within the formal curriculum' and proposed the possibility of 'redefining community relations as part of an active citizenship dimension' within the proposed new curriculum (ibid., 2002, 4.2.5, ii and iii). At the level of attitudinal development the 2003 report called for the use of 'strategies that encourage a culture of reflection amongst pupils and teachers' (ibid., 2003, 8.4.3).

In the light of this report it is perhaps surprising that the Northern Ireland Department of Education, who fund the SCRP along with a Core Funding Scheme for community relations support bodies, appear in more recent times to have interpreted their own criteria more strictly in terms of local 'perceived community' diversity (i.e. 'Catholics and Protestants'). This appears somewhat at odds with the publicly expressed purposes of the Department's Community Relations policy – 'to provide opportunities for young people to develop an awareness and understanding of religious, cultural and political diversity within our society... including social, racial, cultural and religious issues' (DE, 2003). It is felt by many support organisations and schools that the changing diversity of Northern Ireland requires a more broadly based approach, not in order to avoid contentious local inter-community issues, but rather to be more inclusive of the range of such issues facing schools today.[2]

---

2   At the time of writing (2008–9) there are strong indications that the Schools' Community Relations Programme may well be subject to significant changes in the near future. Ironically one of the fears is that the current *imbalance* in relation to local and broader issues of diversity may be reversed; this, of course, would be no less an imbalance!

Beyond EMU – Towards Citizenship and 'PDMU'

By the end of the 1990s a new political and civic context was developing in Northern Ireland. Paramilitary ceasefires and political agreements had led to new opportunities for cross-community co-operation and the intro- duction, albeit somewhat haltingly, of a new Northern Ireland Assembly. In the course of the framing of such agreements there was a strengthening of the legislative structures in relation to issues of equality, human rights and community relationships. This has impacted on education in various ways, as has been indicated with reference to the clause in the 1998 Belfast Agreement about the promotion of 'a culture of tolerance' (see above). The legislation resulting from the Agreement also included the signifi- cant Section 75, which required that public authorities should have 'due regard to the need to promote equality of opportunity' and 'good relations between persons of different religious belief, political opinion or racial group' (Equality Commission, 2000 – quoting the Northern Ireland Act, 1998).[3] The establishment of a Northern Ireland Human Rights Commis- sion similarly led to proposals for the development of human rights edu- cation. Coinciding with the research on EMU which indicated the need for a sharper and more cohesive approach focusing on political awareness and democratic participation, the scene was set for significant change to impact on the ways in which the education system was promoting aware- ness of diversity and mutual understanding.

One of the aspects of post-Education Reform EMU which had raised some concern was the desirability and effectiveness of the cross-curricular approach. It has been noted that the official and preferred term was 'Educa- tional Theme', implying a holistic approach, but for some people even this whole-school concept was problematical. The danger with a *theme* that is meant to permeate all aspects of the curriculum and the broader life of the

---

3   Schools, however, are not regarded as public bodies for the purposes of this Act,
     which has led to concerns that some teachers and other educators may take a more
     casual view about the promotion of good relations.

school is that it can easily get taken for granted or lost altogether, perhaps especially at the post-primary level. An area which is meant to be everyone's responsibility can too quickly become *everyone else's* responsibility! This led some teachers and other observers to argue that what was required was a more specific timetabled slot for particular aspects of EMU, perhaps in relation to Personal and Social Education or a civics programme. This issue became very significant in shaping the next stage of the development of education for diversity and mutual understanding.

Partly as a result of the various reports and critiques which noted the inadequacies of the educational theme EMU model, and partly because of the influence of work carried out in the Republic of Ireland and Britain, the proposals for a Revised Northern Ireland Curriculum, initially developed between 1999 and 2002, moved towards a new approach. Long bureaucratic delays and uncertainty about government structures, however, set back the implementation of the new curriculum model until 2007.

While broadly welcoming the opportunities that such a new curriculum would present to the development of this important area of education some observers expressed their concerns that the timetabling of taught 'subjects' could be detrimental to the concept of a whole-school ethos built around the objectives of mutual understanding. The present author wrote that '… it would seem a retrograde step if personal education or citizenship were simply to be seen as a subject with a small percentage of timetabling and as the responsibility of just one or two specialist teachers' (Richardson, 2000, p. 6).

Another concern on the part of those who worked for many years to develop awareness and skills in the EMU model had been to promote a sense of the continuity between former and proposed practice. Sometimes it seemed that those developing the revised curriculum were unaware of any obvious link between EMU and the new proposals, or else were unwilling to acknowledge it. It was suggested that if educators in Northern Ireland were unable to learn from the experience of implementing Education for Mutual Understanding there would be a great danger of repeating these mistakes in relation to any new model built around personal development and citizenship education.

Curriculum Values

In the earliest version of the revised curriculum proposals there was considerable emphasis on the 'underpinning values' and generic skills of the curriculum. Included among the proposed values underpinning the curriculum were 'equality, justice and human rights within our society and our capacity as citizens to resolve conflict by democratic means' (CCEA, 2000, p. 4). In later phases of the proposals the emphasis on values appeared to some to be less evident (CCEA, 2002a; CCEA, 2002b), but as the Revised Curriculum took shape it became clear that the values base as stated in the Curriculum Objectives was very significant. Teachers and schools at all stages and through all areas of learning were charged with a responsibility to develop each young person 'as an Individual; as a Contributor to Society; as a Contributor to the Economy and the Environment', and the terminology used to spell out what was meant by this included key concepts such as 'personal understanding', 'mutual understanding', 'cultural understanding' and 'citizenship'. The documentation indicates that pupils' learning experiences should be 'culturally diverse', and among the 'attitudes and dispositions' that the curriculum is expected to foster should be 'tolerance', 'openness to new ideas', 'community spirit' and 'respect' (see 'The Big Picture' sections for Key Stages 1 and 2 and Key Stages 3 and 4 on the Northern Ireland Curriculum website[4]). It certainly appeared that many of the dimensions of education for diversity and mutual understanding that had previously seemed frustratingly peripheral to the curriculum had now been established firmly within the mainstream.

The decision to introduce 'Personal Development' as a new area of learning also very clearly drew together many of the elements which previously appeared as Educational Themes and turned them into taught units of work. At Foundation Stage and Key Stages 1 and 2 many aspects of EMU, Cultural Heritage and Health Education (which was also one of the six Educational Themes) were included under the two sub-sections

---

4   See <http://www.nicurriculum.org.uk> (accessed 15 July 2010).

of *Personal Understanding and Health* and *Mutual Understanding in the Local and Wider Community*, with a strong emphasis in the latter on issues of relationships, 'rules, rights and responsibilities', diversity ('similarities and differences'), creative approaches to managing conflict and 'learning to live as members of the community' (PMB/CCEA, 2007, pp. 23–6). The retention of the terminology of 'Mutual Understanding' seemed to be a positive indication of the importance of continuity with the former model of EMU as an educational theme, and the late decision to change the name of the area of learning itself to 'Personal Development *and Mutual Understanding*' (PDMU) reinforces this perception. (Personal Development without the 'and mutual understanding' tag also features in the post-primary curriculum.) Guidance documentation issued in 2007 to primary schools outlines nine statutory 'Statements of Minimum Requirement' for PDMU, at least five of which relate very specifically to the mutual understanding strand: Relationships; Rules, Rights and Responsibilities; Managing Conflict; Similarities and Differences; and Learning to Live as Members of the Community (CCEA/PMB, 2007).

In support of PDMU a range of new primary school resources were developed. Stemming from the *Values in Education in Northern Ireland* report (Montgomery and Smith, 1997), CCEA developed *Primary Values*, which uses children's stories to explore values and attitudes relating to Identity, Interdependence and Conflict, on a scale ranging from personal, through local to the global dimension, 'to contribute to respectful and democratic discussion with others' (Montgomery and Birthistle, 2002, p. 2). In particular it promotes the use of 'A Community of Enquiry', based on Matthew Lipman's approach to developing philosophical enquiry with children (Lipman, 2003) and also Circle Time techniques. The Council for Curriculum, Examinations and Assessment (CCEA) has also developed attractive resource boxes for each primary year group entitled *Living.Learning.Together* to provide ideas and relevant activities for PDMU (CCEA, 2007–9), and these have been very well received by teachers.

During roughly the same period (2001–7) a new series of primary school human rights education resources was under development by a cross-border consortium led by Amnesty International and supported by Ulster Teachers' Union and the Irish National Teachers' Organisation. The 'Lift

Off' programme, widely piloted and eventually published in the form of three resource books plus a support website (Cross-Border Human Rights Initiative, 2003, 2005, 2007[5]), effectively overcame the earlier perception that human rights was somehow the preserve of the Catholic/nationalist population and was well received during its piloting in several of Northern Ireland's controlled schools. Human Rights education work has also been encouraged through the work of international agencies such as UNICEF (United Nations Children's Fund), offering support for teachers through its website and encouraging schools to take part in its Rights Respecting Schools Award scheme, which is based around the UN Convention on the Rights of the Child.

A substantial Citizenship pilot programme in post-primary schools was undertaken between 1998 and 2002 focusing on the concepts of diversity and interdependence, human rights and responsibilities, equality, justice and democracy and active participation. However, the original proposal, in 2000, to include Education for Citizenship as a discreet curriculum area within Personal Development at Key Stage 3 (and later also including Key Stage 4) was initially set aside in later versions in favour of the incorporation of Citizenship into *Environment and Society*, raising concerns in some quarters that the link with values education and personal reflection could be lost in favour of a didactic civics-based approach. After further discussion in 2003, both *Local and Global Citizenship* and post-primary Personal Development were re-allocated to the newly defined learning area of 'Learning for Life and Work', which also includes Home Economics and Employability (see the section on *Learning for Life and Work* on the Northern Ireland Curriculum website[6]). Consultation on the 2000 proposals had seemed to indicate serious divisions on the question of introducing Citizenship Education, despite clear precedents in both the Republic of Ireland (CSPE – Civic, Social and Political Education – introduced in the mid-1990s) and England (where Citizenship Education was proposed and established for all Key Stages following the 1998 Crick Report). Neverthe-

5   See <http://www.liftoffschools.com> (accessed 25 June 2010).
6   See <http://www.nicurriculum.org.uk/> (accessed 15 July 2010).

less significant funding was earmarked by the Department of Education for the training of teachers in each Education and Library Board area in *Local and Global Citizenship*, and this went ahead in 2002 in order to ensure that over a three to four year period there would be trained teachers in all post-primary schools by the time the revised curriculum was due to be introduced. (In-service training on a similar scale was not, however, made available for primary PDMU, to the disappointment of some.)

These movements from the peripheries of the schooling system towards the 'mainstream' have impacted positively on initial teacher education (ITE), albeit slowly. In previous decades it was difficult to find space for themes and topics that were not perceived to be within the curriculum proper, and references to EMU and diversity education tended to be located in one-off contact activities and non-contentious student conferences, notwithstanding some attempts at establishing more challenging programmes in several ITE institutions. At the time of writing, however, the opportunities for exploring both personal and professional issues around diversity and intercultural understanding have widened in the teacher education sector and there now seems to be a real possibility of sending into schools more aware and better skilled young teachers in relation to these concerns.

Shared Education in 'A Shared Future'?

As the Revised Northern Ireland Curriculum moved, despite the delays, towards implementation, government policy in Northern Ireland became more firmly committed to the promotion of good community relations, both in its traditional emphasis on local issues and in relation to the growing concerns about racism towards newly emergent diverse ethnic groups in the Province. Stemming from the equality discussions and legislation of the late 1990s the office of the First Minister and Deputy First Minister initiated a consultation process towards the concept of 'a shared future'. The policy document that appeared finally in March 2005 covered many areas of life in Northern Ireland and certainly did not neglect education, keenly articulating the intention that there should be opportunities 'for shared and inter-cultural education at all levels – nursery, primary, secondary and tertiary'. It set a responsibility on all schools to ensure 'through their policies, structures and curriculae, that pupils are consciously prepared for life in a diverse and inter-cultural society and world' (OFMDFM, 2005, p. 24).

Noting that 90 per cent or more of children of school-going age continue to be educated in schools associated with their own cultural/religious community, the policy stresses that 'both integrated and denominational schools have important roles to play in preparing children for their role as adults in a shared society' (paragraph 2.4.5). Citing the potential of new curriculum areas such as Local and Global Citizenship, the document emphasises the importance of schools understanding the causes of conflict in Northern Ireland and further afield and notes that 'to make a real impact it is essential that this work tackles the reality of living in a divided society' (2.4.8). In order to achieve this there will be a need 'actively to prepare teachers and lecturers to educate children and young people for a shared society' (2.4.11). The policy acknowledges the significant work of initiatives based on EMU, Cultural Heritage and the Schools Community Relations Programme:

> These programmes have encouraged children and young people, from the basis of a greater understanding of their own roots, to understand the essence of reconciliation and the importance of building relationships grounded in mutual recognition and trust. In the revised curriculum shortly to be implemented, these themes will continue as integral parts of the Citizenship Programme. (ibid, 2.4.10)

Coming at a time of significant political and curriculum change in Northern Ireland the 'Shared Future' policy seemed to provide a basis for continuing commitment to diversity awareness and mutual understanding as keystones of educational practice in the Province. Nevertheless, at the time of writing it seems clear that the policy has been reconsidered by the two numerically largest parties in the power-sharing government (the Democratic Unionist Party and Sinn Fein) and that it is to be replaced by what some observers fear may be a 'watered down' policy for 'Cohesion, Sharing and Integration' to tackle racism and sectarianism, possibly less sympathetic to some of the key principles of diversity and mutual understanding (of which neither of these political parties had previously seemed to be particularly supportive).

Other initiatives, stemming from the Costello Report (Department of Education, 2004) and the Bain Report (Department of Education, 2006), suggest that greater sharing, partnership and collaboration between schools is possible notwithstanding the continuation of separate parallel systems of schooling. At the same time the integrated education movement has continued to work towards its stated target of ten percent of children in integrated schools by the year 2010 (although in 2009 the figure is still only just above six percent), arguing still that the best basis for building mutual understanding is in educating children together in the same school.

Whatever future changes there may be, and whatever terminology may be given to the next phase in this area of work there is no doubt that the concerns and motivations which gave rise to the introduction of education for community relations, for peace and justice, for cultural diversity, for mutual understanding, will not go away. They are necessary elements of education in any society and most pertinently so in a society like Northern Ireland which continues to express many deep divisions and significantly increasing diversity. Without such initiatives not only education but society in general would be the poorer.

Summary

Over a period of almost four decades educators in Northern Ireland have been seeking ways of responding educationally to civic unrest and violence. After many informal experiments in curriculum programmes and in cross-community contact, the formal education system embraced such work under the terminology of Education for Mutual Understanding and Cultural Heritage, introducing them as educational themes in the Northern Ireland Curriculum of the early 1990s. Despite the significant efforts of many educators in statutory and voluntary programmes it became evident that many teachers and schools were unsure about how to implement EMU or unwilling to attempt to do so. Attempts to sharpen and refocus these areas of work have led to the more mainstream introduction of Personal Development and Mutual Understanding (PDMU) and Education for Local and Global Citizenship in a revised Northern Ireland Curriculum.

References

Belfast Agreement (1998) *Agreement reached in the multi-party negotiations*, Belfast: Northern Ireland Office.

CCEA (1997) *Mutual Understanding and Cultural Heritage*, Belfast: Council for Curriculum, Examinations and Assessment.

CCEA (2000) *Proposals for changes to the Northern Ireland Curriculum Framework (Northern Ireland Curriculum Review, Phase 1 Consultation)*, Belfast: Council for Curriculum, Examinations and Assessment.

CCEA (2002a) Curriculum Review: *Detailed Proposals for the Revised Primary Curriculum and its Assessment Arrangements*, Belfast: Council for Curriculum, Examinations and Assessment.

CCEA (2002b) Curriculum Review: *A new approach to Curriculum and Assessment 11–16*, Belfast: Council for Curriculum, Examinations and Assessment.

CCEA/PMB (2007) *Northern Ireland Curriculum: Personal Development and Mutual Understanding for Key Stages 1 and 2*, Belfast: Council for Curriculum, Examinations and Assessment, Partnership Management Board.

Cross-Border Human Rights Initiative (2003; 2005; 2007) 'Lift Off' Project – in 3 books: *The Right Start*; *Lift Off*; and *Me, You, Everyone*, Belfast and Dublin: Amnesty International, Irish National Teachers' Organisation, Ulster Teachers' Union.

DE (2003) *Jane Kennedy Announces £3.5m for Community Relations* (Department of Education New Release: 19 August 2003), Bangor: Department of Education (Northern Ireland).

DENI (1988a) *Education in Northern Ireland – Proposals for Reform*, Bangor: Department of Education for Northern Ireland.

DENI (1988b) *Education Reform in Northern Ireland – The Way Forward*, Bangor: Department of Education for Northern Ireland.

DENI (1992) *Educational, Cross-Curricular Themes: Objectives*, Bangor: Department of Education for Northern Ireland, Belfast, HMSO.

DENI (1998) *Towards a Culture of Tolerance: Integrating Education* (Working Party Progress Report, November 1998), Bangor: Department of Education for Northern Ireland.

DENI (1999) *Towards a Culture of Tolerance: Education for Diversity* (Report of the Working Group on the Strategic Promotion of Education for Mutual Understanding), Bangor: Department of Education for Northern Ireland.

Dunn, S., and Smith, A. (1989) *Inter-School Links*, Coleraine: University of Ulster Centre for the Study of Conflict.

ETI/DE (1999) *Report on the Educational Themes: Primary Inspections 1998–99*, Crown Copyright 1999, Bangor: Education and Training Inspectorate, Department of Education.

ETI/DE (2000) *Report of a Survey of Provision for Education for Mutual Understanding (EMU) in Post-Primary Schools (Inspected: 1999/2000)*, Crown Copyright 2000, Bangor: Education and Training Inspectorate, Department of Education.

Equality Commission (2000) *Guide to the Statutory Duties… arising from Section 75 of the Northern Ireland Act 1998*, Belfast: Equality Commission for Northern Ireland.

Flanagan, T., and Lambkin, B. (1993) 'Religious Identity and Integrated Education', in Moffatt, C. (ed.), *Education Together for a Change*, Belfast: Fortnight Educational Trust.

FOCUS (2000) *Who's Who in Education for Diversity? – 2001–2002*, Belfast, the FOCUS Group (final edition of a regularly revised booklet).

Harland, J., et al. (1999) *The Real Curriculum at the end of Key Stage 2 – N.I. Curriculum Cohort Study*, Slough, National Foundation for Educational Research (on behalf of the NI Council for Curriculum, Examinations and Assessment).

Harland, J. et al. (2002) *Is the Curriculum Working? The Key Stage 3 Phase of the N.I. Curriculum Cohort Study*, Slough, National Foundation for Educational Research (on behalf of the NI Council for Curriculum, Examinations and Assessment).

HMSO (1989) *Statutory Instruments: The Education Reform (Northern Ireland) Order*, Belfast: Her Majesty's Stationery Office.

Leitch, R. (2001) 'Victims or Mentors? Metaphors for Twenty-first Century Children', in Gardner, J., and Leitch, R. (eds), *Education 2020: A Millennium Vision*, Belfast: Blackstaff Press, Queen's University Belfast Graduate School of Education.

Leitch, R., and Kilpatrick, R. (1999) *Inside the Gates: Schools and the Troubles*, Belfast: Save the Children Fund.

Lipman, M. (2003) *Thinking in Education* (2nd edn), Cambridge: Cambridge University Press.

Mawhinney, B. (1989) 'Letter to Jonathan Bardon from Brian Mawhinney', 19 January, repr. in *Cultural Heritage: A Cross-Curricular Theme*, Belfast: Northern Ireland Curriculum Council.

Montgomery, A., and Smith, A. (1997) *Values in Education in Northern Ireland*, Coleraine: School of Education, University of Ulster; Belfast, Council for Curriculum, Examinations and Assessment.

Montgomery, A., and Birthistle, U. (2002) *Primary Values: A literacy based resource to support the Personal Development Programme in primary schools*, Belfast: Northern Ireland Council for the Curriculum, Examinations and Assessment.

NICC (1989a) *Education for Mutual Understanding: A Cross-Curricular Theme*, Belfast: Northern Ireland Curriculum Council.

NICC (1989b) *Cultural Heritage: A Cross-Curricular Theme*, Belfast: Northern Ireland Curriculum Council.

NICC (1989c) *Cross-Curricular Themes: Consultation Report*, Belfast: Northern Ireland Curriculum Council.

PMB/CCEA (2007) *Personal Development and Mutual Understanding for Key Stages 1 and 2 (Guidance Material)*, Belfast: Partnership Management Board and Council for Curriculum, Examinations and Assessment <http://www.nicurriculum. org.uk/docs/personal_development/training/PD-Guidance.pdf> (accessed 25 June 2010).

Richardson, N. (2000) 'What is Happening to Education for Mutual Understanding?', in Bell, A. and Richardson, N. (eds), *Who's Who in Education for Diversity?*, Belfast: The FOCUS Group.

O'Connor, U., Hartop, B., and McCully, A. (2002) *A Review of the Schools Community Relations Programme 2002: A Consultation Document*, Bangor: Department of Education.

O'Connor, U., Hartop, B., and McCully, A. (2003) *A Research Study of Pupil Perceptions of the Schools Community Relations Programme*, Coleraine: University of Ulster School of Education.

OFMDFM (2005) *A Shared Future – Policy and Strategic Framework for Good Relations in Northern Ireland*, Belfast: Office of the First Minister and Deputy First Minister.

Smith, A., and Dunn, S. (1990) *Extending Inter-School Links*, Coleraine: University of Ulster Centre for the Study of Conflict.

Smith, A., and Robinson, A. (1992) *Education for Mutual Understanding: Perceptions and Policy*, Coleraine: University of Ulster Centre for the Study of Conflict.

Smith, A., and Robinson, A. (1996) *Education for Mutual Understanding: The Initial Statutory Years*, Coleraine: University of Ulster Centre for the Study of Conflict.

NORMAN RICHARDSON

5 Critiques and Objections

It is hardly surprising that educational initiatives concerned with mutual understanding and cultural diversity have stimulated criticism and controversy in view of their concern with attitudes, beliefs, feelings and behaviour in the context of community division and violence in the contested society that is Northern Ireland. The same is no less true in other places in relation to multicultural education, human rights education, peace education and other members of the 'intercultural family' as indicated in Chapter 1. Similar criticisms are often voiced about other strategies, outside of formal education, relating to community relations and peace and reconciliation processes, not least in countries or regions where there is a history of conflict, disputed identity or perceived injustice and oppression. The existence of such objections is at the very least an indication that these processes have been noticed and, to some extent, taken seriously.

This chapter considers some of those objections during the period from the mid-1980s when government interventions began to come into play in relation to what might then have been termed 'community relations education' in Northern Ireland.

An analysis of the documented criticisms (from pamphlets, letters to the press and occasional academic articles), taken alongside discussion with teachers and others over a number of years, suggests that there are about six loose categories of criticism or objections, with considerable overlap. These are social, cultural, religious, political, educational and practical.

Throughout these categories there are three common themes, albeit expressed in quite varied ways by different critics:

> such initiatives are perceived as *manipulative*;
> such initiatives are perceived as *propagandist*;
> such initiatives are perceived as *superficial* or *irrelevant*.

It will be the purpose of this brief chapter to examine these criticisms and to offer some constructive observations on the points raised. An indication of some of the key educational research which has pointed to weaknesses in such work and in its implementation has already been given in Chapter 4.

A Survey of the Criticisms

Some of the earliest critiques of educational processes designed to encourage inter-community understanding frequently focused on religious anxieties and, in particular, on opposition to perceived ecumenical religious activities between Protestant and Catholic children. These often appeared as letters to the press, such as in the case of an inter-church publication encouraging the exploration of different Christian traditions in Ireland (ICC/ICJP, 1985). Under the heading 'Religious Education package criticised', a statement by Independent Loyal Orange Institution indicated that:

> ... the Grand Lodge has recently concluded an investigation into a religious educa-
> tion package published jointly by the Irish Commission for Justice and Peace and
> the Irish Council of Churches – the material is entitled 'Looking at Churches and
> Worship in Ireland.' The statement adds: 'Our investigation leads us to criticise the
> package on the following grounds: 1. The ecumenical character of the stated aims
> and content; 2. The assertion that Roman Catholicism is part of Christian tradition;
> 3. The superficial analysis of complex religious issues; 4. The involvement of Nuns
> and Priests in producing educational material for Protestant children; 5. Historical
> inaccuracies with regard to the reformation; 6. Deceit and confusion with regard to
> the Mass and the Lord's Supper, and other distinctive doctrines. We therefore warn
> Protestant parents of the dangers of this insidious and unprofessional package. Our
> institution has circularised the other loyal orders and various Church Bodies... to
> join with us in our condemnation and to bring pressure to ensure that the material
> is totally rejected. (Coleraine Chronicle, 1985)

This sense of a fear of religious and political syncretism and of attempts to 'reconcile the irreconcilable' was clearly but more extensively evident during the late 1980s and early 1990s, when Education for Mutual Understanding and Cultural Heritage were beginning to make some public impact as a result of legislation in the Education Reform (Northern Ireland) Order, 1989. A series of pamphlets was produced by the Free Presbyterian Church of Ulster and widely distributed in some parts of Northern Ireland, reaching school principals and boards of governors. Their forthrightly antagonistic tone inevitably caused some concern, not least on the part of teachers and those developing programmes and processes in Education for Mutual Understanding.

The pamphlets accused those promoting EMU of attempting to exert undue influence by forcing children to take part in activities to which Protestant parents would be opposed. Furthermore, they accused teachers and others of deliberately keeping parents in the dark or misinforming them about what was going on. The following extracts give some indication of the tone of these criticisms:

> (An) ... assault has been launched against the Protestant children of our Province in order to brain-wash them into accepting ecumenical concepts. That attack is contained in the policy of the Department of Education known as 'Education for Mutual Understanding'... The whole exercise is reprehensible because it is in violation of the rights of parents. It is a deliberate attempt to by-pass parents in order to mould the minds of children in accordance with the religious and political ambitions of the ecumenically-minded Dr. Mawhinney [then Minister of Education at the Northern Ireland Office]. It is not only unethical but it is very close to, if not altogether, illegal. The Free Presbyterian Church intends warning every Protestant parent in Ulster about what is going on behind backs and doing all in its power to stop this plan to 'kidnap' Protestant children. ... Protestant parents must not allow their children to be brainwashed into accepting a share of the blame for the terrible events in Ulster when the blame lies fairly and squarely with the Roman Catholic community. ... It is proposed to amalgamate Protestant and Roman Catholic pupils in various school activities. They will attend each other's schools and exchange teachers. They will also engage in joint extra-curricular activities such as sports outings and joint trips. In all these arrangements no effort is to be made to inform the parents or to ask if they approve. ... In the light of these facts I call upon the Protestant parents of Ulster to take a stand now for their own rights and their children's freedom before Dr. Brian Mawhinney and the ecumenical educationalists march their children off into the oblivion of a Roman Catholic education system. (Foster, 1988)

A similar leaflet in the same series parodied the EMU acronym, calling it *EMU: Exercise in Mutilating and Undermining Protestantism*, and claimed that its purpose was the 'De-Protestantising' of Ulster: '... EMU is allied to

Romanism. EMU forces ecumenical joint worship services. EMU refuses any conscientious objectors. EMU threatens education disadvantage on any parent who does not co-operate. EMU forces on children Roman priests – the next step is the confessional box' (Free Presbyterian Church pamphlet, c. 1989).

At the same time a certain amount of local pressure was put on schools that were participating in the Cross-Community Contact Scheme (as it was termed at the time), and there are indications that this was organised by those involved in issuing the anti-EMU documents. One primary school principal in Co. Tyrone received the following letter:

> Firstly I would like to object to receiving letters asking permission for various activities to be permitted signed by a Principal of a Roman Catholic school along with other teachers.
> Secondly I would like to put on record my disgust at your school's continuing participation in the Government's Education for Mutual Understanding. This political blackmail does not help the problem in this province.
> We should be seeking to portray the true biblical teaching to our Roman Catholic friends rather than joining with what is anti-biblical ecumenism.
> ... I know that I am not the only one who would like to register their objection but perhaps they feel intimidated. ... I know I will not be popular for writing to you, but I am concerned. (Quoted with the permission of the recipient)

While for the most part this strident campaign had a limited impact on schools, not least because the vast majority of principals *had* discussed the matter with both parents and governors before embarking on cross-community contact programmes, there were a few serious situations in which local objectors were able to influence the course of events. In 1991, for instance, a small County Armagh primary school received national press publicity when a number of parents withdrew their children 'in protest over growing activities with pupils from the nearby Catholic school'. The *Belfast Telegraph* reported one parent as saying: 'No-one really objected to the children meeting in school but when it got to the stage of joint teams for sporting events it was felt the school had gone too far' (*Belfast Telegraph*, 21 September 1991). Various meetings were held between parents, governors and the Education and Library Board, but the situation was unresolved, and as a result a teacher's job was threatened due to the drop in pupil numbers. While other schools have had to deal with small numbers of parental concerns over cross-community contact plans, including occasional withdrawals, incidents at the extreme of the 1991 County Armagh situation were very much the exception.

While this level of opposition to such work seems to have diminished in intensity, similar criticisms do re-emerge from time to time in the pages of the local press. A recurring feature is a belief among some members of the protestant/unionist community that contact and curriculum work of this kind represents a deliberate attempt to destroy their culture. In 1994 a Protestant minister complained to the Belfast Telegraph about '... the efforts of the Department of Education in Northern Ireland to undermine the heritage and ethos of the Protestant religion' (Belfast Telegraph, July 1994). Around the same time a statement by the education spokesperson for the Democratic Unionist Party, Sammy Wilson (later a minister in the Stormont Assembly), launching their education manifesto, urged parents to resist education for mutual understanding, which he described 'as a "blatant misuse" of schools, more suited to Stalin's Russia, Hitler's Germany or a "loony left" council' (Belfast Telegraph, 15 March 1993). On another occasion the same politician claimed that 'in reality cultural heritage and EMU is a programme for cultural genocide directed against unionists' (*Sunday Life*, 8 March 1992).

Objections of this kind have been almost exclusively heard among some sections of the protestant/unionist community. There has been little evidence of such opposition to curriculum programmes and inter-school contact from catholic/nationalist parents, and in general Catholic schools have been perceived as supportive of such activities, encouraged, indeed, by the Church hierarchy and the Council for Catholic Maintained Schools. (Such support in itself, of course, may have served inadvertently to confirm the fears of some of the critics from the protestant/unionist community.) It has been suggested that the Catholic school authorities are in a much more homogeneous situation thereby enabling them to encourage participation in such work, although more cynically others have suggested that support for EMU and associated work within the Catholic sector has been a corollary of the Church's opposition to the development of integrated education. Where there has been criticism from the catholic/nationalist community this has not been couched in religious and cultural terms, but it has more usually indicated a nationalist political perspective which perceives such schemes as a diversion from 'the real issues' or as a 'papering over the cracks of injustice'.

The clearest and most public expression of this critique was made by Fr. Martin O'Callaghan (a senior figure in Catholic teacher training) in a number of articles around 1989. O'Callaghan emphasised that he was

> wholeheartedly in favour of those elements of the EMU programme which consist in the enhancement of pupils' self-esteem; personal, social and moral education; social and life skills; understanding of conflict and conflict resolution; multicultural education; international education, etc. [and] of having children from Catholic and non-Catholic schools meet... to co-operate in meaningful work and thereby to get to know and respect each other.

His concern, however, related to what he saw as a simplistic analysis of the Northern Ireland conflict as one relating to lack of understanding and subsequent intolerance and division, thereby requiring increased understanding of each other's cultural traditions which would in turn lead to decreased intolerance and division. This, he claimed,

> carries a hidden political agenda. No blame is attached to political or economic structures: the fault lies with individual people and their internal attitudes.
> The government's analysis does not represent the real nature of the Northern Ireland problem. The real problem is... political discrimination and economic discrimination... [that] continues to be perpetrated even though the vast majority of individual members of the dominant group do not wish to be unjust people and do not personally act in an unjust way towards anyone.
> ... The proper role of education in helping to solve the Northern Ireland problem consists in enabling the children who will form the next generation, firstly, to understand the unjust societal structures which cause people in dominant and subordinate groups alike to nurse prejudice and mistrust to the detriment of all and, secondly, to work to change those structures. The central issues which need to be addressed and explored are not 'different cultural traditions' but issues of justice, inequality (poverty) and class.

If the EMU programme is not drastically amended to take account of these issues...
the real problem will continue to fester unacknowledged, and the situation will
continue to worsen.

What I am against is the government offering us, as an analysis of the problem, a viewpoint which is no more than the product of its own sectional interests. (O'Callaghan,
1989)

Some years later a similar critique was made by John McQuade of the
Ulster People's College, though with greater emphasis on the weaknesses
of the perceived over-individualistic approach of EMU and similar community relations processes:

Underpinning many of these initiatives is the assumption that communal conflict
can be alleviated, or eliminated, by a combination of educational programmes which
promote cross community contact and greater understanding of 'the other tradition',
and measures designed to tackle social and economic inequalities.

... the argument appears to suggest that communities in Northern Ireland have acted
irrationally, that they have mutually misunderstood each other and that they can be
reconciled through appropriate educational experiences. ... The conflict in Northern
Ireland is not based on a series of misunderstandings about the beliefs of the other
community, rather it is based on a fundamental dispute over the ideas of sovereignty
and nationality... that is, the constitutional position of Northern Ireland.

... It is important to emphasise that what we have witnessed in Northern Ireland over
the past 25 years has been a communal conflict and not simply a conflict between
groups of individuals. ... It is difficult to conceive of any sense in which individual
reconciliation can translate into communal reconciliation... (which) can only occur
when communities can subscribe to a shared notion of justice and where there is at
least some consensus...

... Community relations projects have failed to produce reconciliation or mutual
understanding, not because they have been inadequately funded or poorly targeted,
but because they have been working with a set of assumptions about the conflict
which do not bear scrutiny. (McQuade, 1996)

The criticisms articulated by McQuade have been expressed over many
years in one form or another. Community Relations work in general has
also been subjected to the accusation that it is misdirected because it tends
to emphasise the similarities, especially between individuals, and to ignore
the differences, especially between groups. While this attitude of 'politeness

between nice people' may prevail in some quarters, however, it has long been rejected by those who recognise that real and hard issues have to be part of the agenda of community healing just as they are part of community division.

Perhaps the most challenging critiques of these initiatives, however, are those which suggest that they are based on unsound or inadequate *educational* principles and practice. At a simple level this has expressed itself in the fears of some teachers that they are being unfairly and unrealistically expected to achieve a level of community harmony which governments and others have failed to do over many years. The problems and pressures of the divided society of Northern Ireland, it is sometimes argued, go too deep for schools to be able to make any impact on personal, group or community attitudes. Thus some educators have responded with caution, others with antagonism, especially in the light of the heavy weight of expectations of all kinds which are laid on teachers. Others have argued that an inevitably superficial, ineffectual and bland approach to such issues may only serve to reinforce prejudice rather than to alleviate it. Such concerns are not infrequently expressed in the form of cynicism about the inter-school cross-community activities which have been funded under the auspices of the Schools' Community Relations Programme. It has often been suggested, sometimes from within the teaching profession, that many schools have inadequate motives and are simply interested in extra funding rather than the development of improved community relationships between pupils.

Occasionally teachers have been accused of failing to tackle such work with sufficient seriousness and engaging only half-heartedly, rendering it superficial and ineffective. Concerns of this kind were taken up by the Community Relations Council in 1995 in a submission to the Department of Education which was intended to offer constructive criticisms. As it was reported in the press, however, under the bold headline 'EMU scheme has failed, says Council', the impression was given that the Council was sniping at the whole idea:

> Fears that the government's own bird of reconciliation – EMU – may be moving towards extinction have been put to it by the Community Relations Council. Critics believe that the scheme is open to abuse and that the money for helping to cross the sectarian divide is sometimes being used simply to fund school outings.
>
> The council claimed that only one third of Northern Ireland's 1,200 schools are actively involved in cross community contact schemes... And EMU... suffers from inadequate training for teachers, with aspects 'likely to be ignored or dealt with superficially', said the council. ... Several teachers have told Education Telegraph they feel that schools often pay lip service to the cross-community contact scheme.... One spoke of pupils from different schools travelling on different buses to a joint outing. Yet, once there, they ate their sandwiches separately, toured the centre in their own groups and returned on their own bus. They then asked the EMU teacher to sign a form to confirm an integrated educational trip took place. Actual contact: Nil.
> (*Belfast Telegraph*, 3 March 1995)

This particular newspaper article was evidently widely read at the time, and was much quoted by teachers and the broader public, sometimes simplistically as 'evidence' that 'EMU has failed'. The Press Officer of the Community Relations Council responded with a letter setting their Report in context and insisting that they were among those 'who are constructively critical because they wish (EMU) to succeed' (*Belfast Telegraph*, 17 April 1995). His letter was also critical of the common press confusion between the voluntary cross-community contact scheme and Education for Mutual Understanding in the curriculum. Nevertheless, it was the original emotive article rather than the well-argued response which gained public attention and almost certainly damaged the public perception of Education for Mutual Understanding.

While it is often perceived that curriculum work for diversity and mutual understanding is fully compatible with structural initiatives to develop integrated or shared schools, there has occasionally been friction between the movements based on the suggestion that to work within the existing divided systems was a conservative strategy which accepted the status quo rather than challenging it. In this view EMU and similar initiatives only served to detract from the impetus for a more radical transformation. Flanagan and Lambkin have argued that the supporters of segregated education are anxious to show that they recognise the problems of segregation and to demonstrate that they wish to attend to these problems:

> They are implementing the government's... initiative which seeks to increase contact
> between Protestants and Catholics to break down suspicion and mutual misunder-
> standing between the two sides. *They are preserving separation by conceding a degree*
> *of integration.*
> ... Catholics and Protestants become more friendly but they retain their separate
> schools and with them their separate religious identities. They become friendly
> through sharing some educational experiences, *but not too friendly*. ... EMU and Cul-
> tural Heritage are in practice a 'weak' form of integration. ... (they) could amount to
> little more than window dressing for continued, albeit better informed segregation.
> (Flanagan and Lambkin, 1993; author's italics)

In a rather damning phrase, those promoting the 'weak-form integration'
while retaining separate schools are ultimately designated by these writers
as 'covert separatists'.

Taken together with the various research programmes (noted in Chapter 4) these indicate something of the range of critiques of diversity and
mutual understanding initiatives over a number of years. It is important
to note, however, that as such work has moved more into the mainstream
of educational provision many of these criticisms have subsided.

Reflections on the Objections

These critical approaches to the ideals of education for diversity and mutual
understanding have been surveyed here with minimal comment so far, and
simply to attempt to demolish these arguments would be unhelpful for a
number of reasons. Firstly, some of the comment has been offered by people
who share the broad aims of such work even if they do not fully accept the
premises or processes on which they perceive it to be based. Secondly, some
of the criticisms are genuinely related to a concern for improved practice
rather than for a negation of the idea. Further, even in the case of those
strident criticisms which are overtly antagonistic and sometimes destructive, it is important to recognise genuine anxieties and fears on the part
of some sections of the community which must be taken seriously and, as

much as possible, addressed honestly and sensitively. Thus the reflections that follow are offered in order to move the discussion forward positively if at all possible.

One of the principal obstacles confronting those attempting to develop good practice in such work has been the constant confusion between curriculum initiatives and inter-school cross-community contact programmes. It has often been pointed out that contact is but one strategy in this process; nevertheless there is a persistent impression, evident from the examples above, that contact is the whole picture, and this has made it difficult to discuss the much broader concept of mutual understanding without getting distracted by attempts to clarify what it is not. While there are many examples of good practice in contact programmes which are carried out with broad educational and community approval, some work of this kind has inevitably been poor or superficial. Because inter-school contact may have a relatively high public profile (not least because schools *are* expected to notify parents) the poor examples are prone to publicity and may be held up (for whatever reasons – innocent or malign) as typical. It is important to emphasise that valid work in this area is not totally dependent on the inclusion of contact; indeed, where contact is superficial it may well stand in the way of effective mutual understanding. Skills in other areas – building up of self-esteem and relationships and developing awareness of differences and creative approaches to conflict – must be part of contact work if it is to have any possibility of impact.

Among the more strident criticisms was the suggestion that teachers are engaging in such work without consulting parents or, in some, cases, in direct opposition to parental wishes. If this was the case, however, it was completely contrary to official advice since the initiation of the Department of Education's Cross-Community Contact Scheme in 1987 (see, for example, DENI, 1995, p. 11).[1] To fail to advise parents is undoubtedly counter-productive, and the vast majority of schools have recognised that parental views must be respected. At the same time there have been many

---

1   In September 1996 the operation of this scheme was transferred to individual Education and Library Boards and renamed *The Schools' Community Relations Programme*.

cases where initial parental objections and anxieties subsided when it was recognised that curriculum and contact programmes are unthreatening and educationally sound. This relates very closely to the trust which is built up between a particular school and its local community. Some schools, indeed, have made significant and effective efforts to involve parents in the curricular and inter-school process thereby deepening and enhancing the quality of such work.

One of the central purposes of education for diversity and mutual understanding is surely to help children and young people to be aware of human diversity and a range of differing opinions, and to encourage sensitivity and respect for those differences, whether these relate to local community divisions or to wider issues of race, ethnicity and disability, etc.. These qualities have not always been exemplified in Northern Ireland society – as in other parts of the world – and sometimes opposition to such work stems from unease or cynicism about attempts to encourage such qualities in young people. As formative and influential institutions, schools have to do more than just verbally advocate such qualities – they have to exemplify them. An ethos in which diversity is accepted and respected is crucial, not only for pupils but for the wider community as well. It is important for schools to recognise that this is a key socialising function of schools – a statement of what they are about in terms of preparing young people to live in a diverse world. In the real world schools will achieve this only haltingly and to varying degrees, but they should not be afraid to work on the belief that what we may describe as 'an ethos of respect and mutual understanding' is a key function of any good school.

Teachers may come to this area with a range of personal convictions, religious, political or humanitarian persuasions and motivations, but ultimately their only substantial justification for work in this as in any other educational field must be educationally grounded and related to the well-being of pupils and the wider school community. If teachers are clear about this, then there is no need to fear indoctrination or manipulation, because such approaches are educationally and professionally unacceptable. On this basis teachers must respect the various backgrounds and positions from which pupils and their families have come. This does not prevent education from being challenging and raising questions – for these too are fundamental to the very idea of education – but ultimately the process is open-ended. It is not the role of teachers to work to mould children to their own views, and if this is recognised it should allay some fears even when the process is a challenging and demanding one.

It has sometimes been claimed that EMU and similar initiatives were simply government ploys to shift responsibility for 'solving' the problems of Northern Ireland. But, as argued in other chapters, government came late onto the scene, and the concept took shape largely as a result of the work of teachers, voluntary agencies and academic institutions, and was often informed and inspired by similar work elsewhere in the world. It was fundamentally a set of educational responses to division and conflict in society. Government support had certainly been sought and was welcomed when at last it came, because it helped to give the work a higher profile and a certain status, as well as gradually introducing funding opportunities, but it remains fundamentally an educational strategy, and should be judged on whether it is good education rather than on the political motives of any government.

Fears of attempted manipulations by governments or other political forces have led some to criticise educational work of this kind as an attempt to gloss over or 'whitewash' really divisive community issues by focusing only on friendly individual relationships. Many have argued that this is too simplistic in tackling the problems of sectarianism and injustice. Such criticisms have indeed been directed at the entire span of community relations or 'peace and reconciliation' work, sometimes under the familiar slogan of 'no peace without justice'. If this is a corrective to naive assumptions that divisions can be solved merely by polite inter-personal contact and an emphasis on how people are similar, then it is a valid and fair point. Many educators have recognised that education must help children and young people to understand differences as well as identifying similarities. Difficult issues about justice cannot be shirked, although some degree of inter-personal and inter-group trust is essential if such explorations and discussions are not to be counter-productive. Those who regard justice as essential *before* peace can be achieved might usefully reflect on the concept of peace not so much as an *end* but rather as a *process* which is essential to the creation of an agreed and fair society. The achievement of justice for one community may create injustice for another unless the *processes* of peace are in operation. These must surely involve awareness of and respect for the feelings and values of others; considerate behaviour; the development of co-operation and trust; the promotion of creative and non-violent approaches to conflict management; negotiation towards *mutual* justice. If there can be 'no peace without justice', then it is surely no less true that there can be *no justice without peace*.

It is unhelpful to portray education as a panacea for social and political problems. Overstating the significance of education has sometimes led to cynicism and disillusionment. Education of any kind is a long-term process. Especially in relation to attitude development and social skills, it is often indirect and difficult to assess in terms of clear-cut results. Education functions in the context of society, not in splendid isolation. Thus it is important not to expect too much of education, and certainly not in the short term. It is one approach, one strategy, among several. We need to be realistic about education and what it can achieve, though without diluting our ideals and visions.

While education for diversity and mutual understanding is inevitably only a partial response to the complexities of human divisions – in Northern Ireland and the wider world – it is nonetheless important in that such processes offer reflective approaches to tackling important issues. To perceive these processes as some kind of misdirected 'liberal do-goodism' would be to dismiss the genuine concerns of many teachers, parents and others for finding ways of attending to a broken society and trying to create something better for future generations. In the broad scale of things this work is still at an early stage, and it is still very much a process of learning, sometimes by mistakes, and building up new approaches, new skills, new awareness and new experience.

The late Professor Frank Wright, a political historian, wrote about such work as fundamentally *experiential* for teachers and learners alike. In partial response to the critique made by Martin O'Callaghan, he wrote:

> What is needful is that there should be space for people to share experiences which may have been very hurtful to them. ... Part of the point in coming together is to create bonds of trust and the only thing there can be in the beginning is our trust

in each other's good faith. Until we know something of their reality, how it feels to be in their shoes, we have nothing to set against our stereotypes. ... In the meeting together we learn about each other's feelings and experiences. What is merely preached at us – that which does not correspond to our own experiences or to what we learn from the stories others tell us of their own experience – teaches us little. ... If we explore our histories together with people who have experienced the opposite side of the fear relationships new history may eventually flourish, but the content of what is formally taught is probably much less important than the spirit in which it is taught. (Wright, 1990)

References

Belfast Telegraph (1991) *School Divided by Sectarian Row*, Noel McAdam, 21 September.

Belfast Telegraph (1993) *DUP Calls for Resistance to School Plans*, Noel McAdam, 15 March.

Belfast Telegraph (1994) *'Secret' School Visits: Claim*, July.

Belfast Telegraph (1995) *EMU Scheme has failed, says Council*, David Watson, 13 April.

Coleraine Chronicle (1985?) *Religious Education Package Criticised*, approx. June.

DENI (1995) *Cross Community Contact Scheme 1995–6 (Schools)*, Bangor: Department of Education for Northern Ireland, Department of Education for Northern Ireland.

Flannagan, C.E.T., and Lambkin, B.K. (1993) 'Religious Identity and Integrated Education', in Moffatt, C. (ed), *Education Together for a Change*, Belfast: Fortnight Educational Trust.

Foster, I. (1988) *The Danger Threatening Our Children*, Kilskeery Free Presbyterian Church.

ICC/ICJP (1985) *Looking at Churches and Worship in Ireland*, Belfast and Dublin: Irish Council of Churches, Irish Commission for Justice and Peace, Stranmillis College.

McQuade, J. (1996) 'Justice First Please!', in *Journal* No. 13, Summer 1996, Belfast: Northern Ireland Community Relations Council.

Mullan, R. (1995) 'Cross-community contact scheme has not failed', letter in *Belfast Telegraph*, 17 April (from Information Officer of the Northern Ireland Community Relations Council).

O'Callaghan, M. (1989) 'What's Wrong With EMU?', in *The Catholic Teacher*, November.

Sunday Life (1992) 'Rumpus over history "bias"', 8 March.

Wright, F. (1990) 'Some Problems of Education for Mutual Understanding', in Morrow, D., Wilson, D., Wright, F., and Kaptein, R. (eds), *Finding Ways To Go...: A Discussion Paper About Community Relations in Northern Ireland*, Belfast: The Corrymeela Press.

PART 2

Pedagogy and Practice

ANNE MURRAY

6 A Whole-School Approach To Diversity and Mutual Understanding: A Primary School Perspective

In the early 1990s, when the general requirements were issued relating to the educational themes of Education for Mutual Understanding and Cultural Heritage, it was stated that the aims of all the themes 'should form part of the whole curriculum in schools and all teachers should take responsibility for implementing them' (NICC, 1989, p. 15; DENI, 1992, p. 3). Similarly the more recent Guidance booklet for Personal Development and Mutual Understanding proposes that:

> Planning for Personal Development and Mutual Understanding must take into account your established school ethos, build on the existing good practice and reflect how you and your colleagues can promote the all-round development of your school's children. (CCEA/PMB, 2007, p. 9)

Often, however, a whole-school approach can be like the kiss of death to a school initiative. In practice it means that no-one really takes responsibility for it and everyone presumes that everyone else is doing it. That certainly is a danger. However a whole-school approach is the only approach which makes sense in this context. All teachers must share some of the responsibility for implementing such an important aspect of the school's work. The whole curriculum is involved. This means that school policies in all the curricular and general areas should incorporate the principles of education for diversity and mutual understanding. Such work should be considered as an integral part of the school curriculum and school life in general.

If we examine the type of opportunities pupils are entitled to, it becomes clear that mutual respect and understanding cannot be delivered, taught, imparted or experienced in isolation. The Objectives of the Revised Northern Ireland Curriculum (CCEA, 2007, p. 4) emphasise the importance of developing young people as individuals, as contributors to society and as contributors to the economy and the environment, and they highlight the importance of qualities such as *personal understanding, mutual understanding, cultural understanding, ethical awareness* and *citizenship.* While these are particularly focused within Personal Development and Mutual Understanding (at the Foundation Stage and Key Stages 1 and 2) and Local and Global Citizenship (Key Stages 3 and 4), it is expected that they will also be developed as whole-school objectives.

Selected clauses from the Revised Curriculum documentation clearly spell out the responsibilities of teachers and schools in relation to developing awareness of diversity and mutual understanding:

... teachers should help children to:
- develop self-confidence, self-esteem and self-discipline;
- understand their own and others' feelings and emotions; ...
- listen to and interact positively with others;
- explore and understand how others live; ...
- take responsibility for their actions;
- develop tolerance and mutual respect for others; ...
- become aware of some of their rights and responsibilities; ...
- contribute to creating a better world for those around them;
- develop awareness and respect for the different lifestyles of others; ...
- understand some of their own and others' cultural traditions;
- be aware of how we rely on each other; ...
- become aware of the potential impact of developments upon the lives of others.

(CCEA, 2007, p. 4)

These all have implications throughout the school, involving the whole curriculum and the whole school community. If these ideals are taken seriously they will certainly impinge on the school ethos. They have an effect on pastoral issues and discipline. They challenge schools to consider staff development in a broader context to include personal as well as professional development. This article is based particularly on the experience of one school – an integrated primary school in Derry/Londonderry, Northern Ireland – in working through these ideals and challenges and trying to find appropriate strategies to deal with them.

Positive Whole-School Ethos

What do we mean by ethos? 'Characteristic spirit, prevalent tone of sentiment of a people or community' (Concise Oxford English Dictionary) is one dictionary definition. Many people think of ethos in terms of atmosphere. What does a positive school ethos feel or look like? Pupils in one school described it as a friendly atmosphere. They felt that they had a voice and were listened to. Parents identified 'openness' and 'a spirit of equality' as features of a positive school ethos. They also felt it had something to do with happiness, acknowledging difference, caring, respect and being child-centred. Where there is a well developed positive whole-school ethos, child-centredness will be evident in many different areas of the life of the school.

At a teachers' conference, a group of teachers considered strategies for promoting positive behaviour in the playground (Northern Ireland Council for Integrated Education – NICIE, 1996). They suggested that sunshine, somewhere to sit, some friends, games and a clean, large space to play were among the ingredients for a happy playtime in school. In discussion teachers talked about what ideas currently worked on the (play) ground, for example: peer mediation; adequate supervision to co-ordinate games; an interesting environment with seats, equipment, etc.; a no-bullying policy; timetabled lessons on play (e.g. jacks, skips); induction of lunchtime supervisors; different play areas for different age groups; chalk for pupils to draw with; a reward system for good behaviour.

Elsewhere in the school, child-centredness can be promoted through, for example: ensuring policy is put into practice in the day to day activity and organisation of the school; promoting and ensuring positive and egalitarian approaches and attitudes in the classroom and throughout the school; records of achievement for each child; effective classroom management and organisation; quality teaching and learning – particularly learning; commitment to differentiation in all areas of the curriculum; personal development workshops for staff and pupils; students' councils and/or class meetings to ensure children have a voice and that it is listened to.

These activities associated with child-centredness give children the types of opportunities and experiences which are central to the concept of mutual understanding, as outlined above.

Inclusion and 'The Happy School'

When a school considers its own policy for the development of mutual understanding, the aims and objectives should come initially from the staff followed by an input from governors. A more valuable policy will be developed if this process is inclusive and open so that each person feels she/he has a valuable contribution to make. If a school is to be able to work towards a shared understanding of the principles and practice of diversity and mutual understanding it will be very important and much more meaningful if each person is given a chance first of all to consider what his or her aims and objectives would be in relation to it. The sharing of this in a small group and then feeding the discussion into a large group enables the formulation of a valuable policy.

In the Integrated Primary School where the present writer is principal, a pamphlet was put together called *The Happy School Book* which was actually the school discipline policy. The well considered process involved working through the subject in workshop sessions with all the interested parties including parents, teachers, governors, pupils and support staff. This was a vital part of the policy. It took months to do all the consultation and most of a year to put the booklet together and even then it was considered a draft document in many ways because all felt that it should be reviewed regularly to ensure the policy was working in practice and was a reality for the children in school on a daily basis.

The Happy School Book contained reasons why good behaviour should be promoted in school. It contained negotiated class and school rules couched in positive terms instead of 'Thou Shalt Not...' language. It contained a bullying policy which gave advice on bullying to the victim, the bully and the parents of both victims and bullies. It was illustrated by the children and its title came from an inspired parent. *The Happy School Book* was about inclusion. It included the views and feelings of all those involved in the school community.

Where inclusive policies of this kind are implemented in schools it will be much easier to emphasise the importance of respect for diversity among children of all age groups, because such respect is intrinsic to the very nature of the school.

Effective work in areas such as self-esteem and conflict resolution cannot be delivered by documentation alone. The process of involving and *including* all the players in the process of agreeing policies and methods of delivery and review are of vital importance and significance.

It is generally considered that the key issues in this process are centred on:

- respect for self and others
- dealing creatively with conflict
- awareness of interdependence
- awareness of diverse cultural traditions
- openness to diversity
- respect for differences
- inter-/trans-Nationalism.

The most basic issue appears to be the first one – the development of respect for self and others. If schools manage to give this the consideration it deserves, then people become much more open to exploring the other aims.

Whole-School Self-Esteem

According to the official documentation of the Revised Northern Ireland
Curriculum, the development of primary-age children's self-awareness
and self-esteem is central to the processes of Personal Development and
Mutual Understanding (CCEA/PMB, 2007). However, schools which
begin to give serious consideration to how they are going to help pupils
develop self-esteem discover very quickly that the starting point cannot
be the pupils. It has to begin with the adults in the school community and
in particular teachers, classroom assistants and staff who come into daily
contact with the pupils.

Teachers aim to help children develop confidence in their own work
so that pupils can accept success and failure, evaluate their own strengths
and weaknesses, recognise their contribution to social situations and take
responsibility for themselves and the consequences of their actions. This
is a tall order! How many teachers feel comfortable in their own ability
to do all these things?

Factors in Developing Self-Esteem

One of the main difficulties with developing self-esteem is that it requires
experiential learning and lots of positive reinforcement to be effective. If
self-esteem could be acquired as the result of a handwriting exercise or a
handout, schools would be full of people with high self-esteem. Unfortunately it is not that simple. In many of the activities designed to develop
self-esteem people are required to engage actively in exercises which may
seem awkward and uncomfortable at first. Acknowledging their ability
and talents and capabilities aloud and in company is not an easy thing for
most adults to engage in. But that is exactly where many have to start to
develop their own self-esteem.

Culture is another factor which may inhibit the development of self-
esteem. Many people in Northern Ireland are from traditional Protestant
and Catholic backgrounds and both traditions, until fairly recently, have

focused significantly on the negative rather than the positive side of religion (a sentiment that is certainly not unique to Northern Ireland). 'The sin of pride' looms large in many people's psyche and the net result has been that the people brought up in such a negative atmosphere find it difficult to recognise, acknowledge or proclaim their better qualities. In contrast many Americans seem to have recognised the value of self-esteem some time ago and it is more central to the ethos of their schools. Our religious-cultural baggage makes it difficult for us to develop freely this very important area of self-esteem.

Self-esteem cannot be developed in isolation. It really does require a whole-school approach. Individuals or classes can do lots of work developing self-esteem. Some primary classes start each day with an affirmation circle or song – each person in the class gets an opportunity to say something positive about themselves or others or to sing a song such as 'Today is a day for smiling'. This is a great way to start the day and set a positive tone in a classroom. However if this is not understood, acknowledged and supported throughout the whole school community, the effect is limited. If other members of the teaching and support staff do not understand what is going on by way of promoting positive atmosphere and building up each child's self-image they can actually do damage to the process by using a negative comment rather than a constructive one.

Self-esteem work must also be ongoing and developmental. It has to take place every day. It has to happen everywhere – in the staff room, in the classroom, in the playground, in the canteen, in the Principal's office and be supported, where possible, at home. It has to concern everybody – teachers, pupils, support staff, governors and ideally parents. This experience does not necessarily come either naturally or easily to parents any more than it does to teachers or pupils and schools can play a very important role in children's lives by working with parents to help them develop their own self-esteem thus supporting the work going on in school. In one school the parents' meetings start with an affirmation round in which parents have to tell one another about some of the things they admire about their children.

It has become clear to educators that not only is self-esteem crucial for underpinning learning in general, but that it is also crucial in the process of developing in children the capacity to build respect and celebrate diversity.

There are many complex implications of all this self-esteem development work. Schools need to be open enough to examine their own practice. Teachers need to be prepared to take risks and move out of their comfort zones perhaps in order to develop themselves personally as well as professionally. Change rarely occurs without some discomfort whether physical, mental, emotional or spiritual.

A Case Study in Whole-School Self-Esteem

The Integrated Primary School and Nursery featured in this article takes its mutual understanding brief very seriously and does a great deal of work in the area of building self-esteem throughout the school community. A programme which encourages the development of self-esteem has been set in place from Nursery right through to Primary 7. The process starts with the teaching staff and they begin each year with an in-service training (INSET) element which includes personal development. These sessions are experiential in nature and the staff did not embrace them easily. They acknowledge that the workshops which make them examine their own attitudes and feelings about their own self worth are both difficult and at times downright uncomfortable. However, they also consider them to be the most valuable training they have ever done on a personal level as well as being beneficial to building a spirit of teamwork among the teachers.

Circle Time is not just a classroom activity for the children. Teachers use Circle Time to affirm each other and the work they do with the children. For example, if the weekly staff training topic happened to be looking at some aspect of Science then the meeting might start with an affirmation round in which each teacher talked about something which was particularly successful in Science which she or he had done in class with the children. This ensures a positive note – it affirms the teachers, focuses on the pupils and their learning, spreads good professional ideas and builds the spirit of teamwork within the staff. All teachers would have the opportunity to facilitate staff sessions like this and it helps develop them both personally and professionally.

The children are consistently affirmed all the way through school. Within their classroom teachers help them discover their unique talents and qualities and encourage them to share these with others. Plenty of praise and then some more is used on a daily basis and this is supported with motivational or positive stickers and certificates given by the teachers and the Principal who keeps a large stock in her bottom drawer which she is happy to dispense at any time of the day. Children's successes are highlighted and rewarded. A positive discipline policy is in place which supports the work in the classroom and good behaviour is rewarded. Good classroom management and organisation are encouraged so that children get every possible chance to learn in a positive atmosphere. Additionally the work of the School Council gives the children a real sense that they have a voice and that they are heard.

Dealing with Conflict

Once self-esteem is being addressed, schools find that it is in some ways a natural development to move into the other central areas of mutual understanding. Once people are happy about who they are and have developed a positive high self-esteem, then they are ready to move on and look outside themselves at other people. Conflict resolution can be a useful area to explore once children have developed a healthy self-esteem. The aims of respect and promoting positive approaches to dealing with conflict are closely interlinked and some schools now undertake a programme of Peer Mediation which examines this whole area in an experiential way (Murray, 1996; see also Tyrrell and Farrell, 1995; Tyrrell, 2002).

Our school became involved in a Peer Mediation project in which pupils began to explore the issue of conflict and its resolution. The older pupils of P6/P7 (aged 9–10 and 10–11) began training in Peer Mediation by participating in experiential workshops in which they considered self-esteem, differences, the nature of conflict, the skills involved in mediation and actual practice in role playing mediation of conflicts. They took part in exercises which helped them focus on difference in fun ways such as *All Change*, a circle game where participants had to change seats if they belonged to a group of people who wore white socks or had black hair or who were male, etc. They played listening games to increase their listening skills: games in which they listened intently to a partner and retold the story, and games in which they ignored their partner and didn't use good listening skills and then discussed how it felt to be ignored. They role-played conflict sketches and took the part of the people in conflict, the peer mediators and the observers. These were very sophisticated skills which these young people were acquiring and the personal development involved in the training programme was astonishing and immensely beneficial.

After a six week training period pupils gave mediation presentations to support staff, other classes and parents. They were then organised into teams and on a rota basis worked in the playground during lunch and playtime, dealing with small scale disputes and conflicts. The training during the project developed their confidence as well as giving them an insight into dealing with conflict. The end product of peer mediation training is undoubtedly beneficial to schools; the process, however, is invaluable!

Interdependence

It is much easier to examine the notion of interdependence in the family and in the community once the groundwork has been done on self-esteem. When the pupils have looked at themselves and others in the context of conflict resolution, it is easier to look at the day to day realities of conflict in the home and in the community. The notion of interdependence with each other may be explored with more confidence.

Even when children are studying an apparently innocent topic such as 'People who help us', uncomfortable and potentially contentious issues may arise, such as Child Protection and the school's relationship with the police.

As well as knowing about how families interact, children need to be aware of personal safety skills and to have some training in them in order to combat abuse by adults from within or without the family circle. Programmes such as *Kidscape*[1] are about empowering children and high self-esteem is a prerequisite for such a programme.

The role of the police in a divided society like Northern Ireland may be problematic to some when the community police officer is one of the people included in the 'People who help us' topic. Teachers and school governors need to be confident about how to ensure their policy is inclusive in terms of contentious issues and ensure that parents are aware of what that policy is.

Diversity, Human Rights and Widening Horizons

As pupils move on through the school, they begin to widen their horizons. When the basic self-esteem work has been started early on and continues as a backdrop to their learning, teachers may find pupils more receptive to examining issues of diversity on a broader canvas both national and international. A useful feature of studying this wider context is that it helps pupils put themselves and their community into perspective.

Many schools have external links with schools in other countries. Our integrated school has been involved with a national school in County Kildare through the University of Ulster's 'Dissolving Boundaries' project[2] which links schools in Northern Ireland and the Republic of Ireland through videophones in each host school as well as by email. Children also had an opportunity for a face-to-face meeting with their partners from the south. The project is curriculum based and helps youngsters to begin to look outwards to their nearest neighbours on the island of Ireland.

1　<http://www.kidscape.org.uk> (accessed 25 June 2010).
2　See <http://www.dissolvingboundaries.org> (accessed 25 June 2010).

Other projects such as 'On the Line' linked schools along the zero longitude line and we enjoyed the services of a Ghanaian artist in residence who shared her artistic skills in art, creative writing, geography, cookery and dance. The whole school community enjoyed the fruits of the project through a very colourful exhibition of children's work, music and dance including learning to dance sitting down during a special Ghanaian Evening. The importance of projects like these is evident given the growth of racial attacks on African and Chinese families in Northern Ireland. One Chinese family lasted only a few months at our school due to attacks on the family home. We need to raise awareness of issues like this and prepare our children for a multicultural world. The increased presence of foreign nationals, including families whose first language is not English, has led to a number of new initiatives in many Northern Ireland schools, including, for example, multicultural evenings and, more importantly, a greater readiness to address issues of diversity in the curriculum.

Many schools have become involved with the UNICEF Rights Respecting School Award. This award process is a very valuable means of enabling schools to evaluate their policies and practice in regard to children's rights, in their own school first, and then encouraging them to look outwards towards the issue of children's rights across the world.[3]

Another valuable award scheme is the International School Award, organised by the Westminster government Department for Children, Schools and Families (DCSF) but supported in Northern Ireland by the British Council. There are different levels of commitment and this enables schools to plan a programme over time to enhance their awareness of the global picture and consider opportunities to celebrate diversity.

3   See <http://www.unicef.org.uk/resources/index.asp> (accessed 25 June 2010).

Process

In the Revised Northern Ireland Curriculum there is a strong emphasis on the importance of 'Whole Curriculum Skills and Capabilities', and 'Thinking Skills and Personal Capabilities'. Particularly relevant are the sections on:

> *Working with Others* (including listening actively and sharing opinions; understanding how actions and words affect others; taking personal responsibility; being fair; respecting the views and opinions of others; working collaboratively); and
> *Being Creative* (including making new connections between ideas/information; learning from and valuing other people's ideas). (CCEA, 2007, pp. 8–9)

This Revised Curriculum, which is much more skills based than before, lends itself well to being more child-centred. The focus on skills such as being creative and working with others is more about process than product. The new areas of learning of The World Around Us (History, Geography, Science) and Personal Development and Mutual Understanding provide excellent opportunities to explore issues and challenges in relation to diversity and mutual understanding.

The actual *whole-school processes* involved in the development of mutual understanding and positive approaches to diversity, however, are crucial to the success of such work in any school and in all types of schools. Obviously the body of knowledge taught is important but the ways in which skills are developed within a supportive ethos are every bit as significant.

As always the process needs to start with the teachers in order to ensure that they are prepared to help deliver a skills-based curriculum. The prescriptive and content-based curriculum that has been in operation for the past twenty years in N Ireland has actually deskilled teachers to a certain extent. In an increasingly diverse N Ireland society, we need to devote more time, energy and expertise to the areas of mutual understanding and diversity. This was emphasised in the publication of a report by a NICIE Working

Party on the theme of 'Integrating Through Understanding': 'The challenge for teachers in [the integrated school] setting is to foster positive relationships among pupils in the context of cultural difference... Teachers need to be given the opportunity to develop the sort of skills more commonly associated with the community relations sector' (NICIE, 2001, p. 15).

Specific training for teachers and support staff, as well as sharing good practice within and across schools, will be crucial as we move forward into a more multicultural future both here and across the world.

Whole-School Diversity and Mutual Understanding for All School Types

Various publications have been issued over the years dealing with aspects of diversity and mutual understanding in integrated schools. An article by the present author on 'Education for Mutual Understanding in Practice' (Murray, 1996) reflected on the implementation of what was then one of the educational themes. A NICIE working party report entitled 'Integrating through Understanding' encouraged integrated schools to see mutual understanding as 'central to the integrated ethos' (NICIE, 2001, p. 2). More recently, however, the integrated schools have attempted to emphasise that the principles that they employ in their own sector are no less important for other schooling sectors. The Integrat*ing* Education project published a brief set of recommendations on 'including everyone in our schools' (NICIE, 2008b), emphasising the central importance of whole-school ethos. At around the same time a new edition of a former publication was issued to promote 'an anti-bias approach to education in Northern Ireland', emphasising a whole-school approach:

> The anti-bias approach relates to the whole set of school experiences from which children can learn. Such experiences may be provided for children deliberately as part of the 'formal curriculum'... or incidentally as part of the 'informal curriculum'... However, they may also arise more or less unconsciously as part of the 'hidden curriculum'. (NICIE, 2008a, p. 9)

Some teachers may still find it difficult to embrace the ideals behind education for diversity and mutual understanding. There is an implicit challenge in how it is developed. By its very nature it has to involve a whole-school approach. The concept of mutual understanding weaves its way through the taught and hidden curriculum. Above all it requires openness on behalf of those who are delivering it, as well as those to whom it is delivered.

Realising Dreams

As we move into the twenty-first century, we see much to celebrate in terms of diversity and mutual understanding. The election of the USA's first African-American President, Barack Obama, was a hopeful beginning to 2009 and a great step forward since the time when slavery, and later segregation, was acceptable. It was a moment when Martin Luther King's 'dream' became more of a reality.

However, the news across the world and wars still being fought indicate how difficult we still find it to live together and accept each other's differences. In Northern Ireland the news brings us regular reports on sectarian and racial incidents and we need to continue to be proactive in educating ourselves and our children about the importance of diversity and mutual understanding if we are to become a more cohesive society. Education has a big part to play in this process.

References

CCEA (2007) *The Northern Ireland Curriculum – Primary*, Belfast: Northern Ireland Council for the Curriculum, Examinations and Assessment.
CCEA/PMB (2007) *Personal Development and Mutual Understanding for Key Stages 1 and 2*, Belfast: Northern Ireland Council for the Curriculum, Examinations and Assessment, Partnership Management Board.

DENI (1992) *Educational (Cross-Curricular) Themes: Objectives*, Bangor: Department of Education for Northern Ireland.

Murray, A. (1996) 'EMU in Practice', in *Developments in Integrated Education (NICIE Annual Report 1995–6)*, Belfast: N.I. Council for Integrated Education.

NICC (1989) *Cross-Curricular Themes: Consultation Report*, Belfast: Northern Ireland Curriculum Council.

NICIE (1996) *Primary Schools Resource Pack*, Belfast: Northern Ireland Council for Integrated Education.

NICIE (2001) *Integrating Through Understanding (Working Party Report)*, Belfast: Northern Ireland Council for Integrated Education.

NICIE (2008a) *ABC: Promoting an Anti-Bias Approach to Education in Northern Ireland*, Belfast: Northern Ireland Council for Integrated Education.

NICIE (2008b) *Elephant, Bee and Other – Including Everyone in our Schools (Recommendations from the IntegratING Education Project)*, Belfast: Northern Ireland Council for Integrated Education.

Tyrrell, J. (2002) *Peer Mediation: A Process for Primary Schools*, London: Souvenir Press.

Tyrrell, J. and Farrell, S. (1995) *Peer Mediation in Primary Schools*, Coleraine: Centre for the Study of Conflict, University of Ulster.

JERRY TYRRELL WITH SEAMUS FARRELL

7   Dealing with Conflict and Prejudice

Editors' Introduction

Jerry Tyrrell, who died too young in December 2001 after some months of illness, was one of the pioneers in Northern Ireland of what we might today call 'education for diversity and mutual understanding'. From the mid-1980s, in Derry/Londonderry, Jerry led a research-based project that was rooted in practical, activity-based learning and he and his team worked in schools and other places around Northern Ireland and further afield, planting ideas and fresh ways of working, including the introduction of peer mediation processes. Originally sponsored by the Religious Society of Friends, the 'Quaker Peace Education Project' was based in the University of Ulster's Magee College campus and changed its name in the early 1990s to 'The EMU-Promoting School Project'. The editors and other contributors to this book all knew Jerry Tyrrell, and some worked very closely with him and learned a great deal from the experience. Many of Jerry's 'experimental' workshop approaches are now taken much more for granted and have found their way into the curriculum and the practice of many teachers and schools.

Jerry's work on this chapter (intended for a much earlier publication date) was almost complete at the time of his death and was checked over and finalised by his friend and close colleague, Seamus Farrell. The material in the chapter is no less relevant than when it was originally penned, though one or two of the references (for example, to the educational theme of *Education for Mutual Understanding*, or *EMU*) reflect a slightly earlier stage in the development of this field of work. These references have been left unchanged, so as to reflect the context of when they were written, and Jerry's chapter is presented here with only a few other very minor amendments, mostly as suggested by Seamus Farrell.

*

Conflict

> Conflict is neither good nor bad, but intrinsic in every relationship from
> marriage to international diplomacy. Whenever two or more people are
> gathered, there is conflict or potential conflict. The real issue is not the
> existence of conflict but how it is handled.
>
> — DARBY, 1995

Darby's definition underlines the inevitability of conflict. Conflict happens, in the classroom, in the playground, in the staff room, in the community, in the world. The inclusion of issues relating to conflict within the aims and objectives of Education for Mutual Understanding has provided teachers with opportunities to de-mystify 'conflict' and 'conflict resolution' for their pupils:

> [The] Aims of Education for Mutual Understanding... [are] ... to appreciate how
> conflict may be handled in nonviolent ways. Key objectives... [are that] ... pupils
> should develop a knowledge and understanding of conflict in a variety of contexts
> and of constructive and nonviolent ways of dealing with it. (DENI, 1992)

Tom Leimdorfer has suggested, disturbingly, that 'Society educates young people at best haphazardly and at worst quite destructively as far as conflict is concerned' (Leimdorfer, 1995). Education for Mutual Understanding creates an opportunity for teachers to rectify this situation. An important starting point is to link conflict to the pupils' own lives, and approaches to establishing this link are outlined in this chapter.

A 'Workshop' Approach

This chapter will focus on *informal* approaches to developing conflict resolution skills in the classroom. Ideally this involves a workshop approach where for example the pupils and teacher sit in a circle and, where possible, work is done in small groups and/or in pairs, as well as with the whole class.

Conflict resolution skills are difficult to teach as an abstract subject detached from the life of the class, emotionally or physically. The original objectives of EMU also stated that 'pupils should know and understand that people affected by conflict can experience differing emotions and reactions' (Department of Education for Northern Ireland – DENI, 1992). The emotional aspect of conflict sometimes makes teachers apprehensive about conflict resolution skills training. However, although conflict is a serious subject, looking at alternative approaches to its resolution doesn't have to be intense. There are different ways of approaching the subject, adapted to an individual teacher's style and confidence.

However, ambivalence towards the subject is exacerbated when conflict is only talked about or focused on when there has been a breach of the school rules, or when a particular class or individual has presented with patterns of anti-social behaviour. Inevitably conflict then tends to be seen as negative and the teacher's role tends to be reactive. Sometimes, like a rapid reaction force, an outside agency is brought in, in the hope that it can provide a 'quick fix'. There is a danger in only seeing a conflict when and where it breaks out, and not being aware of what brought it to a head. 'In all lively classrooms and playgrounds conflicts arise and what isn't allowed to surface there will appear with a vengeance later' (Hopkins, 1995).

Above all a school is a community and the nature of the relationships within it, between pupils and teachers, teachers and each other, teachers and ancillary staff, pupils and pupils etc., creates the culture in which conflict is found.

The aims and objectives of EMU help create the latitude whereby teachers can become proactive concerning conflict. A culture is where things grow, and by creating a culture in which creative responses to conflict are allowed to flourish, work done in preparing the pupils with skills to handle conflict can have a profound influence on whether the response to conflict is positive or negative. As Darby says, it is how we respond to conflict that determines whether it has a destructive or a constructive impact.

Mapping Out the Conflict

It is useful as a starting point to identify when and where conflict happens and how it is dealt with in the school. One way of doing this is to make a *Conflict Map*, adapting the following exercise used on a primary school staff in-service training day.

Ask the staff to brainstorm (see below) different types of conflict in school. Give each type of conflict a colour code. Invite staff to indicate types of conflict and where each happens, using coloured dots on a map of the school enlarged to the size of a flip chart. Similarly a circle divided into segments to indicate the hours of the school day can be used to illustrate when conflicts happen. Further questions can reveal how and by whom different conflicts are dealt with. This exercise often points up the amount of time that teachers have to spend dealing with conflict. Teachers by the very nature of their jobs work in isolation, and it can be reassuring for younger teachers that even experienced teachers have to deal with conflict on a regular basis. This reinforces the reality that *conflict exists*, and helps to offset the idea that the very existence of conflict is in itself a sign of failure.

A similar exercise focussing on the school rules allows pupils to acknowledge that rules help prevent and deal with conflict, and underlines the need for everybody in the school to adhere to them for the good of the community. Older students could be encouraged to discuss the school's EMU policy in relation to its discipline policy. This is particularly relevant when deciding what the ground rules are for a training workshop or lesson on conflict resolution skills.

Conflict and Classroom Control

If pupils are to be encouraged to develop conflict resolution skills of their own, this will unavoidably lead to questions about how teachers exercise control in their class. By the very nature of mandated learning, the teacher in his/her style of 'conflict management' has to maintain a balance between control and giving the pupils a measure of independence, in order to get through the curriculum. By handing over the responsibility for dealing with conflict – even partially – to students, traditional methods of control are challenged.

The issue of control is a key one to address if the principles of Education for Mutual Understanding are to be anything other than cosmetic. If mutual understanding is to be at the heart of the school ethos, then the essence of the relationships within the school must reflect this. Anything less than a real whole-school policy may lead for example to situations where a pupil goes from a workshop on affirmation, communication and co-operation in one classroom to a situation where she or he is 'bawled out' in front of his or her peers by another teacher for some alleged misdemeanour.

Ground Rules

Letting go of control can feel threatening to a teacher. However the benefit in terms of 'ownership' of the rules can lead to the class being more responsible for its behaviour, whilst still leaving the teacher as the ultimate authority. If the class makes the rules for the workshop, it is more likely that they will keep them. It is quite likely that the teacher has already negotiated class rules. At one secondary school for example, the class rules include, 'respect other people and their property', 'no putdowns', and 'listen'.

With the objective of ensuring that the workshop is a safe, enjoyable and useful experience for everybody concerned, the class can be invited to brainstorm ground rules. If the concept of a 'brainstorm'[1] is alien to the class, it is useful to demonstrate the process by asking them to come up with as many uses as possible for an everyday object such as a coat hanger.

---

1   Since this chapter was written, the terminology of 'brainstorming' has been criticised in some quarters as being offensive to people with epilepsy, though the point is questioned elsewhere. The term is retained here, as used regularly by Jerry Tyrrell and his colleagues, but is in no way intended to give offence.

People call out ideas, without comment or discussion for a set period, usually only a few minutes, and the ideas are all written up on the board. The aim is to demonstrate that there is often more than the 'obvious' idea, in this case 'to hang clothes', that one person's idea can spark off another person's ideas, and that the seemingly crazy idea, 'to help get into a car' can be feasible. Only later are the ideas evaluated for suitability.

The process of agreeing ground rules for a workshop in itself involves the conflict resolution skills of *listening*, *negotiation* and *compromise*. When a list of ground rules has been generated they can be grouped, and consensus amongst the class sought for them. Ideally the teacher negotiates the workshop ground rules with the class, within the parameters of the school rules, in order that the class takes ownership of them, and indeed of any sanctions that are agreed.

One series of workshops with year 11 pupils was faced with a recurrent breaking of ground rules. Taking a lead from the world of football, the adult facilitators were provided with yellow cards and red cards. A minor infringement of a ground rule was responded to by a yellow card; two yellow cards led to the pupil being removed from the circle, whilst the red card itself led to the misbehaving pupil being asked to leave the room. The sanctions had been previously agreed by the group.

It may be appropriate with younger pupils to be more directive (rather than involve them in generating ground rules) and to suggest the following seven:

Observe Confidentiality

As with all the rules it is worth taking time to explore the rules with the pupils in order that they can (a) understand them, (b) adapt them where necessary, (c) agree to them. Confidentiality needs to be negotiated, so that the pupils are clear about the difference between 'good' secrets and 'bad' secrets. It may be appropriate to rewrite it as 'Keep good secrets'. This means nobody talks afterwards about anything personal that was said in the workshop, even to the person who said it. The teacher needs to be thoughtful around informing pupils if there are things she or he is legally bound to pass on – information about abuse for example.

You May Pass

This rule may jar with a teacher and seem like a licence to opt out. As a teacher your discretion is necessary; it may make sense to say that this only applies to not sharing something of a personal nature, rather than not participating in an activity. Or make it clear that if they don't participate in a particular activity they have to sit quietly and not disrupt it for anybody else. However, if the pupils are given a real choice they are more likely to participate wholeheartedly; it is difficult to get the best out of a mandated group of people, young or old.

It's Okay to Make Mistakes

Creative responses to conflict sometimes require us to act differently from previously. We may give an opinion about something for the first time, and show our ignorance. Since evolution is a process of learning from our mistakes, mistakes are necessary. This rule encourages the acknowledgement of our own mistakes and learning from them whilst being treated with respect.

Volunteer Yourself Only

A number of these ground rules are as much a struggle for the teacher as they are for the pupils. The idea that when a volunteer is needed you put only yourself forward and try not to coerce anybody else, is somewhat disconcerting for a teacher who is loath to wait for people to come forward.

No Putdowns

Low self-esteem is a key issue to be addressed in people generally, and in young people in particular. Whether it is name-calling or individuals referring to themselves as being 'stupid', the outcome is the same. The 'slagging' or banter has the effect of inhibiting us from looking differently, thinking differently or speaking differently from the image/stereotype of what people think we should be like. It also prevents us from reaching our full potential.

In small groups during one workshop, all the pupils had to agree on what sanctions would come into play if ground rules were broken. One small group said that if anybody put down somebody that person had to affirm the person they had put down, in front of the small group.

Look for and Point Out Positive Qualities in One Another

This is the corollary of 'No putdowns'. If you ask a class to brainstorm a list of 'putdowns' and then a list of positive qualities, the latter list is usually considerably shorter than the former. There are various exercises to help pupils to develop a 'vocabulary of affirmation', and to practise using it. We live in a culture where usually the only effective affirmation of a person takes the form of a eulogy when he or she is dead. It is a skill to say things that are true, kind and important about someone else, and it has a powerful effect when you are in conflict with someone. One skill in conflict resolution is the ability to separate the person from his/her behaviour. If we can remember and remind ourselves of the good in others, it helps us to remember that we are good ourselves, and vice versa.

One activity that has been developed to illustrate the effect of putdowns and affirmation, *Dummy Bump*, is described later in this chapter.

One Person Speaks at a Time

The way a teacher traditionally enforces this is to require the pupils to put up their hands if they want to ask a question. Without this agreement, the pupils are liable to talk at the same time, or interrupt each other. Yet in a discussion, or a brainstorming exercise, communication becomes somewhat stilted if the 'hands up' rule is enforced. In order to get used to taking turns, an exercise can be employed whereby, for example, a 'magic microphone' is used, so that only the person holding the microphone (which may be a toy or any suitable safe object) is allowed to speak. This is artificial, of course, but unlike 'hands up' each person learns to take responsibility for choosing when to speak rather than the teacher. One other variation is that each pupil has three matches, so that each time they speak they surrender a match. When they have surrendered all three they cannot take part any more in the discussion.

By getting agreement on these ground rules, and also a consensus on what to do if any are broken, the teacher is ensuring that the class takes on owner-ship. Then everybody has a vested interest in keeping the rules; otherwise the informal nature of the workshop process will not be possible. If it proves impossible to establish these ground rules as they stand, it is worth adapting them to suit the 'culture' of the class. For example one method used for settling primary school pupils in readiness for the next activity is the 'Quiet Please' sign. It can be made to look like the 'Stop' sign carried by the 'lollipop' man or woman (the school crossing attendant). One side reads 'Quiet Please', the other 'Thank you'. When the pupils' attention is required, the *Quiet Please* sign is displayed, and when the class is ready, the sign is turned to show *Thank you*. For older pupils, a more sophisticated approach is necessary, which may be as simple as a raised hand, requiring everybody to follow suit as they notice it.

Why is it so important to involve the pupils in establishing ground rules? In a sense the *content* of a workshop is secondary to the *context* and the *process*. There is a vast array of conflict resolution skills activities, involv-ing communication, co-operation, affirmation and problem solving. For them to have more impact than say, Christmas party games, a context has to be implemented whereby a safe and enjoyable environment is created, for the teacher as well as the pupils. In addition the point of the exercises has to be drawn out, most effectively usually, in the pupil's own words.

Teaching Skills for Dealing with Conflict

Having established the ground rules, how should we develop the workshop approach? If we can show young people how to handle a small conflict well, it leads to them having the competence and confidence to handle a bigger conflict better. There is need to remember that the conflicts that are important are those that are important *to pupils*: 'It is a common mistake for teachers to ignore, belittle, or resist solving the very real problems which exist in children's lives, whether at home, in the classroom or in the wider community' (Hicks, 1988).

Our job as adults is to recognise that when pupils are upset because of something we regard as trivial, *that* is the key issue for them at that moment. Equally if we give pupils the skills to handle the conflicts which do affect them directly on a daily basis, we create a climate where they can begin to empathise with others not directly connected to them.

The ability to empathise or 'walk in someone else's moccasins' is a key skill in conflict resolution. Conflict has been defined as an indication of the need for change. Empathy and the recognition that sometimes it is ourselves that need to change lie at the heart of conflict resolution strategies.

This is worth bearing in mind, because dealing with conflict often requires a flexible response, a creativity that we sometimes do not have the time or the energy for, particularly when conflict resolution is synonymous with crisis management.

If we only respond to conflict when it breaks the surface, then we fail to recognise that we are only seeing the tip of the iceberg. Dealing with the visible conflict without dealing with the issues below the surface is not dealing with the conflict effectively. It does not acknowledge what is below the surface. This is like lopping off the tip of the iceberg only to have another 10% of the remaining floe break the surface again.

To continue the analogy of the iceberg, when a conflict breaks the surface, what is often below the surface is a *lack of communication*, *non-cooperation* and a *low self-esteem*. Activities which address these issues by positively emphasising *communication*, *co-operation* and *affirmation* help the pupils develop conflict resolution skills. (A publication by UNICEF,

1995, provides examples of conflict resolution training in affirmation, communication and co-operation skills in different conflict situations throughout the world.)

This chapter began with the statement that the teacher is in an ideal position through EMU to de-mystify conflict and conflict resolution. Although not normally an explicit part of his or her training, conflict and its resolution are an integral part of his or her everyday experience. A primary school teacher, faced with five pupils with competing stories about upsets during the lunch break as she or he embarks on the first lesson of the afternoon, has neither the time nor the disposition to give adequate attention to each of the complainants. Summary justice involves the apportioning of blame as best we can, often leaving aggrieved pupils in its wake, and an aggrieved child is unlikely to be a willing participant in subsequent lessons.

A secondary school teacher faced with a fight going on between two girls may not have the time to investigate the events that led up to the contretemps. At the other end of the schooling ladder, a Primary 1 teacher is likely to have fine-tuned antennae to sort out those conflicts that require her intervention and those that can be allowed to carry on unattended.

Teachers have by the nature of their vocation opportunities for dealing *creatively* with conflict. The school community is about relationships, and relationships depend on co-operation, communication, and mutual respect or affirmation. The rapport between a teacher and his or her class provides opportunities for creating a co-operative atmosphere. This means that when a conflict arises, the pupils have the skills to deal with it constructively. These skills have been described as *conflict literacy*, a literacy that is as necessary in life skills as is ordinary literacy. As a teacher exploring approaches to conflict, it is useful to become aware of your own style of dealing with conflict. The four traditional responses are co-operation, compromise, confrontation and avoidance.

It goes without saying that a teacher is one of the most powerful role-models a child has, and the way you respond to conflict has a significant effect. Having a clear idea of your own responses is also helpful when sharing your experiences with your pupils. There are a number of exercises that can be used in this regard.

Whilst there is no hard and fast rule about 'teaching' conflict resolution, it has to be acknowledged that there is an emotional life to most conflicts between people. It is generally true that when we are hurting we stop thinking, and it therefore isn't surprising that it is difficult to remember a strategy for dealing with conflict when we are in the middle of one, let alone devise a new strategy.

For this reason it is worth practising strategies for dealing with conflicts. The use of realistic role-plays can be particularly important. Another useful approach is the 'I-Statement'.

The 'I-Statement'

For one child to say to another 'You're always bossing me about' leaves the other with little room for manoeuvre and insufficient information to change his/her behaviour even if she or he wanted to. When this is turned into an 'I-Statement' the same child would say '*When you* tell me what to do, like you did just then, *I feel* that you are bossing me...' This gives more scope for dialogue.

The I-statement exercise is one you can do in a classroom, with pupils at their desks. Invite them to think of arguments they have had and the words they have used. They can then explore ways of changing the dialogue into I-statements and then role-play the situation. Practising using I-statements is one way of giving pupils skills for defusing a conflict rather than escalating it.

Prejudice

According to the 1992 Northern Ireland Curriculum:

> Pupils should know about and understand the nature of prejudice... within the individual, the family, the peer group, the school and the community. This should be examined within a variety of contexts, for example, culture, disability, economic background, sex, race and religious persuasion. They should know that suffering can be caused by many things such as words, gestures, symbols and actions. (DENI, 1992)

A useful starting point for exploring prejudice is to draw on the experience of pupils. Name-calling usually ranks high in the order of conflicts that present themselves in schools. It is probably the most tangible way in which prejudice is expressed, focussing on what is different, and then putting someone down for it. 'Specky four eyes' or 'fatso' may seem relatively innocuous, but (even without a repetitive barrage) name-calling can ruin self-confidence and self-esteem.

'Dummy Bump'

An exercise called *Dummy Bump* looks at the effects of put-downs and affirmation. It is a powerful tool for generating small group discussion about bullying, name-calling and experiences of discrimination and prejudice generally. It starts with the class brainstorming words or phrases that make them feel good, and these being listed on a blackboard or flip chart.

When the list has dried up, the class generates a list of names that makes them feel the opposite, for example, awful, humiliated, upset. (It is stressed that for this exercise the rule about putdowns is waived). Everything they call out is written up, using asterisks to disguise expletives, if necessary. Experience tends to show that the most hurtful phrases are not necessarily those associated with 'bad language'. Usually the list of putdowns is longer than the list of words that make them feel good.

At this stage Dummy Bump is introduced. (She or he can be either an adult dressed up or drawn on the whiteboard/chalkboard. If the dressing-up option is taken it is important that an adult takes the role of Dummy Bump, as the character will be on the receiving end of verbal abuse.) For primary school pupils Dummy Bump has big feet that he sometimes falls over – hence the bump on his head; large ears, a giant nose, a fat tummy, huge hands... etc. For secondary school pupils Dummy Bump can be adapted to be the current equivalent of a 'nerd'.

The story of Dummy Bump is then told, illustrating that she or he is happy-go-lucky, good natured, clumsy etc. At a critical moment in the story, for example getting on the school bus, the class are given the go ahead to call Dummy Bump names. As each name is called out, a piece of Dummy Bump is rubbed out, or if in character, Dummy Bump reacts as if hit by each putdown, and curls up into a ball, in a corner.

The class is then asked how they think Dummy Bump feels, and if they have ever felt like that. Prompted to think of things to make Dummy Bump feel better, someone will usually come up with 'Say nice things'. As the class do so, Dummy Bump is redrawn on the blackboard, or grows in stature from a tiny ball.

This exercise has a lot of scope for exploring issues that are close to home for the pupils. For example in a small group discussion afterwards, one of the pupils made the point that members of the Chinese community who attended the school had been treated like Dummy Bump. It gives the teacher the opportunity to assist the class at looking at its own diversity, and what it would be like to welcome diversity. There are several exercises such as 'Up/downs', and 'First thoughts' that also serve to acknowledge difference and welcome diversity.

There is a myth that young children are too young to know what prejudice is – but any child who has had to wait in a shop while an adult in the queue behind him or her is served, knows what discrimination means. With sensitivity and support it is possible to draw on the experiences of the pupils to explore the effects of prejudice.

One such activity involves asking the pupils to think of groups they belong to that they know have suffered from discrimination, or have been treated with less than one hundred per cent respect. If there are two more people voting for such a group, it is constituted, and they are asked to come up with a list of things they never want to hear said, done or thought about their group. To stimulate the pupils' thinking it may be useful for the teacher or leader to share his/her own experiences.

Through learning about each other's life experiences, and relating them to discrimination in other parts of the world, through drama, literature, current affairs, etc, it is possible to encourage empathy. It is possible to focus attention on the effects of discrimination on particular groups, disabled people for example, and think of strategies for bringing it to public attention.

A Whole-School Approach

By linking conflict and prejudice to the pupil's own life experiences one can also illustrate that conflict resolution is also relevant to the pupil's day to day life. Training a whole class in conflict resolution skills not only increases the corporate conflict literacy of the class, but paves the way for the possibility of providing a mediation service *for* the pupils, *by* the pupils. This is the strategy of *peer mediation*, already well-established in the United States and which has now been applied in a small but growing number of schools in Northern Ireland, Britain and elsewhere in Europe. (For a fuller treatment of peer mediation see Tyrrell, 2002: *Peer Mediation: A Process for Primary Schools*, Souvenir Press, London)

Increasing awareness of the effects of prejudice and developing conflict resolution skills can have a long term effect on the class. It means that before any conflict breaks the surface there will be some measure of understanding as to how it will be dealt with. A whole-school approach to diversity and mutual understanding requires some consensus about dealing with conflict, and ideally a universal provision of conflict resolution skills. A programme that identifies existing good practice and draws on the creativity of the school community to improve the ways in which conflicts are handled can have a profound effect.

In conclusion, you may start 'small', but think big, so that work with an individual class can become a pilot project for the whole school. It is important to involve at an early stage as many of the staff as possible. As schools develop policies in this area and monitor their implementation, the accessibility of conflict resolution skills is a useful indicator of the integration of mutual understanding within a school.

In the medium term by providing your pupils with some of the skills necessary to resolve their own conflicts, as part of EMU as a cross-curricular theme, you are also likely to reduce the number of conflicts you have to deal with. Hopefully it will reduce your stress as well!

References

Darby, J. (1995) *What's Wrong With Conflict?* Coleraine: University of Ulster Centre for the Study of Conflict.

DENI (1992) *Educational (Cross-Curricular) Themes: Objectives.* Bangor: Department of Education for Northern Ireland / HMSO.

Hicks, D. (1988) *Education for Peace*, London: Routledge.

Hopkins, B. (1995) 'Transforming Conflict in Schools' (flyer).

Leimdorfer, T. (1995) 'Teaching Creative Responses to Conflict' in *Citizenship*, 4(2).

Tyrrell, J. (2002) *Peer Mediation: A Process for Primary Schools*, London, Souvenir Press.

UNICEF/ODEC (1995) *Children Working for Peace*, London: United Nations Children's Fund / Oxford Development Education Centre.

MARY POTTER

8   Creating Safe Spaces for Exploring Diversity

> Children will always need safe spaces for learning. They will always
> need launching pads from which to follow their curiosity into the larger
> world.
>
> — SENGE, 2000, p. 4

The language of safety is widely used in relation to children and young
people, evidenced specifically in concepts such as Child Protection and
the Rights of the Child. Alongside this it is likely that the creation of safe
space, physical and emotional, within the school context will be both an
intention of school staff and an expectation on the part of parents, guard-
ians or carers. Hopefully, it will also be the lived experience of the children and young people themselves. This safety is important not only in
itself, but also because it is a key factor in ensuring that effective learning
can take place. The creation of a supportive learning environment is the
responsibility of all school staff, across all curriculum subjects as well as
other aspects of school experience.

Curriculum changes in Northern Ireland and elsewhere, focusing
attention on issues of citizenship and respect for difference, have raised
particular challenges for both the commitment to and the understanding
of safe space which may be held. The themes such as identity, diversity and
conflict which are encompassed in education for diversity and mutual
understanding have frequently been deemed too unsafe to address within
the school context, particularly when they engage with issues that would
be viewed as contentious. On the other hand, an understanding of the
purpose of education as playing a part in equipping children and young
people for life in Northern Ireland – or, indeed, anywhere else in the global

village – demands that cognisance is taken of the day-to-day realities of their lives, their communities and wider society. Because this learning, therefore, demands taking steps outside what both teachers and pupils (along with others in the wider school community) may feel comfortable with, it necessitates a particularly clear understanding of the nature of the supporting safe space and of the ways in which it can be nurtured.

Essentially, what is needed is a space which is safe for children, young people and adults alike, whether participant or teacher/facilitator, where everyone is enabled to reflect individually and together on the themes which are raised and to apply that learning to their life experience. This space is likely to be characterised by a valuing and respecting of individuals, the building of trust between group members, inclusive and equitable approaches, and open and honest discussion. It will be safe, not in the sense of being risk-free, but rather being a place where people feel supported to take appropriate risks in building relationships, in talking about their personal experiences and views and in exploring areas of potential and actual conflict.

Safety or Avoidance?

During the early years of the Northern Ireland Troubles an understanding of schools as 'havens of peace' arose with the intention of keeping sectarian conflict outside the school gates (Cairns, 1987, p. 161). This kind of language continues to be heard, and there is a danger that it implies that the issues themselves can also be left outside the gates; that children, young people and adults somehow set down their out-of-school identities and concerns when they enter the school in the morning and pick them up again on their way out in the afternoon. Clearly, this is an unrealistic expectation, but it is unsurprising in a situation in which many people seek to avoid the difficult issues raised by the sectarian conflict. By contrast, Leitch and Kilpatrick (1999) have argued that such issues must be dealt with *Inside the Gates*, in order 'to prepare young people for the political context in which they live' (p. 50) and in response to concerns expressed by young people themselves.

This culture of avoidance, whether it has at its centre religion, ethnicity, sexuality and/or other areas perceived as contentious, in itself seems to stem from an understanding that safety can be best ensured by steering clear of themes which will potentially highlight differences or cause conflict. In this sense, it is always safer to talk to 'your own' (those who are perceived as similar to you in terms of culture, politics, religion, race, etc.) than to those whose background, experiences and views are likely to be different. In their work on sectarianism in Northern Ireland, Liechty and Clegg discuss how this can be evidenced within Protestant/Catholic inter-community groups where diversity and dissenting voices can be stifled by a false inclusivity which seeks to emphasise 'how well we get on' at the expense of acknowledging genuine differences and even tensions within a group (Liechty and Clegg, 2001, p. 170). However, it can equally be the case at an intra-community level where a perceived threat from an external group in conjunction with a deep need for belonging can lead a group to suppress their differences in order to create a strong impression of group unity (Liechty and Clegg, 2001, p. 171).

The difficulty with these versions of safety is precisely that they ignore the differences and issues which exist in reality below the surface. Similarly, to focus school experience only on academic subjects and perceived 'safe' areas of personal development potentially minimises the effectiveness of learning and its application to the broader context of people's lives. While recognising that no aspect of education is neutral and that general principles of safe space such as respecting and valuing individuals apply across the board, particular structures and ways of working need to be put in place to enable the exploration of 'real life' issues, some of which may well be controversial. This exploration can be challenging for adults as well as for children and young people, but it is important not least because, as Cambron-McCabe and Quantz suggest: '... all learning begins when our comfortable ideas are found to be inadequate... the diversity of ideas that comes with the diversity of people is one of the best ways to create this necessary condition of learning' (Cambron-McCabe and Quantz, 2000, p. 319).

In a partisan context such as Northern Ireland, although equally relevant in other places where some form of segregation is the lived experience, Wilson makes the additional point that, 'Reflective meeting spaces can be points of contrast through which people question old established patterns of separation' (Wilson, 2007, p. 50), enabling people to see new possibilities in terms of understanding and relationship, and the building of a shared community and society.

Recognising Fears and Concerns

While acknowledging the value of this work, there needs to be an equal recognition that the concerns and fears which are held in relation to this kind of learning are genuinely felt and often for very good reasons. Many, if not all, of these are likely to apply whether the group members all come from similar backgrounds or whether there is significant diversity within the group, although the strength of the feelings will probably be stronger in the latter case. The tendency to have conversations about politics, religion, race, etc. only with those who come from the same background and perspective can create a vicious cycle of deepening fears as to what the consequences will be if the risk is taken to hold the conversations with those from different backgrounds. At the same time, it is important not to assume similarity or uniformity within a group of people who are perceived to come from the same background; particularly if the facilitator's assumption of this is apparent to the group, as it will heighten individuals' fears, for example, of expressing a different view or of telling a story about a life experience that might in some way set them apart from others. The concept of 'multiple identities' recognises the need to get beyond a single stereotyped label, enabling people to reflect on the wide range of aspects that make up their sense of who they are and a rich spectrum of differences even with people with whom they share a common label. Examples of work around multiple identities with primary school children can be found in CCEA's revised curriculum materials for Personal Development and Mutual Understanding.[1]

Within the context of exploring identity and sectarianism in Northern Ireland, some of the fears expressed or demonstrated in various ways by group participants have included the following:

- fear of not being listened to or respected;
- fear of being laughed at, mocked or embarrassed;
- fear of being misunderstood;
- fear of giving offence;
- fear of harming (new) friendships;
- fear of being 'forced' to talk about difficult/sensitive/personal issues;
- fear of isolation, being a 'lone voice';
- fear of 'letting the side down' or breaking the united front presented by the rest of the group;
- fear of being shown up as ignorant of their own or others' traditions;
- fear of issues being talked about outside the session or group;
- fear of verbal or physical attack, either during the session or afterwards.

As well as the specific experience of the group process, some of these fears are likely to relate also to the participants' broader context – for example, events and relationships within their local community and wider societal or political developments which have an impact upon them.

For teachers these concerns may also span the professional dimensions of their roles as facilitator and as member of a school staff team, possibly including:

---

1   See, for example, CCEA (2006), 'Unit 6: Learning More About Others – Valuing and Celebrating Cultural Difference and Diversity' in *Living.Learning.Together: Personal Development and Mutual Understanding (Key Stage 2, Year 5, Strand 2)*, Belfast: CCEA.

- concerns about curriculum pressures and how this work fits into those demands;
- concern about not having the skills or resources to carry out the work;
- lack of experience in this kind of facilitation or with group work methodologies;
- concerns about giving away too much personal information;
- concerns about the consequences of raising issues which were previously hidden or ignored;
- concerns about what to do if emotions such as grief or anger are strongly expressed;
- fears about losing control of the situation or of physical violence among or from pupils;
- fears of parental or other external criticism/intervention;
- fear of lack of support from senior management or other staff and of being left in an isolated or vulnerable position.

Part of the creation of safe space will be about the addressing of these fears, recognising with honesty that some of them may not be allayed in full but ensuring that at least some basic structures are put in place so that the risk taking involved is appropriate and adequately supported.

A Whole-School Model

The most effective structure for enabling staff and pupils to explore themes within the framework of education for diversity and mutual understanding is a whole-school model which has a core commitment to an ethos based on, for example, equity, respect for and understanding of diversity, building interdependence and developing positive ways to approach conflict. This commitment needs to be demonstrated particularly by the school's senior management team and Board of Governors, but also by all of those who form part of the school community. It will be evidenced through such aspects of school life as how people (and from how diverse a range) are welcomed as members of the school community or as visitors, the way in which the staff team (teachers and support staff) work together, the way decisions are made, the restorative approaches to behaviour/discipline issues,[2] the atmosphere in the staffroom, the place parents have in the life of the school, etc. It will have to be shaped in relationship with the local community as well as wider social and political developments, and these will at times place particular restrictions on what is possible. Clearly, therefore, as highlighted by Booth et al. in their work on inclusion in schools, this is likely to be a 'set of never ending processes' (Booth et al., 2000, p. 12), a work in progress, as different schools will have different starting points, and its dynamic and relational nature will reveal new challenges and possibilities at different times.

Individual teachers are likely to have much greater confidence to raise issues and address conflicts within the staff team as well as to carry out work with their classes where they are operating within this kind of whole-school commitment and approach. It means, for example, that:

- the work is given a recognised place within the overall prioritising of teaching and learning so that teachers are not left feeling that if they do specific work around diversity and controversial issues they will be penalised in some way for not adequately covering other prescribed areas of curriculum content;
- if a parent expresses concern or criticism of work being done in the classroom on a theme such as sectarianism, the teacher can be certain that she/he will have the support of the senior management team in talking with the parent and will not somehow be scapegoated;

---

2   Restorative approaches to behaviour/discipline issues build on restorative justice principles which recognise the damage caused to relationships through conflict of any kind. As well as an emphasis on prevention through creating an inclusive and respectful environment, they seek to develop ways in which people finding themselves in the role of victims or offenders can be reintegrated into the school community. For further information see, for example, the work of Belinda Hopkins and others at <http://www.transformingconflict.org> (accessed 15 July 2010).

- teachers will be supported with sufficient development and training opportunities to enable them to build the skills which they need to facilitate intentional work in the classroom, to respond to topics which arise (for example, as a consequence of local, national or international events, or reports in the media) and to address incidents of prejudice, discrimination or bullying. Ideally, this will include opportunities to reflect on their practice and discuss concerns/issues through a supervision type model;
- teachers will have the practical support they need in terms of both financial and physical resources, adequate planning and evaluation time, etc.

Most crucially, it means that the children, young people and adults will experience and be part of a holistic model which demonstrates what the core values look like in practice. This is the strongest context within which specific work around diversity themes can take place. Although the language of teacher and class/pupils is used, most of the principles and strategies outlined below will apply whether the facilitator is working with a group of adults, for example a staff team or group of parents, or a group of children or young people in a class or inter-school setting. (For more information on developing a whole-school model, see Chapter 6.)

Equipping the Teacher

With regard to specific classroom-based work on diversity themes, the primary responsibility for creating safe space lies with the teacher. In this context, the teacher is a group-work facilitator, and needs to give as much attention to the process as to the content of the programme. Above all else, this requires a significant amount of personal preparation for the task and experience involved.[3] Clearly, not all of this will happen in advance of beginning the work because for the teacher, as for the pupils, it is a learning process. However, aspects will include the following:

1. Self-reflection

Teachers need to give honest attention to their own value base, life experiences and attitudes. This involves recognising and acknowledging how these impact on, for example, the way they relate to pupils, the teaching and discipline styles they use, the information they may share about particular historical or contemporary events, and fears they may have about exploring certain issues. While recognising that there will be times when it is appropriate and beneficial for teachers to share something of their own views and feelings about a particular issue or event, their role as facilitator means that their exploration of personal feelings needs to take place elsewhere. As Taylor describes: 'Active facilitation requires a balance in recognising and responding to the emotional content of discussion while maintaining a sense of separateness necessary to facilitate versus participate... the role of the facilitator is to provide a context for the discussion to occur and to act as a container for emotional expression' (Taylor, 2002, p. 146).

2. Personal Development

This need for space for teachers to explore their own feelings, experiences and attitudes has often been emphasised as crucial to their preparation to teach in these sensitive areas. In the view of Halstead and Taylor (2000, p. 15), 'Teachers need to be clear about their own values and attitudes in order to be aware of their practices and to reflect critically on their role

---

3   These themes are explored in detail in N. Lynagh and M. Potter (2005), *Joined Up: Developing Good Relations in the School Community*, Belfast: The Corrymeela Press.

as values educators'. This point was made even more forcefully in CCEA guidance material on EMU and Cultural Heritage:

> Teachers themselves need space to consider how their own values, attitudes and cultural background influence what and how they teach. They need to consider how to guard against unwitting or unconscious prejudice, the advancement of personal standpoints or selectivity in their choice of evidence. (CCEA, 1997, p. 7)

In addition to individual reflection, one way of doing this is to instigate some structured or informal conversation around the issues in question with friends or colleagues who have views and life experiences different to the teacher's own. Alternatively, this kind of opportunity could be provided through staff development sessions, possibly working with other local schools to broaden the diversity of the staff group. As well as deepening personal understanding and relationships, this experience has the potential to allow the teacher to feel the fears and other emotions which the children or young people may also hold. It also provides the teacher with meaningful insights into other perspectives and the life experiences which have shaped them. If the teacher is working with a group where all the children or young people come from similar backgrounds, the teacher will then be equipped to provide alternative perspectives on a given subject where group members may not feel able to do so. This, in turn, demonstrates that the teacher values the reflection process and does not expect the children or young people to take risks which she/he has not also experienced in some form.

Such a process enables the teacher to increase the young peoples' knowledge base in relation to, for example, historical events, flags and symbols, political structures, different world religions, the ethnic and cultural diversity of people living in the local community, etc. This needs to be qualified, however, by recognising that the teacher is not expected to be an expert and that responses such as *'I don't know the answer to that question, but I will try to find out for our next session'* or *'I don't know the answer to that question – is there someone here who would like to investigate that for us and report back at our next session?'* are an appropriate part of the facilitation process.

3.   Skills Development

Some of the experiences outlined above will include the ongoing development of skills such as self-reflection, critical thinking and self-expression. Given that it is important that the teacher should model the behaviour and skills which they would like the children or young people to develop, this is a valuable starting point. However, there may also be specific training support which the teacher needs in areas such as active listening, positive ways of approaching conflict and other aspects of facilitation in order to feel competent and confident in their role as facilitator and to then share these skills with their class members. Where teachers feel that they need specific support in developing facilitation skills, or where they are working with a group that they find particularly challenging, there may be opportunities for co-working with another member of staff or an external facilitator, perhaps from a voluntary organisation which specialises in one or more of the themes being explored.

Setting the Context

Beyond the teacher's personal preparation, there is a range of other aspects which need attention. It is likely that the most effective methodology for whole group discussion within a programme will involve working in a circle. From a safe space point of view, this enables the development of trust (for example, a child or young person in the front row of desks may worry about the reactions from the back row if they are expressing an opinion or talking about a personal life experience), helps build a sense of team and belonging, and encourages both personal and group responsibility.

As suggested above, some of this work is likely to be intentional in nature (for example, a planned lesson or module). At other times it may arise in a way that needs an immediate response as a result of an external event or as a consequence of an incident of prejudice, discrimination or bullying within the school. However, even in the latter cases the considerations outlined below are important, as is the ongoing experience of the kind of facilitation process which is described. For example, if a class regularly uses Circle Time to explore classroom issues, playground/lunchtime conflicts, etc. the forum for addressing these situations is already in place. Time taken to build positive relationships, to develop skills and to familiarise pupils with these kinds of ways of working is well spent and, in fact, crucial in providing a framework for the exploration of more challenging issues. (The use of Circle Time is discussed in more detail in Chapter 9.)

1.   Building Positive Relationships

It is crucially important that the teacher builds a positive relationship with the children or young people within the class group, which values each one of them and gets to know their individual talents, interests and needs. The teacher also needs to develop an understanding of the community and cultural contexts within which they live, something which is particularly important if the teacher lives outside the area in which the school is situated or comes from a different background to some or all of the pupils. This can involve being aware of particular events and relationships within local communities which may have a direct impact on individuals or groups of pupils and, for example, which may affect the level of risk taking involved in exploring certain issues or meeting with groups from different backgrounds. It also means giving attention to cultural differences, which may have implications for the way in which individual pupils participate in particular activities.

Allied with this positive relationship building, is the challenge of avoiding 'preconceived judgements [of pupils], often unconscious, based on past experiences, catchment areas or family reputations' (Mosley, 1996, p. 15). In discussing the specific example of sectarianism, Liechty and Clegg point out how easily 'responsibility for sectarianism is... assigned to everyone but oneself and one's own people, and especially to the relatively few people directly and obviously involved in violence, intimidation and provocation' (Liechty and Clegg, 2001, p. 18). This highlights again the importance of self-reflection because any temptation to scapegoat children and young people, and the communities from which they come, even if verbally unexpressed, will jeopardise the relationship and undermine group members' sense of safety and willingness to engage fully with the process.

The children and young people themselves also need opportunities to build positive relationships with each other, so that the trust is developed which will enable them to participate fully as the work becomes more challenging. Some of the strategies which can assist with this are outlined in a later section. Each child or young person will participate in a group in different ways and recognising the roles which they may take on at different times and their different learning styles will help the teacher to ensure that they are all able to participate and to learn.

2. Developing a Programme

As with all other areas of lesson planning, this work needs to have a clear purpose and an understanding of intended learning outcomes. However, probably the biggest challenge here is the fact that the teacher is less in control of the process than they might be in some other aspects of their work. There are a number of reasons for this:

- The material for this work is drawn largely from the life experiences of the group members and is dependent to a significant extent on what they choose to bring to the process;
- Linked to this is the fact that the teacher does not come to the process as an expert with knowledge to share with pupils. While maintaining the facilitator's role, the teacher is also a listener and a learner, recognising what each of the children or young people brings to the group;
- There is an emphasis on the process itself rather than on completing a specific task. This requires a high degree of flexibility on the part of the facilitator and a strong sensitivity to the needs and feelings within the group;

- Given these circumstances, it is also highly appropriate to enable the group members to share in programme planning (and evaluation) as the 'experts' on their own life story and situation;
- This different style of working means the teacher may wish to consider using his or her first name, at least within the context of name games, introductory activities and exploring personal identity.
- One or all of these factors may challenge the teacher's sense of safety. Therefore, feeling reasonably confident about their facilitation skills and having a positive relationship with their pupils will help to ensure that this dynamic space is safe for both teacher and pupils.

The children or young people will also feel safer and more able to participate fully if the programme designed: has a clear purpose with which they are able to engage; is genuinely relevant; provides a range of learning opportunities which will match their different learning styles; is appropriate for their age group, ability range, cultural backgrounds, etc. (for example, if there are children or young people with disabilities within the group, it will be important to ensure that all activities are, or are adapted to be, inclusive and enable the participation of all group members); is developmental in nature and builds from the level of previous experience.

3.   *Practical Considerations*

Although safe space is about far more than the physical surroundings, these and other practical considerations will play an important part and need to be considered by the teacher within the overall session planning. Three particular factors which will need to be covered are the physical setting, the time available and the gathering of appropriate resources. Each of these raises a number of questions:

The physical setting

For a class group working on their own, the best place to do the work will probably be their own classroom as this is likely to be the place in the school where they feel most at home. This also recognises that the work is integrated within the life of the classroom and is not something additional or exceptional. The question will need to be explored in more depth, relating to the specific circumstances, where two or more groups from within a school or from different schools are meeting together.

On a very practical level, the teacher also needs to consider aspects such as whether the space is big enough for the planned activities, and whether a circle of chairs needs to be set up and put away for every session. While an assembly hall, for example, will provide plenty of space for games and for a circle on the floor, some group members may feel overwhelmed by such a big space, or feel that their voice is too exposed when they express a personal view.

The time available

For individual sessions, this is likely to be more flexible within a primary school than within a post-primary school context, but in both cases the balances between flexibility and other curriculum demands need to be maintained. The bell ringing for the next class/break/end of school is usually a non-negotiable limit and it is crucial to ensure that the programme has reached an appropriate point of closure before this happens. Whether planning an individual lesson or a module/series of lessons, it will be important to think about how much time is needed for the different aspects of introduction, relationship and trust building within the group, exploration of the themes, and evaluation and closure. The appropriate depth to which the discussions can be taken will depend in part on the time available to ensure that each of the preparation and ending steps is sufficiently developed.

Gathering resources[4]

There are many resources available which can support this kind of work, in terms of books or packs outlining exercises, games and activities. Having such resources to draw upon will enable more creative programme planning

---

4   For some relevant resources, see, for example, the Community Relations Education Northern Ireland website: <http://www.creni.org> (accessed 25 June 2010).

and will support the facilitator in introducing a range of learning opportunities. It is important that the teacher familiarises her/himself thoroughly with a particular activity before introducing it to a group. This will include paying specific attention to its appropriateness for that group and for the programme in which the group members are participating.

4.   Reflection and Evaluation

The teacher needs to consider in advance how she/he will reflect on and evaluate both individual sessions and the overall programme. It is also important that the children or young people are actively involved in the process. Having established the purpose of the work and the intended learning outcomes, these can be used as indicators to measure the learning which is taking place. Sample stories (always respecting confidentiality), examples of developing skills and team work are forms of evidence which will enable both teachers and pupils to see where learning is taking place, to value the work, and to feel confident that it is an important use of their time.

The Facilitation Process

Just as progression needs to be demonstrated within a series of sessions, within each individual session there needs to be a clear sense of purpose for the different activities used, and any changes made to an original plan. While the pupils are being encouraged to take responsibility for their own learning, it is the facilitator who keeps the group focused on the overall purpose and ensures that the safety of the space is maintained. Within this role, there are a number of general principles which apply as well as a number of strategies which can be used.

1. General Principles

The facilitator needs to pay attention to aspects of the process which will ensure that it is as positive and as safe an experience as possible for all those involved. This will include responsibilities such as:

- giving attention to the ground rules established at the beginning of the process and appropriately calling the group members back to those when necessary;
- establishing an atmosphere of respectful listening and ensuring that everyone gets some opportunity to contribute to the discussion if they want to;
- working at a pace which is appropriate for the group;
- paying attention to the body language and 'mood' within the group. This might include being aware when someone is experiencing strong emotions but is unable to express them vocally within the group, or when a group as a whole needs a short break for whatever reason;
- enabling the group to take new directions or move on if they get stuck in a particular discussion;
- bringing the group back to the core purpose/theme if the discussion becomes inappropriately side-tracked;
- keeping watch on the time and ensuring that group members also know what time is available to them.

Some of these circumstances may raise anxieties for individuals or for all group members, so it is important that the teacher supports pupils to develop the skills to express these and works with the group to come up with some strategies which will help them re-establish an atmosphere of safety.

2. Establishing Ground Rules

In order for both the teacher and pupils to feel safe, it is important that clear ground rules are established. This is true of all ground rules, but in some cases such as 'appropriate confidentiality', the commitment of group members to keeping the rule, balanced by individuals taking responsibility for what they choose to say, is crucial for safety outside the programme as well as within it. In this regard, the development of trust and respect is crucial, as people's willingness to engage with the process is in part commensurate with their confidence in fellow group members to commit to the agreed ground rules. The teacher as facilitator also needs to have confidence in this before supporting the group to progress to more challenging themes.

The ground rules are likely to be most effective if the group members are involved in deciding what the rules should be, although how this is done may depend somewhat on the age group involved. Group members are also more likely to keep ground rules when they understand the reasoning behind them. In terms of creating safe space, a contract has a number of uses – it enables the group to clarify their purpose and hopes for their time together; it enables the group to make clear the values which they want to underpin their work together; and it helps to ensure that people know what is expected of them in terms of participation, behaviour and learning.

Ultimately, however, it is a key tool for helping to create a setting where people feel safe enough, for example, to discuss more controversial or difficult issues, to take appropriate risks around sharing personal experiences and views, and to listen with openness to other people's experiences and views without feeling defensive about their own. (The development and content of a possible contract is discussed in more depth in Chapter 7: Dealing with Conflict and Prejudice.)

3. Purposeful Use of Games

Sometimes the perception of games is that they are 'just a bit of a laugh' and within the context of education and learning, not really very useful or not a priority when thinking about the use of time. However, as demonstrated in CCEA's *Active Learning and Teaching Methods for Key Stage 3* (2007), they can be purposeful exercises which have clear learning outcomes, and very useful tools when trying to create 'safe space'.

Some of the reasons for using games in this way are that:

- Games are fun – they can help people relax and have a laugh together, perhaps as an icebreaker activity at the start of a process, or as a closure exercise to release tension after a more difficult discussion;
- Games can enable people to get to know each other – they can allow people to learn each other's names, to talk to each other, to find out information about each other and do something together which is non-threatening and good fun;
- Games can enable individuals to become a group – they can help people to become aware of each other and of each other's skills, needs, contribution to the group, etc., encouraging people to support each other and work together;
- Games can involve everyone – they can allow everyone to participate, including those, for example, who may not feel so confident about speaking out in a discussion setting;
- Games can enable people to experience success and affirmation – they can create opportunities for people to demonstrate different talents and to succeed in a way which they might not experience, for example, in an academic classroom setting;
- Games can enable people to develop skills – they can create opportunities for people to use skills such as listening, communication, co-operation/teamwork, aspects of leadership, problem solving, etc.;
- Games can enable people to learn – they can raise people's awareness and understanding of all kinds of issues, e.g. their own sense of identity, diversity within a group, etc., providing a more light-hearted introduction to deeper discussion or more demanding exercises exploring the theme.

As with all programme or lesson activities, it is important that the games chosen are appropriate for the group concerned. Not all games will achieve all of the outcomes listed above, and a game that is effective and fun for one group may not be safe or appropriate for another. To be most effective, games need to be chosen carefully so that:

- They are appropriate for the ages, cultural backgrounds, gender mix, physical and learning abilities, etc. within the group;
- They are appropriate for the stage in the group's life (i.e. how well people know each other and how comfortable they feel together as a group);
- They are physically safe. Attention will need to be given to the above points, plus factors such as the size of the group, the physical environment, and the facilitator's skills and confidence;
- They fit within the values reflected in the contract or learning agreement you create with the group. For example, a game which leaves one person feeling left out and laughed at, will not 'match' the values of respect, being supportive to each other and participation which are being encouraged within the group. Given that the games are an integral part of building the group, games which encourage competitiveness may not be appropriate;
- They are purposeful. The games are an integral part of the overall learning experience and need to be included with particular learning or developmental outcomes in mind. As with any other aspect of a programme, thorough planning and preparation is important.

4.   Developing Skills

Clearly, these kinds of challenging discussions require quite high levels of skill for those who are participating. In order that children and young people feel safe and confident to participate effectively, time within the early stages of the process can valuably be given to their initial development. These are the skills which the facilitator also needs to develop and they include self-reflection, active listening, the clear expression of personal views, emotional literacy, empathy, critical thinking, and positive ways of working with diversity and conflict. Of all of these, active listening is probably the most important starting point for both the teacher and the pupils because, as Prendiville explains: '... developing and employing the skill of active listening helps to create an atmosphere in which members feel they are an important part of the group. When people experience active listening they are more inclined to bring their skills, experiences, expertise and ideas into the group relationship' (Prendiville, 1995, p. 34).

Valuable groundwork can be done through the use of relevant games, Circle Time activities, scenarios and role plays, to name just a few of the tools available. If the understanding and basis of the skills are established early on, they can be more effectively developed through the experience of participation.

5. *The Importance of Closure*

In any session exploring diversity themes, it is likely that people's emotions will be touched, some tension and anxiety may be experienced, and some strongly conflicting views may be discovered within the group. In order to ensure that people are able to leave the session feeling relaxed, with their relationships affirmed and the discussion appropriately brought to a close, it is important that sufficient time is always allocated for closure. In some cases, this will mean resisting the temptation to let the 'fantastic discussion' continue 'just another five minutes'! The pupils will also have useful contributions to make in terms of evaluating the work, and part of the closure at the end of a session or at different points through a module will need to include some time for that.

Ways of achieving closure can include one or a combination of the following:

- Calling the group's attention to the time five to ten minutes before the end of the discussion/exercise so that they have a clear conception of the time frame within which they are working;
- Using a closure exercise which allows group members to say something about how they are feeling at the end of the session;
- Using a closure exercise which allows group members to affirm their relationships with each other;
- Using a closure exercise which allows the release of any tension, for example, a game which involves laughter and having fun together.

Beyond the Classroom

If the themes explored and the learning that takes place are genuinely relevant to the lives of the children or young people, it is unlikely that the experience for them will end with the closure of the final session in a programme. Most learning involves some level of change, and if the facilitator looks honestly at their value base and the intended purpose of this kind of work, it is probable that there is an explicit element of change intended. This might be something such as challenging prejudice and discrimination, encouraging pupils to relate more positively to those who come from backgrounds different to their own, and trying to take different approaches to conflict situations. Critical thinking is a good example of the way in which even the skills involved carry inherent change possibilities because it enables people to 'identify and challenge assumptions and explore and imagine alternatives' (Jeffs and Smith, 1990, p. 9).

In some circumstances, particularly for young people who are less powerful than adults but more independent than younger children, there may be a number of difficult consequences to this. Some participants may experience a significant change in their ways of thinking and relating to people from backgrounds different to their own. This may be a challenging experience which raises feelings of uncertainty and even anxiety, and there is the possibility that they will find themselves in conflict at some level with family members, friends, peers and others in their community. For some, even to participate in a programme with people from a different community may make them vulnerable within their own community, regardless of whether or not they demonstrate changes in attitudes or behaviour as a result of their participation.

In discussing sectarian conflict in Northern Ireland, Fitzduff comments on one potential consequence of participation, stating that, 'In many cases… talking with our "enemies" can be a dangerous idea – it may complicate our view of the situation, and of any possible solution, and hence diminish our energy to take part in the fight. Possibly the loneliest people in Northern Ireland are those who cannot, or will not, accept the "simplified" version of the struggle as publicly espoused in their communities' (Fitzduff, 1999, p. 187).

This re-emphasises the crucial importance for the teacher to think clearly through the purpose of the work, the likely learning and change outcomes, and the support structures which exist. While recognising the reality of the limitations which a school will face within its particular community and societal context, safety must be appropriately attended to beyond the actual programme. As Lorenz points out in relation to anti-racist work with young people, 'the credibility of any programme rests on its ability to follow through the changes that it may have triggered, particularly where those changes lead to inevitable conflicts and frictions' (Lorenz, 1996, p. 159).

Beyond the actual programme there are possible structures and ways of working which will contribute to the safety of children and young people involved. The whole-school model allows for a broader context of support and a wider range of structures as people work through the implications of their learning and resulting changes in attitudes and behaviour. Informing parents and others (for example, local youth workers) about the work being undertaken, and, where possible and appropriate, involving them in the process will broaden this support structure still further.

Throughout the programme, the facilitator needs to hold a balance between acknowledging the genuine fears and concerns which may be held and encouraging the participants to recognise the potentially positive outcomes of their participation and learning. The development of skills within the programme should be transferable to the rest of life, and the facilitator needs to ensure that these connections are sufficiently made.

The ethos of encouraging people to take responsibility for their own learning needs to be supported by discussion which helps them to contextualise this within their longer term experience. Part of this will also involve helping them to develop their awareness and understanding of the implications of the social and political context at a local and wider level.

The facilitator and others within the school need to be available to offer appropriate individual support on both an informal and formal basis. The more formal support might include follow up sessions with the class or group and one-to-one opportunities within the form tutor or other pastoral support structures, and there may be opportunities to provide training and support to older pupils so that they can take on a mentoring role for younger pupils. Informal and more formalised peer support structures can be developed through the programme (where hopefully a sense of team has been strongly built) and beyond.

*

Ultimately, as Senge affirms, 'Genuine learning occurs in the context of our lives, and the long-term impact of any new learning depends on its relationship to the world around us' (Senge, 2000, p. 41). This learning, however, will only be truly effective where the learner feels supported and confident enough to engage in the process. No space will be completely secure and the learning is about risk taking, but the creation of a space which is inclusive and equitable, where individuals are valued and respected, where trust is built and where open and honest discussion can take place opens up new possibilities for positive relationships, the development of new skills and relevant, 'real life' learning.

References

Booth, T., et al. (2000) *Index for Inclusion: Developing Learning and Participation in Schools*, Bristol, CSIE.

Cairns, E. (1987) *Caught in Crossfire: Children and the Northern Ireland Conflict*, Belfast: Appletree Press.

Cambron-McCabe, N., and Quantz, R. (2000) 'Guiding principles for preparing transformative educational leaders', in Senge, P., et al. (eds), *Schools That Learn*, London: Nicholas Brealey Publishing.

CCEA (1997) *Mutual Understanding and Cultural Heritage: Cross-curricular Guidance Material*, Belfast: Council for Curriculum, Examinations and Assessment.

CCEA (2007) *Active Learning and Teaching Methods for Key Stage 3*, Belfast: Council for Curriculum, Examinations and Assessment.

Fitzduff, M. (1999) *Community Conflict Skills*, Belfast: Community Relations Council.

Halstead, J.M. and Taylor, M. (2000) *The Development of Values, Attitudes and Personal Qualities; a review of recent research*, Slough: NFER.

Jeffs, T., and Smith, M. (1990) 'Using Informal Education', in Jeffs, T., and Smith, M., *Using Informal Education*, Buckingham: Open University Press.

Leichty, J., and Clegg, C. (2001) *Moving Beyond Sectarianism: Religion, Conflict and Reconciliation in Northern Ireland*, Dublin: Columba Press.

Leitch, R., and Kilpatrick, R. (1999) *Inside the Gates: Schools and the Troubles*, Belfast: Save the Children.

Lorenz, W. (1996) 'Pedagogical Principles for Anti-Racist Strategies', in Aluffi-Pentini, A., and Lorenz, W., *Anti-Racist Work with Young People: European Experiences and Approaches*, Dorset: Russell House Publishing.

Lynagh, N., and Potter, M. (2005) *Joined Up: Developing Good Relations in the School Community*, Belfast: The Corrymeela Press.

Mosley, J. (1996) *Quality Circle Time in the Primary Classroom*, Wisbech: LDA.

Prendiville, P. (1995) *Developing Facilitation Skills: A Handbook for Group Facilitators*, Dublin: Combat Poverty Agency.

Senge, P., et al. (2000) *Schools That Learn*, London: Nicholas Brealey Publishing.

Taylor, J.E. (2002) 'Facilitating Difficult Discussions: Processing the September 11 Attacks in Undergraduate Classrooms' in *Analysis of Social Issues and Public Policy*, Washington, DC: The Society for the Psychological Study of Social Issues.

Transforming Conflict website (Belinda Hopkins) <http://www.transformingconflict. org> (accessed 15 July 2010).

Wilson, D. (2007) 'Coming of Age at Last? Youth Work, the Good Relations Legislation and the Shared Future Policy in Northern Ireland' in *Youth Studies Ireland*, 2(1).

KATHRYN EDGAR

9   Circles for Learning: Circle Time in Diversity and Mutual Understanding

Introduction

Circle Time is now extensively used by a wide variety of people in both the voluntary and the statutory sectors in Northern Ireland. This chapter seeks to provide the reader with

- a rationale based on the underpinning principles of Circle Time drawn from literature on the subject;
- a sense of how the strategy can be used in the classroom;
- some practical suggestions for its management; and
- particular references to the application of Circle Time to develop mutual understanding and engagement with diversity issues.

While reading the chapter will give an overview of Circle Time it is no substitute for as much practical training in the strategy as the reader can acquire. To enable the personal acquisition of skills, knowledge and understanding best suited to your setting it is advisable to draw training from a variety of sources. If Circle Time is to be a rewarding experience for all, focused planning and the monitoring and evaluation of Circle Time in the reader's group of people, young or old, is essential to ensure that the individual needs and interests of the group are being addressed. A structured and planned approach to Circle Time encourages a self-evaluative attitude which is central to the improvement of quality learning and teaching.

Background

This chapter is based on the author's use of Circle Time for over fifteen years as a strategy to develop positive relationships that are open, honest, meaningful and genuine. In personal research (Edgar, 2000) it was discovered that Circle Time was used by a wide variety of people, for a wide variety of purposes by many who had little or no formal training and very little knowledge of underpinning theory or values. The vast majority of those who used Circle Time attested to its values but the research did identify the need for training, monitoring and evaluation of practice and the need for focus and planning when conducting Circle Time sessions. Much of the material in this chapter will reflect this research and subsequent experience in Circle Time training and its monitoring and evaluation (1999–2005) in the South Eastern Education and Library Board area (Northern Ireland); the Train the Trainers course delivered by Jenny Mosley; and practical experience gained from working with cross community groups of Year 7 children (1995–2008).

Many teachers have identified their first introduction to Circle Time as being through the voluntary sector in informal situations associated with cross-community groups in the Schools Community Relations Programme (formerly the Cross Community Contact scheme) and currently under review. 'Circle' activities allowed young people from different communities to explore similarities and differences through co-operative games and team building activities to promote mutual respect and trust. It has been my own experience that this has worked equally well both in and outside the classroom situation and equally well with young children; teenagers; and adults. Circle Time in the classroom is used in a more formal way and with less emphasis on games, than for instance in the informal atmosphere of a residential or out of school experience. This, however, can be equally effective in promoting mutual respect and in instilling a sense of ownership, participation and responsibility within the young people themselves not only for behaviour but for the way a class functions. It encourages a sense of responsibility for wanting to maintain warm relationships with both peers and teacher. It encourages and can develop a sense of personal responsibility towards learning. From an early age young people can see themselves as participant members of a class and of a school, with roles and shared responsibilities for its management. This aim for Circle Time is inherent in the whole Northern Ireland Curriculum aim 'to empower young people to develop their potential and to make informed and responsible choices and decisions throughout their lives' (CCEA, 2007, p. 4).

The Northern Ireland Curriculum began its implementation process in 2006 and will be completed in the academic year 2009–10. A new Area of Learning within the curriculum is Personal Development and Mutual Understanding (PD&MU) and the resource *Living.Learning.Together.* uses Circle Time as an important strategy to support the learning and teaching of PD&MU.

Circle Time has long been used in cross-community contexts as a strategy to promote both personal and mutual understanding, a sense of interdependence and the skills of conflict management. I am convinced that Circle Time is equally valuable in the classroom situation for young people of all ages from pre-school to post primary. In so doing we are preparing the children of tomorrow to be better placed to have the necessary skills to be tolerant and to accept the increasing diversity within our community, as highlighted by the Department of Education and the Education and Training Inspectorate:

> Teachers have the pivotal role in promoting tolerance in their classrooms: they are responsible for creating the climate within which children learn and for methods of teaching and learning which encourage self-esteem and mutual respect. (DENI, 1999, para. 49, p. 24)

> The rising number of racist attacks, and the continuing sectarian divisions, suggest that there is still a great deal more to be done to counteract prejudice and fear in parts of Northern Ireland. (ETI, 2007, p. 10)

The Role of the Teacher

It is the relationship between a child and his/her teacher that is crucial and provides the experience which determines whether the child's perception of school will be either positive or negative. As a teacher, the words we may use *today* have significant potential to influence how pupils view themselves *tomorrow*. As scholastic achievement focuses more and more on measurable outcomes so teachers are in danger of concentrating on what Lawrence (1988) refers to as the 'non human' aspects of teaching. As he goes on to point out

> ... education is not just about learning cognitive skills. It is also about helping children to learn about themselves, to be able to live peacefully with themselves, and with others, and to help them develop into competent, mature, self motivated adults... There can be no substitute for the enthusiasm, warmth and spontaneity of the personal encounter. (Lawrence, 1988, p.xii)

The pupil-teacher relationship is very important in developing self-esteem and Circle Time can play a positive role in that development. According to Lawrence, however, the *application* of self-esteem activities alone will not enhance self-esteem. The personality and the communication skills of the teacher are vital in this process. In this first edition of his book, Lawrence drew attention to the relationship between the self-esteem of the teacher and the self-esteem of the pupil and showed how teachers with a high sense of self-esteem tended to produce pupils who also showed a high sense of self-esteem. In considering 'positive climate' as a key factor for effective junior schooling, Mortimore et al. (1993) claim that:

> Positive effects resulted where teachers obviously enjoyed teaching their classes, valued the fun factor, and communicated their enthusiasm to the children. Their interest in the children as individuals, and not just as learners, also fostered progress. Those who devoted more time to non-school chat or small talk increased pupils' progress and development. (p. 16)

Carl Rogers (1983) clearly describes with 'feeling and passion' the necessity for teachers to be facilitators rather than instructors and the conditions necessary to facilitate learning, suggesting that '... one of the most important of these conditions is the attitudinal quality of the interpersonal relationship between facilitator and learner' (p. 133). This interpersonal relationship is clearly and explicitly described with vibrant examples in his book 'Freedom to Learn in the 80s' and is summarised by him as the following:

> First of all is a transparent realness in the facilitator, a willingness to be a person, to be and live the feelings and thoughts of the moment. When this realness includes a prizing, a caring, a trust and respect for the learner, the climate for learning is enhanced. When it includes a sensitive and accurate empathetic listening, then indeed a freeing climate, stimulative of self-initiated learning and growth, exists. The student is *trusted* to develop. (p. 133)

Conflict between teaching as being pupil-centred but results-driven becomes more manageable when the *how* of teaching and learning is addressed through Circle Time. So often the emphasis in teaching can be on content rather than process. Circle Time is one strategy used to address this often-neglected part of the curriculum – hidden or otherwise. As we look to the *how* of learning and teaching so we must consider the *how* (the *process*) of Circle Time. An understanding of the theory and practice must be an integral part of its development in the classroom otherwise it risks becoming either as content driven as the formal curriculum or a piecemeal approach which will not realise its full potential. Cameron (1998) suggests that what both young people and their teachers require is an approach which is holistic: 'It must be rooted in research, drawing on the full range of educational knowledge. It must take account of how we think and how we learn. Without such roots, no development can be credible' (p. xii).

Each teacher needs to take time to study the rationale for Circle Time and the personal implications before committing to its use in the classroom. It is only when a teacher *truly* empathises with the underpinning values and beliefs of Circle Time and feels comfortable in its use that both teacher and pupils will benefit.

A Rationale for Circle Time

The right to an opinion and the right to voice that opinion are central to the ethos of Circle Time. This is exemplified in Article 12 in the United Nations Convention on the Rights of the Child (United Nations, 1989) which affirms that children have the right to express their views freely on all matters that concern them and that those views must be taken seriously.

Circle Time has its origins in various traditions and practices and is often associated with the Native American way of communicating in a circle or with the legendary King Arthur and his Knights of the Round Table. In Japan 'Quality Circles' have been used to improve quality of performance in the workplace by encouraging workers at different levels to contribute ideas and opinions as to how best a job can be done. Circle Time is also found in Northern European countries. In his article 'Getting Round to Clarity: What Do We Mean by Circle Time?' Lang (1998) explores the traditions of Circle Time and its practices: 'The North European tradition has two significant strands, one which is particularly concerned with the personal and social development of younger children, as in Scandinavia, and one which has a strong pedagogic element, the Jenaplan model' (p. 6). He goes on to add: 'The American and Northern European models of circle time involve two potentially very different conceptions. In the first, psychological theory forms the basis of the model, whilst the second is formed from a pedagogic theory.' (p. 6)

Lang's article also describes the Italian use of a version of Circle Time modified from a variety of sources to encourage group empowerment among disaffected pupils in Italian schools. He writes that 'this Italian model is unique, both in that its theory was specifically selected taking the situations in which it was to be used into account, and that the actual methodology was developed in the same way' (p. 7).

It is in America that Circle Time is recognised to have been first used as 'The Magic Circle' in 1960s and 1970s and developed from ten years of experience by Jim Ballard in his book 'Circlebook: A Leader Handbook for Conducting Circletime – A Curriculum of Affect' as 'a set of guidelines for conducting circletime, a curriculum of affective growth and human relations skill development'.

Ballard (1982) clearly sets out the basic human education assumptions on which the book is written and circletime should be conducted, as the following:

- Human beings are constituted not bad, at least neutral, and probably good;
- The seeds of growth are inside people;
- People can always do more than they are presently doing to become more than they presently are;
- Each of us can be nicer to herself/himself than she/he tends to be;
- Each of us is, in the end, alone and responsible;
- We are always choosing our own lives;
- Fear is our major limiter;
- Human behaviour arises out of needs;
- Awareness brings responsibility;
- Listening is uniquely powerful in building awareness. (pp. 2–4)

Ballard's model of circletime has three major goal areas:

- awareness – knowing who I am;
- mastery – knowing what I can do;
- social interaction – knowing how I function in the world of others. (ibid.)

His rules for circletime are:

- everyone gets a turn who wants one;
- everyone who takes a turn (shares verbally to the task) gets actively listened to (feedback). (ibid.)

In this way children choose what they want to say but also learn that others are responsible for what they hear. Responsibility for what is heard rests with the listener, not the speaker. In this way children begin to learn the skills of empathy as they clarify their feelings so that others can understand. Ballard sees circletime as 'a listening laboratory' with a specific set of listening skills:

- Being totally *there* with the other person;
- Showing that you understand;
- Focusing on the speaker's needs;
- Letting the speaker have his or her feelings... (ibid. p. 13)

He continues by giving examples of what the 'skill of listening' is not:

- Really? I don't agree.
- And then what happened?
- Well, let me tell you about my operation!
- You shouldn't feel that way... (ibid.)

And then gives examples of the listening skill in action:

- In other words, you are saying...
- If I'm understanding correctly, you felt...
- You don't like it when...
- Sounds like you feel... (ibid.)

Children as well as teachers are encouraged to give feedback and it is this feedback which both increases the self-awareness of the speaker and develops empathy in the listener. Active listening is a vital skill in the development of empathy and consequently in respect for diversity. It is a skill which requires considerable practice and if children are to learn the skill effectively it also needs to be consistently modelled by all teachers in the school and not just in Circle Time. For this reason schools need to give its use serious consideration. Effective use of Circle Time needs to be a part of a whole-school ethos and not confined to thirty minutes per week. Jenny Mosley (1993, 1996, 1998) emphasises the importance of Circle Time as one part of a whole-school system which values everyone and which is manifested in every aspect of school life.

Disparity between Current Writer Consultants

The main current writer consultants on Circle Time – Mosley (1993, 1996, 1998), White (1992) and Bliss, Maines and Robinson (1995) – recognise the humanistic influence of Ballard either directly or through the work of Maslow (1968) and Rogers (1983) all of whom refer to the individual's ability for growth and acceptance of personal responsibility for choices, in addition to the importance of a sound sense of self-esteem to facilitate in this development.

It is interesting to note the differing perspectives of the current writer consultants. Bliss et al. (1995) acknowledge the influence of Ballard and adhere to his aims. Like Ballard they do not see circle time as an arena for the solving of problems but rather as an opportunity to develop skills in self-awareness. To quote Ballard (1982): 'The teacher does not bring to the circle a "something-is-wrong-and-needs-fixing" problem mentality' (p. 12). As a result, Ballard instructs: 'ask no questions, make no analysis, no judgement. Do not pry, interpret, comment, moralize, teach, interrogate, or piggyback your own story ("I know what you mean because I...")' (p. 17)

In contrast the 'conference' section of the Curry and Bromfield (1994) model is seen as a crucial element and while it suggests that children should offer their ideas, the 'teacher should also have an input in order to steer the discussion in certain directions if necessary, so that children see the point of the exercise.' (p. 20). This is also in contrast to the Mosley (1993, 1996) model in which children are encouraged to question each other to solve problems with the prompt: 'Would it help if...' (1996, p. 56). Mosley sees problem solving as an integral part of her Quality Circle Time model but contrary to the other Circle Time models Mosley (1993) while emphasising the importance of self-esteem develops its links with positive behaviour (p. 6). It is, however, Mosley's (1999) development of 'The Jenny Mosley Whole School Quality Circle Time Approach – an ecosystemic model' (p. 12) that identifies her approach as being a more holistic model than those described by White, Bliss, Robinson and Maines or Curry and Bromfield and it is this model which 'can help improve and maintain high standards of behaviour and discipline' (DfEE, 1999, p. 7).

In his article Lang (1998) acknowledges the influence of psychologists advocating the importance of classroom discussion as having 'much in common with current circle-time practice'. He refers to the influence of Glasser (1965, 1969) who:

> introduces the idea of classroom meetings: the social-problem-solving meeting, concerned with students' social behaviour in school; the open-ended meeting, concerned with intellectually important subjects; and the educationally diagnostic meeting, concerned with how well students understand the concepts of the curriculum. Glasser (1969) is very specific in his recommendation that classroom meetings are best conducted in a circle. (Lang, 1998, p. 5)

A circle is collegial and provides an environment where the views of all participants in a group are accepted and valued equally in an atmosphere of mutual respect and trust. This has important implications for education where according to Preedy (1993) '... effective schools as well as having good examination results, are also characterised by a positive ethos, shared values and good relationships among staff and pupils' (p. 2).

Influences from Current Educational Thinking

While they do not refer specifically to Circle Time in their writing, a very sound basis for developing the process is evident in the work of William Glasser on Choice Theory, Howard Gardner on Multiple Intelligences and Daniel Goleman on Emotional Intelligence.

While Glasser does not use the term 'Circle Time' the values and attitudes of his classroom meetings are supportive of the Circle Time model. Enjoyment of an activity is in itself a valid objective and is identified by Glasser (1998) as an inborn need but Circle Time should have – and indeed has – greater potential than mere enjoyment. It also needs to be both meaningful and purposeful. Used effectively it provides opportunities for developing the other basic needs identified by Glasser:

- to belong – to feel accepted as a valued member of a group or class;
- to gain power – power to control part of one's life and to be able to do things competently;
- to be free – to choose and to feel at least partly in control of self.

Infringement of any of these basic needs causes conflict and can affect behaviour.

If Circle Time is concerned with mutual respect and trust, and if everyone in the circle is to be valued equally with an appreciation of diversity then Howard Gardner's theory of multiple intelligences must be part of any current rationale for the use of Circle Time. Gardner identified seven intelligences in 1983 and added an eighth in 1997. Recognition of these learning styles enables a teacher to respect and value individual learning styles while at the same time seeking to activate or develop areas where learners are less adept. The identified intelligences are:

- Linguistic
- Logical – mathematical
- Musical
- Spatial
- Bodily kinaesthetic
- Interpersonal
- Intrapersonal
- Naturalist

Circle Time fits clearly into current educational thinking on Emotional Literacy and Daniel Goleman argues that learning and intellect in the academic sense are not enough to ensure successful and fulfilling lives. He cites research 'that social intelligence is both distinct from academic abilities and a key part of what makes people do well in the practicalities of life' (Goleman, 1996).

Goleman considers the five domains of emotional intelligence to be the following:

- Knowing one's emotions
- Managing emotions
- Motivating oneself
- Recognising emotions in others
- Handling relationships

In her notes to discussion and implementing the Community of Enquiry as a pilot project using Primary Values (CCEA, 1999) Alison Montgomery outlined the following:

Factors which foster the thinking child:
- Building self-esteem
- Reaching each child
- Listening with care
- Being positive
- Being genuine
- Being clear
- Being a learner too.

She also points out that 'there is a close connection between the development of the moral dimension and the development of reason. It is not just a question of *What is Good?* That is important, but even more important is an ability to answer the question: *Why should I be / do good?*' (ibid.)

In her Conceptual Framework, Montgomery (1999) clearly establishes the values and attitudes which the project is designed to develop among which are: self-esteem, self-confidence, self-respect, acceptance, empathy, trust, understanding, co-operation and tolerance. The resource uses the strategy of Circle Time as one of the suggested elements for developing these values and attitudes.

Reading through the values and underpinning principles of each of these writers/educationists many common themes can be identified. Perhaps the most important are the need to value ourselves and others, and the importance of active listening skills. West Kidlington Primary School, Oxfordshire under the leadership of its principal, Neil Hawkes, has evolved a set of values which it has put into practice in the school. Hawkes has since been appointed by the Oxfordshire Education Authority with a comprehensive brief that includes developing a values-based approach to teaching and learning in schools. The identified values for West Kidlington Primary School are the following:

quality	co-operation
unity	understanding
peace	honesty
happiness	appreciation
hope	courage
patience	love
caring	friendship
humility	thoughtfulness
simplicity	tolerance
trust	responsibility
freedom	respect. (Farrer, 2000)

What Happens In Circle Time?

To understand how practice can reflect the aforementioned rationale the following outline gives a brief overview of what happens in Circle Time:

- All participants sit in a circle facing inwards;
- The teacher is the facilitator and sits in the circle on the same type of seat as the pupils;
- Everyone in the room should be a member of the circle;
- All have equal responsibility and participation;
- All members draw up a list of ground rules for the group to determine the behaviour desired for the group;
- A suitable object can be held in turn to determine whose turn it is to speak;

- The object is passed around the circle and each in turn is given time to speak on the theme being considered e.g. 'I feel valued when…';
- Anyone can pass if s/he wants to but will be given another opportunity to participate at the end;
- Everyone takes a turn to speak and listen to each other without interruption;
- The language used is positive, encouraging, praising and supportive; everyone is valued equally;
- There are no 'wrong' views or opinions – all are accepted equally;
- Anything discussed in Circle Time is confidential to the group – within the constraints of Child Protection issues.

Examples of how this translates into actual Circle Time sessions are given in the Appendices. Writer consultants on Circle Time each have their own structure for how Circle Time should be conducted and these can be accessed in their books on the subject. The sample structure given is drawn from a variety of sources, tested through time and experience and rationalised in Appendix 1. It is important that those facilitating Circle Time follow a structure with which they are comfortable and which addresses the individual needs of the group with which they are working.

Rules for Circle Time

Ideally the group will form its own rules/contract/agreement but as a general guide the following have been found to be effective:

- One person speaks at a time;
- We do not use 'put downs';
- We may pass;
- We listen when others are speaking.

In recent training it has been found that rules can be effectively introduced according to need and as and when required. In the case of 'We may pass' it was often found that children tended to make frequent use of this rule if introduced prior to experiencing Circle Time. The empathic skills of the facilitator are essential in sensing the nature of a 'silence'. Is it 'I'm thinking' or 'I don't know what to say' or 'I'm really embarrassed and cannot think' or...? Some teachers have found it useful to offer choices in these situations: 'Would you like me to come back to you when you have had time to think?' or 'Would you like someone to help you?' or 'Would you like to whisper your answer to... and s/he could tell it to the Circle?' By giving choices the child can give a chosen response to the circle, taking ownership of his / her own feelings, identifying his / her own needs and in so doing be a participant member of the group. To develop an emotionally safe atmosphere for the group, especially one inexperienced in Circle Time it can be beneficial for the facilitator to acknowledge the feeling of fear: What am I going to be asked to do? What will I say if I don't know what to say? Will I say the 'right thing'? Will others laugh at me? Creating a safe atmosphere initially is vital and it is important for the facilitator to acknowledge understandable fears and to give sample answers to allay such fears e.g. When I don't know what to say, I might say: 'I don't know, I'm still thinking' or... (give own examples). It is useful for the facilitator to model this early in the session but no one should ever be made feel compelled to respond. Circle Time is about open communication and open, honest communication promotes co-operation which in turn promotes affirmation and positivity.

It is of vital importance to fully explore the issue of 'put downs' and to bear in mind the findings of Cremin (2002) who writes:

> Some of the worst examples of Circle Time that I have seen have been where a member of staff doesn't feel confident, and relies too heavily on the session plan without taking account of how the children are responding to what is being taught. On one occasion a teacher was asking children to share how they feel about bullying whilst one child was clearly being bullied in the circle by children who wiped the talking object after she had held it so that they would not get her germs!

Both verbal and non-verbal 'put downs' need to be fully and explicitly explored: words, inappropriate laughter, sniggering, booing, shouting, inappropriate gestures, rolling of eyes, sighing, inappropriate yawning, use of nicknames, not using a person's preferred name, to name a few. Of course, this does not apply solely to pupils. Teachers, too, need to explore positive ways of working with pupils and addressing their areas for development which do not leave them feeling 'put down'. The best way is to have a Circle Time about the topic (see Appendix 2).

As a facilitator think also about how you respond to another's fears. To brush aside someone's fear (which has no doubt taken great courage to expose and express) is to negate that fear. It may not be yours but if someone has verbalised a fear it needs to be valued as such. Ballard (1982) gives excellent examples of how to respond as a listener and of what should be considered inappropriate responses, some of which have been given earlier in the chapter.

Circle Time is a right to speak with a responsibility to listen for *all* who participate, pupils *and* adults. Perhaps the greatest challenge for the teacher is to listen without making verbal judgement or evaluation. It is an ideal strategy for developing the necessary listening skills referred to in the work of Ballard (1982) to value others and to experience the self-esteem necessary to enable us to value ourselves so that we may value others. If we are to ask young people to explore their feelings then teachers need to be prepared to face their own strengths and weaknesses, joys and uncertainties. According to Rogers (1983): 'Only slowly can we learn to be real. First of all, one must be close to one's feelings, capable of being aware of them. Then one must take the risk of sharing them as they are, inside, not disguising them as judgements, or attributing them to other people' (p. 127).

Self-esteem comes not only from having our opinions listened to in a group but also from the confidence experienced from sharing such opinions in the group. It is an ideal way of exploring what we need to say and do, and in what manner we should say it and do it to communicate clearly, openly and honestly so that we can both understand and be understood; so that we can ensure that the message given is the message received and that it is done so in a way that is assertive but not aggressive. When exploring values we need to think about what these values look like. What do they sound like?

How will others know they are our values? Do we apply them consistently and with all people? What words will we use? What body language will give the required message? How will our tone of voice convey the desired meaning? What actions will support our words? Above all we need an inner conviction that positive values should be at the heart of all that happens in the classroom and in the school. Circle Time is as much about process as about content and those using Circle Time need to be as conscious about the implicit messages they are propounding as the explicit.

Cremin (2002) states: 'It is very hard for a teacher to make a success of Circle Time from reading a book without any experience of doing it with peers.' This reflects the observations made by Edgar (2000):

The success of Circle Time will only be as successful as the skills, self-awareness and sensitivity of the facilitator to:

- create the certainty of a safe environment for all;
- empathise with the participants well enough to develop a challenging session where open and honest discussion leads to growth and forward movement from wherever that particular group may be;
- create opportunities for discussion of controversial issues – for this is where real growth will happen – not only for participants in the circle but also, in the longer term, for people in Northern Ireland in general as they learn to become more confident in discussing such issues openly;
- manage conflict creatively;
- plan structured Circle Times.

To ensure confident, competent facilitators, quality trainers will require:

- Well-developed practical skills (in addition to knowledge and understanding);
- The confidence and competence that come from experience and practice;
- The ability to establish an open, warm relationship;

- Time in teacher training to develop the appropriate interpersonal and intrapersonal skills;
- Appropriate training...

Before beginning Circle Time teachers need to ask themselves:

- What training do I need?
- What further personal development would I need to enable me to do this?
- Where can I start that I will feel comfortable and ensure a safe emotional environment for the class?
- Is this for me?

Basically, Circle Time is about being a participative member of a group, about taking responsibility for what we say through using 'I' statements. It is experiential and can be transformational. If we communicate with someone we will have a relationship with that person. By the very nature of human interaction we will also have conflict in our relationships. Conflict is a natural part of life. It is how we deal with it, which will make it either a constructive or destructive experience. In trying to make sense of current educational thinking and to make a case for joined up thinking Edgar (2000) perceives Circle Time to have three sequential and cumulative elements: the development of positive relationships; problem solving; curriculum.

The link between positive relationships and conflict management is made by Bodine and Crawford (1999):

> Developing a cooperative context within the classroom and school is essential. Emotional intelligence is not developed in isolation, but in interactive circumstances. Responsible citizenship does not occur in a vacuum, but rather in a community. A sense of community, sharing commonalities and caring for others, is an overriding environmental prerequisite if individuals in the community are to learn to live in civil association with others. (p. 91)

Using Circle Time to Engage with Mutual Understanding and Diversity Issues

It is always easy to emphasise our similarities and to 'gloss over' our differences but it is our work in exploring difference, in exploring controversial issues, difficult though it may be, that develops better understanding. When diversity is sensitively approached and the risk of exposing our true feelings about a subject is recognised and supported, in a manner in which all responses are equally valued and acknowledged, then true growth can result. At a talk in Belfast in July 2000, Jane Elliott (teacher of the famous *Blue Eyes/Brown Eyes* discrimination lesson in Riceville, Iowa) stated that her response to the attitude of 'In the dark we are all alike' would be, 'If you think that, *you* are in the dark'. So it is for those who maintain that we should emphasise our similarities and that children are unaware of their differences. Connolly et al. (2002) report on the cultural and political awareness of three to six year olds in Northern Ireland. The research found that

> From the age of three, Catholic and Protestant children were found to show small but significant differences in their preferences for particular people's names, flags and in terms of their attitudes towards Orange marches and the police. ... Just over half (51 per cent) of all three year olds were able to demonstrate some awareness of the cultural/political significance of at least one event or symbol. This rose to 90 per cent of six year olds. (p. 5)

Connolly et al. point out that the influence of schools is only partial and that the youngest children come to school already influenced by family and the local community. However, the authors go on to point out the significant rise in sectarian statements between the ages of five and six – the first couple of years of compulsory schooling. The authors state that: 'At the very least, therefore, schools need to ensure that they develop and foster an inclusive ethos. They certainly have a responsibility to encourage meaningful cross-community contact and to create an environment within which difference and cultural diversity are valued and respected' (p. 51).

In counteracting the argument that this would be counter-productive Connolly et al. respond: 'The answer to that is that it simply depends upon how it is done. What is being suggested here is simply that children are encouraged to learn about and explore the diversity of traditions and cultures that surround them. This ultimately reflects a good, well-rounded education' (p. 52).

Circle Time is one strategy by which diversity can be sensitively and constructively explored and discussed. When Circle Time has been developed throughout the school and when positive relationships are well established and conflict management is understood and consistently practised by *all* then Circle Time can have a sound curricular basis. For instance a Primary 7 class may be reading a class novel which focuses on issues of difference and division (such as *Far Away Home* by Marilyn Taylor, 1999; or *The Boy in the Striped Pyjamas* by John Boyne, 2006 – both of which deal with aspects of the Holocaust). This can provide a good context for discussing issues of diversity in relation to the book and for extending that discussion to a local and closer context in Circle Time. 'Primary Values' (CCEA, 2002) provides a variety of contexts for the discussion of controversial issues for primary school children of all ages, including two stories relating to specific Northern Ireland diversity by Dave Duggan (*Scrapbook Summer* and *The First Ship in the Sea*). When piloted, teachers found that many of the stories used in this resource could be used by all key stages and discussed at different levels depending on age. *Living.Learning.Together* (CCEA, 2006–9) gives examples in the various year groups of how Circle Time can be used to explore issues in Personal Development and Mutual Understanding.

Visits to neighbouring churches (at the very least both Catholic and Protestant, no matter what the denomination of the school) can be part of Religious Education and Circle Time is an ideal vehicle for discussion regarding the similarities and differences. The churches chosen should reflect the religious differences within the class, school and local community. In visiting the different denominations and learning about their individual practices one learns to understand about others through personal experience rather than handed down versions, often prejudiced. In addition, one learns even more about one's own faith as it is compared and contrasted with others. An example of a Circle Time to follow a church visit is included in Appendix 3.

Other issues such as graffiti, symbols, stereotyping, prejudice, fact and fiction, exploitation of children in the workplace, the Holocaust, bullying, disability and environmental issues are all important topics for discussion, particularly when related to the curriculum and translated into a local context. There are many excellent resources available such as the Brighton and Hove PSE Advisory Team (2001a; 2001b) whose working group

> aimed to address the needs of children's different lives, now and for the future, starting from the children's perspectives, then encouraging them to relate to the wider world in an empathetic and empowering way. So the children would not only learn *about* Britain's multicultural society, they would also explore their own opinions, attitudes and values. (p. 1)

When Circle Time has a context and can be related to real life; when it is planned and focused and when everyone in the circle feels valued and able to be open and honest, in an atmosphere of mutual respect and trust, then learning about diversity and the effect we have on each other will take place. Communication improves, co-operation results and affirmation is valued. We always need to remember that violence can be evident as much in the words we use and in the non-verbal ways we interact with others as in the physical abuse we often associate with the term. As Gandhi (1925) so aptly said: 'I object to violence because when it appears to do good, the good is only temporary – the evil it does is permanent'.

Circle Time is a way of exploring diversity and developing understanding. It is a way of helping participants express how they feel and learn how others feel. The skills, knowledge and understanding gained can raise the self-esteem of the participants enabling them to voice opinions in an assertive manner, empowering them to recognise and to challenge prejudice and stereotyping not only within themselves but also in the workplace and in their daily lives.

*

Ballard (1982) in clarifying his basic 'human education assumption' quoted earlier in the chapter stated 'awareness brings responsibility'. Gandhi put it like this: 'You must be the change you want to see in the world'

References

Ballard, J. (1982) *Circlebook: A Leader Handbook for Conducting Circletime – A Curriculum of Affect*, New York: Irvington.

Bliss, T., Robinson, G., and Maines, B. (1995) *Developing Circle Time*, Bristol: Lucky Duck.

Bodine, R.J., and Crawford, D.K. (1999) *Developing Emotional Intelligence: A Guide to Behavior Management and Conflict Resolution in Schools*, Illinois: Research Press.

Boyne, J. (2006) *The Boy in the Striped Pyjamas*, London: Definitions/Random House.

Brighton and Hove PSE Advisory Team (2001a) *Personal and Social Education: Cultural Diversity and Identity, Key Stage 1: Years 1–2*, Brighton: East Sussex Education Department.

Brighton and Hove PSE Advisory Team (2001b) *Personal and Social Education: Cultural Diversity and Social Justice, Key Stage 2: Years 5–6*, Brighton: East Sussex Education Department.

CCEA (2007) *The Northern Ireland Curriculum: Primary*, Belfast: Council for the Curriculum, Examinations and Assessment.

CCEA (2006–9) *Living.Learning.Together*. Belfast: Council for the Curriculum, Examinations and Assessment.

Cameron, D. (1998) 'Foreword: Quality Circle Time – the heart of the Curriculum', in Mosley, J., *More Quality Circle Time*, x–xv, Wisbech, LDA.

Cremin, H. (2002) 'Circle Time; why it doesn't always work', in *Primary Practice No. 30*, Spring 2002.

Curry, M., and Bromfield, C. (1994) *Personal and Social Education in Primary Schools Through Circle-Time*, Staffs, NASEN.

DENI (1999) *Towards a Culture of Tolerance: Education for Diversity – Report of the Working Group on the Strategic Promotion of Education for Mutual Understanding*, Bangor: Department of Education for Northern Ireland.

DfEE (1999) *Social Inclusion: Pupil Support* (Guidance Notes) – Circular 10/99, July 1999, London: Department for Education and Employment.

Edgar, K.E. (2000) *Circle Time: The Theory and Practice in Northern Ireland*, unpublished dissertation, School of Education, The Queen's University of Belfast.

Edgar, K.E. (2006) *Mutual Understanding in the Local and Global Community: Teachers' Understanding and Perceptions*, unpublished dissertation, School of Education, The Queen's University of Belfast.

ETI (2007) *The Chief Inspector's Report 2004–2006* (Executive Summary) Bangor: Department of Education.

Farrer, F. (2000) *A Quiet Revolution: Encouraging positive values in our children* London: Rider.

Gandhi, M.K. (1925), from *Young India* (journal), 21 May.

Gardner, H. (1993) *Frames of Mind* (2nd edn), London: Fontana Press.

Glasser, W. (1965) *Reality Therapy*, New York: Harper and Row publishers.

Glasser, W. (1969) *Schools Without Failure*, New York: Harper Colophon Books Harper and Row publishers.

Glasser, W. (1988) *Choice Theory in the Classroom*, New York: Harper Perennial.

Glasser, W. (1998) *The Quality School Teacher: A Companion Volume to The Quality School*, New York: Harper Perennial.

Goleman, D. (1996) *Emotional Intelligence*, London: Bloomsbury Publishing.

Lang, P. (1998) 'Getting Round to Clarity: What Do We Mean by Circle Time?' in *Pastoral Care in Education*, 16(3), 3–10.

Lawrence, D. (1988) *Enhancing Self-esteem in the Classroom*, London: Paul Chapman.

Lingard, J. (1972) *Kevin and Sadie: Across the Barricades*, Harmondsworth: Puffin Books.

Montgomery, A. and Birthistle, U. (1999) articles:
  'Primary values: A literacy based resource for the Primary School: Information'
  'Identity: Key Stage One-Two: A Conceptual Framework'
  'Interdependence: Key Stage One-Two: A Conceptual Framework'
  'Conflict: Key Stage One-Two: A Conceptual Framework'
  'Primary values: Community of Enquiry: Notes on approach to discussion'
  in *Primary Values: A literacy based resource for Primary Schools (Piloting Version)*, Belfast: Northern Ireland Council for the Curriculum, Examination and Assessment.

Mortimore, P., Sammons P., Stoll, L., Lewis, D., and Ecob, R. (1993) 'Key Factors for Effective Junior Schooling' in Preedy, M. (ed.), *Managing the Effective School*, London: Paul Chapman.

Mosley, J. (1993) *Turn Your School Round*, Wisbech: LDA.

Mosley, J. (1996) *Quality Circle Time in the Primary Classroom*, Wisbech: LDA.

Mosley, J. (1998) *More Quality Circle Time*, Wisbech: LDA.

Mosley, J. and Sonnett, H. (2002) *101 Games for Self-Esteem*, Wisbech: LDA.

Rogers, C. (1983) *Freedom to Learn in the 80s*, Merrill, Ohio.

Taylor, M. (1999) *Faraway Home*, Dublin: O'Brien Press.

United Nations (1989) *Convention on the Rights of the Child* – adopted by the United Nations General Assembly on 20 November 1989, London: United Nations Children's Fund <http://www.unicef.org/crc/> (accessed 15 July 2010).

White, M. (1992) *Self-Esteem: Its Meaning and Value in Schools – How to Help Children to Learn Readily and Behave Well*, Cambridge: Daniels Publishing.

Appendix 1
Suggested Framework and Rationale for Circle Time

Intended Learning Outcomes

Intended Outcomes are essential to
- focus the activity;
- address the individual and specific needs of each class;
- develop continuity and progression from previous sessions;
- encourage 'risk taking' within a safe environment.

Welcome and Introduction

It is important to make a positive statement about the forthcoming session so that children know that both they and the activity are valued by the teacher. It is also an opportunity for the teacher to link it to a previous session or to identify the focus for the current session.

Mixing Up Using Silent Statements

Changing places:
- separates cliques in a non-threatening manner;
- encourages new friendships and improved listening skills;
- allows the teacher or facilitator to assess the situation and to prepare to be flexible according to the needs of the class or of individuals;
- 'Silent Statements' allows participants to identify with a feeling that they may find difficult to talk about.

Sentence Completion

Sentence completion is a core activity of Circle Time; it
- encourages participation;
- can develop thinking skills;

- explores emotions;
- develops confidence;
- enhances self-esteem;
- identification of personal needs;
- responsibility for self.

Information Sharing Develops...

- active listening;
- empathy;
- awareness of similarities and differences;
- interdependence;
- communication skills;
- it is also a time that enables the discussion of issues that have arisen to be openly and honestly discussed in an atmosphere of mutual respect and trust – issues involving conflict management, co-operation, communication and affirmation;

Closing Circle

Closing Circles or Concluding Games give an opportunity for affirming those in the circle or an activity that everyone has participated in.

Evaluation

- addresses the individual needs of the group;
- ensures that individual needs are being met;
- forms a basis for the next Circle Time and ensures continuity and progression;
- ensures that learning is taking place.

Appendix 2
A Sample Circle Time Script: 1

Rarely can a script be used exactly as it is scripted. Please adapt the following Circle Time to suit the individual needs of your own group, ensuring that all within the group will be able to contribute.

Suggested Learning Intentions

- The circle will recognise the meaning of the term 'put-downs';
- The circle will understand the feelings induced by 'put-downs';
- The circle will know the range of verbal and non-verbal words and gestures considered to be 'put-downs' by the members of the group;
- The circle will be able to interact with others without using 'put-downs'.

Welcome and Introduction

Welcome the group. Comment on the opportunity to get to know each other better so that in knowing how each of us likes to be treated we can work more effectively together.

Today we will learn about the things that other people can do or say to us that makes us feel unhappy, left out or that we are not in some way equal with the others in the group.

Mixing Up Activity

Change places if:

You have ever felt awkward or embarrassed;
You have ever felt awkward or embarrassed in this class;

Someone has ever said something which made you feel you weren't as
good as others in the group because of something you said;
Someone has ever said something which made you feel you weren't as
good as others in the group because of something you did.

Sentence Completion

(Remind everyone not to mention people by name. Use the term
'Someone'...)

I felt put down when... and it made me feel...
(with younger groups this could be completed as two sentences)

Information Sharing

Ask each person to think of a time when she /he didn't feel part of a group.

What had happened? What had others said/done to cause this feeling?
What did she/he think?
How did she/he feel?
What did she/he do?
What did others do?

Share your thoughts with a partner.
Think about a time when you might have put someone down (even if you
didn't mean to).
Brainstorm and record on a sheet all the things that people can do or say
that can make others feel inadequate.
Ask each pair to contribute to a class brainstorm.
Point out how important it is to recognise that something *we* don't find a
put-down (e.g. 'Don't be silly') *could be a put-down for someone else.*
Point out how important it is for others to point out politely when a put-
down is used.

Closing Activity

Pass the hand shake.
(One person starts by shaking the hand of the person on her / his left. That person shakes the hand of the person on her / his left and so the handshake passes around the circle.)

Evaluation

This Circle Time session, if appropriate, could be developed in subsequent sessions to consider, perhaps through role play, how to deal with a put-down.

Appendix 3
A Sample Circle Time Script: 2

This Circle Time is designed to take place when a group comes together after visits to two places of worship.

Suggested Learning Intentions

- The children will be able to compare two different faith communities;
- The children will recognise the similarities and differences between the religions;
- The children will be able to reflect on what they have learned as a result of their visit and recognise differences without any preconceptions.

Welcome and introduction

The welcome will obviously depend on the circumstances in which the visit is taking place e.g.

Two schools from differing communities;
Children from one school representative of differing communities;
Children from one school visiting a variety of churches within their
own local community;
Whatever the circumstances, a reference to the opportunity to learn
more about each other should be made.

Mixing Up

This part of Circle Time can be an opportunity to play an appropriate
game. For instance, this one can be found in Jenny Mosley and Helen Sonnett's book *101 Games for Self-Esteem* (p. 89) and has been adapted for the
purposes of this Circle Time session:

Greetings

Begin by asking the group to use their imagination to think of as many
different ways as possible of greeting someone. It may be useful to brainstorm some ideas from the children's own experiences prior to starting the
game e.g. shaking hands, a high five, elbow to elbow, rubbing noses.

The children need to give a verbal greeting using the child's name too,
e.g. Good morning... Hi there... Hello...

This could also be an opportunity to practice another language and
customs from another culture. The children could share ideas in twos and
decide on what they are going to do and say before the game begins so that
everyone in the circle has an opportunity to walk over to someone else
(preferably someone s/he doesn't know very well) and offer a greeting. It
is also important to remind everyone that each person can give only one
greeting and receive one greeting. In other words, Person A walks across
the circle to person B and offers a greeting. Person A then sits in Person
B's seat and person B walks across to Person A's seat. Person B then moves
across the circle to Person C and makes a greeting. Person B then sits in
Person C's seat and Person C goes to Person B's seat and so on until everyone in the circle has greeted someone else.

Sentence Completion

> Today I learned that...
> Something that surprised me was...
> A question I would like to ask is...

Information Sharing

In twos, talk about a perception that you had about one of the faith communities which was changed by your visit.
> What was the perception?
> Why do you think you thought like that?
> In what way have you changed your thinking?
> What made you change your thinking?
If there is time one person could feed back to the group the topic and salient points of the discussion.

Closing Circle

Another faith community I would like to visit is...

Evaluation

(to be added by the teacher/facilitator shortly after the session)

NORMAN RICHARDSON

10 Teaching Controversial Issues

> ... Controversy is the dynamic, the growth point of any area of knowledge. Any intellectual domain which fails to generate it must soon atrophy and die; and any educational system which seeks simultaneously to initiate its young into the life of the intellect and to debar them from intellectual controversy must condemn their minds to the same paralysis.
>
> — DAVID BRIDGES (1986, p. 37)

In any divided society the introduction into the curriculum of material and processes relating to those divisions may well be regarded by many teachers and others as too difficult and controversial. Teachers may perceive such work as making unfair demands on them for which they have not been trained or otherwise prepared. They will often be concerned about strong feelings on the part of their pupils or their parents, or about the attitudes of colleagues and, indeed, about how to deal with their own personal attitudes.

Such concerns have certainly been felt in Northern Ireland in relation to various educational initiatives in which cross-community issues and relationships have been on the agenda. For some – perhaps many – teachers, the introduction of curricular Education for Mutual Understanding (EMU) presented such a challenge; others were anxious about the 'dangers' of engaging in cross-community contact schemes such as the Schools' Community Relations Programme; more recently similar concerns have been raised in relation to issues around ethnic minorities and racism. Even if some of these initial anxieties were allayed over time thanks to the provision of professional support or training, and teachers began to feel more comfortable in relation to formerly unfamiliar curriculum approaches and content (or, indeed, found other ways of dealing with the situation, such as by avoidance), further curriculum change may well have re-ignited their concerns and created a sense of being de-skilled by the situation.

A good deal of the critique of the introduction of EMU into the Northern Ireland education system in the 1990s centred on the concern that too many teachers were dealing only with the 'softer' aspects of such work and avoiding the 'hard-edged' issues. Many observers recommended that such work needed to be sharpened up in order to help pupils deal with controversial issues in the classroom. Evidence from the Northern Ireland pilot scheme on Education for Citizenship which was initiated in 1998, however, suggested that many teachers were no less anxious about controversial issues in relation to Citizenship than they were in EMU.

The Revised Northern Ireland Curriculum actually focuses even more keenly on dealing with controversial issues through themes such as similarities and differences, racism and sectarianism, inclusion, democracy, justice and human rights as found particularly, though not exclusively, in primary Personal Development and Mutual Understanding and post-primary Local and Global Citizenship (see, for example, CCEA/PMB, 2007a, p. 21). Thus schools, according to a NICIE report, 'are now engaged in preparing young people for life in a world where they can address conflict and controversy rather than avoiding them' (NICIE, 2008, p. 9). It is the purpose of this chapter to propose that controversial local and global issues in the classroom should be seen not as a potential problem but as a learning opportunity; to consider how they may be explored as an important dimension of education for diversity and mutual understanding; and to examine some of the challenges and concerns that this raises for teachers and others.

Controversies about Controversy

A clause of the 1986 Education Act in Britain forbade 'the promotion of partisan political views in the teaching of any subject', and required that 'where political issues are brought to the attention of pupils... they are offered a balanced presentation of opposing views' (HMSO, 1987, para.45b). Behind this seemingly straightforward and even quite reasonable requirement lay a dispute which raged throughout the 1980s. It was truly a controversy about controversy, highlighting fundamental disagreements on the role of education and underpinned by starkly opposing political philosophies.

At the heart of all this was the belief that some – or perhaps many – teachers were abusing their position to promote their own political views. As pointed out in the Crick Report (QCA, 1998, 10.8), however, verified examples of such unprofessional behaviour on the part of teachers were extremely rare. There was particular criticism of 'peace education', which was perceived by the political right as being nothing more than left-wing propaganda. It seemed, in fact, as though the whole concept of tackling controversial issues in schools was being called into question, and in one of the best known of the pamphlets of the period Dr. John Marks argued that 'politically contentious subjects should normally form no part of the curriculum for pupils below the age of 16 and should be rigorously excluded from primary schools' (Marks, 1984, p. 2).

If there has been any enduring benefit from that debate, it is perhaps that it has persuaded those who would promote the teaching of controversial issues in the classroom to give ever more serious and careful thought to their rationale and teaching strategies, and to pay attention to how these are perceived by others, particularly parents and governors. This may not have convinced the more fervent critics, nor is it likely to have made much impact on the very small number of teachers who *have* unashamedly promoted their own views in class, but elsewhere it has provided the valuable extra resource of a pool of literature and experience devoted to making a strong professional case for those who wish their pupils to benefit from tackling controversial issues. Although Northern Ireland was spared from most of this particular dispute, it seems clear that the development of Education for Mutual Understanding gained from awareness of this British experience. Indeed, even the choice of the name 'Education for Mutual Understanding' (and the avoidance of options such as 'peace education') by those charged with the early development of such work (NICED, 1983, p. 2), indicates a caution and an emphasis designed to avoid attracting the same kinds of criticisms.

Diverse Values and Controversial Issues

It will be helpful to define more clearly what is meant by the term 'controversial issues'. The classic definition is that offered in the 1998 Crick Report, which heralded the introduction of Education for Citizenship in England: 'A controversial issue is an issue about which there is no one fixed or universally held point of view. Such issues are those which commonly divide society and for which significant groups offer conflicting explanations and solutions' (QCA, 1998, 10.2). According to Oxfam, these are issues:

> on which people often hold strong views based on different sets of experiences, interests and values. Almost any topic can become controversial if individual groups offer differing explanations about events, what should happen next and how issues should be resolved, or if one side of an issue is presented in a way that raises the emotional response of those who might disagree. (Oxfam, 2006, p. 2)

Few disciplines are free from controversy of one kind or another. Historians differ over how to interpret evidence and events; literature is full of subjective critical debate and sometimes becomes caught up in disputes about good taste or bad language; geographers argue about theories of demographic movement, or even the appropriateness of different map projections; economists engage in sometimes heated debate on the causes of inflation. The sciences, too, include many controversies both of a factual-interpretative nature (for instance, debates around evolution and 'creationism') and in relation to ethics (such as the use of live animals or human embryos in experiments, genetic engineering or the safety of nuclear energy). Garvin's work in Northern Ireland on the need for well thought out pedagogical skills in teaching the many controversial aspects of biotechnology is a good illustration of this (Garvin, 1994, pp. 373–7). Nonetheless, there may be a tendency to gloss over these disputed questions, as Wellington observed:

> ... a discipline in the curriculum is misrepresented if no mention is made of its controversial elements. Such a narrow treatment is likely to omit the 'historical context' and give students a totally false impression of the subject. In my view, science teachers are especially guilty of misrepresentation of science, often presenting it as unproblematic, value free and non-controversial. (Wellington, 1986, p. 3)

In Northern Ireland the key controversial issues are normally reckoned to centre on those concerns which have traditionally divided the communities – history, religion, cultural identity and the political options promoted by various shades of unionism or nationalism. However, many other issues have the capacity for controversy, not least in relation to sexual ethics, family values and social and economic differences. Particular fears may arise in schools when it is perceived that pupils are dealing with sensitive topics about which there is anxiety or suspicion among parents, governors, local politicians and others. Sometimes concern may focus on the teaching methods being used in relation to a particular subject, especially if emphasis is placed on open-ended discovery approaches which encourage children to explore and develop their own moral, religious or political values (as opposed to the notion of simply passing on parental or community views).

Fear of such controversies entering classrooms has at times prompted some politicians and educators to argue that schools should be 'neutral' places. Others, however, have recognised that such neutrality may be both unachievable and undesirable, because the very concept of education is heavily value-laden and thereby prone to controversies of all kinds. Education for diversity, mutual understanding and citizenship certainly cannot be perceived as value-free and neutral, and indeed probably only have real meaning if their innate controversies are recognised and treated as opportunities rather than as problems.

Why Teach Controversial Issues?

In constructing a case for the conscious inclusion of controversial issues within the curriculum of any school, it is hard to resist the temptation to give prior place to the mountaineering analogy – controversial issues should be taught 'because they are there'! Controversy is a normal feature of life, in and out of schools, and if teachers are to prepare children and young people adequately for life in contemporary controversial society, account has to be taken of the real issues about which people feel strongly and in many cases about which they disagree. These are, quite simply, in the words of Lawrence Stenhouse (whose *Humanities Curriculum Project* in Britain offered many important insights into the teaching of controversial issues), 'matters of widespread and enduring significance' which, if neglected, would leave a serious gap in the child's education (Stenhouse, 1970). A similar point was made by Professor Paul Wilkinson in respect of the specific and contentious issue of terrorism. Although he was writing in the 1980s his observations are remarkably resonant of more recent events:

> the dangers in writing for young people about the complex phenomena of international terrorism are indeed daunting: there is the risk of unwittingly glamorising or sensationalising the subject... and there is an obvious temptation to produce simple solutions to the problem of terrorism on the basis of superficial knowledge and glib analysis... Yet the business has to be attempted... Teachers cannot duck their pupils' questions on these events, however horrifying the reality. (Wilkinson, 1982)

This has been a long-standing concern of the Council of Europe, which recommended in 1985 that 'Democracy is best learned in a democratic setting where participation is encouraged, where views can be expressed openly and discussed, where there is freedom of expression for pupils and teachers...' (Council of Europe, 1985, para.4.1). More recently the Council's white paper on Intercultural Dialogue has promoted the fundamental importance of education for democratic citizenship on the grounds that it 'encourages multidisciplinary approaches and combines the acquisition of knowledge, skills and attitudes – particularly the capacity of reflection and the self-critical disposition necessary for life in culturally diverse societies' (Council of Europe, 2008, para.4.3.1). At the time of the government's opposition to peace education and fears of political indoctrination in the 1980s, a similar principle was invoked by the Politics Association in making the case *for* political education, on the grounds that 'a politically illiterate population is much more likely to be duped, manipulated, won over by seductively simple ideas, or to seek remedies outside the system when it fails them' (Jones, 1986).

Just as democracy itself is as much to do with processes as it is with end products, so it is with the teaching of controversial issues based on democratic principles. Pollard has pointed out that apart from their intrinsic importance, such issues deserve a place in the curriculum 'because they provide an introduction to peaceful processes by which such issues can be fully aired and conflicts resolved. This is a very important educational experience for children and thus, in many ways, a condition of the future health of our democracy' (Pollard, 1988, p. 63).

Thus a major aspect of the justification for the inclusion of controversial issues is that it helps both teachers and learners to develop valuable skills and thought processes which have an educational significance well beyond that of any particular topic under discussion. The influential American writers on co-operative learning, Johnson and Johnson, have promoted enthusiastically what they term 'creative academic controversy' arguing that it encourages open-minded listening and more meaningful learning. Controversy, they suggest, also serves to develop better personal and social relationships as well as skills in managing conflict constructively (Johnson and Johnson, 1992, pp. 1:5–1:16).

In relation to History teaching Carmel Gallagher has argued for this approach so that 'pupils should be trained to adopt a critical attitude to information, to think critically and be "constructively sceptical"' (Gallagher, 1996, p. 13). If we accept the criticism, often made, that classrooms have not generally encouraged the development of such skills, then this approach to controversial issues takes on even greater importance. Stradling and others have affirmed a preference for 'some kind of process-based approach to teaching issues which would provide students with a conceptual framework, skills in discussion and a critical, analytical approach to events and public disagreements in order that they can transfer these on to issues and situations which they will encounter later in their adult lives' (Stradling, 1984, p. 5).

In particular young people in a divided society like Northern Ireland need to have recourse to skills which, according to Gallagher, may help them 'to face some very difficult issues; to challenge stereotypical thinking and prejudice with evidence; to develop positive attitudes and values which include tolerance, solidarity and respect for diversity; and to contribute to greater mutual understanding between communities in conflict' (Gallagher, 1996, p. 30).

Northern Ireland's Revised Curriculum (from 2007) has given strong emphasis to the importance of thinking skills and personal capabilities, including communication skills, critical and creative thinking, problem-solving and decision-making, working with others and the development of effective interpersonal relationships (see, for example, CCEA, 2007a, 3.5; CCEA, 2007b, 1.8.2; 2.6). To teach controversial issues is to help to sharpen the sensitivity among young people towards the urgent issues of society, and to equip them with appropriate skills whereby they may learn to listen with understanding to a range of points of view and discuss them rationally 'as the potential basis for forming personal attitudes and values' (Gallagher, 1996, p. 25). Such skills are surely fundamental to the processes of educating for mutual understanding, through which, in Lynch's words, pupils may 'become morally autonomous as well as socially responsible' (Lynch, 1987, p. xii).

Controversial Issues in the Primary School

Teachers and other educationists may be reasonably persuaded by the case for including controversial issues in as much as it relates to older children in second-level schools, but some might hesitate in relation to such an inclusion at primary school level, believing such children simply to be 'too young' to understand the issues or to be able to deal with them. Some studies have indicated reluctance on the part of teachers to destroy the innocence of young children, but more significant may be a broad acceptance among teachers of the principles of 'sequential developmentalism' and 'readiness' which are rooted in the work of Jean Piaget. In recent years, however, a case has been made for the positive development of primary school strategies which will at least help to prepare children for a fuller approach to controversial topics when they are older.

Piaget's influential work on the stages of cognitive development was dominant for several decades, and most teachers would have a good general grasp of its implications, namely that certain forms of thinking are not possible until a child has entered the appropriate developmental stage. Abstract thought, which might be regarded as essential for the discussion of controversial issues, would not, according to Piaget, be possible until a child has reached the *formal operations* stage – normally from around twelve years of age. But the primacy of Piaget was challenged, and serious doubts raised about his methods, and consequently, about the rigidity and validity of his developmental stages, thus opening a liberating door on the perceived self-imposed constraints applied by many primary school teachers in relation to controversial issues. What has been described as the process of 'dethroning Piaget' became increasingly well known through the work of Donaldson (1978) and others, and thus Short could conclude that 'it is [Piaget's] underestimation of children's cognitive abilities that is critical as far as the introduction of controversial issues to the primary classroom is concerned' (Short, 1988, p. 18). Further, the Piagetian assumption that teachers can do little to train or accelerate children's progression through the developmental stages was also challenged, particularly by Vygotsky and Bruner. The latter's significant claim was that: 'the task of teaching a subject to a child at any particular age is one of representing the structure of that subject in terms of the child's way of viewing things' (Bruner, 1960).

Research on the political consciousness of primary school children in England, in which children between seven and eleven years revealed progressive abilities to discuss a wide variety of political issues and concepts, further supported the case for eschewing Piagetian rigidity (Short, 1988, pp. 18–19; Pollard, 1988, p. 69), and this view was supported by the Swann Committee in 1985 (HMSO, 1985, p. 337). Jeffs has argued that children should encounter political questions in the classroom because 'the earlier this process begins the better... It is as ridiculous to delay the teaching of politics until late in the school career on grounds of irrelevance as it would be to refrain from discussing the dangers of cigarettes until just before the age at which they can legally be purchased' (Jeffs, 1988, p. 40).

It is the experience of many primary school teachers that even quite young children have views on all kinds of issues, and are keen to express and develop them. The introduction of the practice of Circle Time in a growing number of schools in Northern Ireland (and many other places) has reinforced this perception (Edgar, 2000). If children are encouraged and given opportunities to articulate their ideas at a young age, and if they come to feel that their views are heard and valued (however immature such views may appear to adult listeners) this can set an important pattern for their later years and it is also part of the crucial process of building a positive self-image. Richard Andrews has made a strong case for the formal teaching of written and spoken argument from the earliest years, on the grounds that *argumentation* (Andrews' specific term) is an important feature in the communication of very young children (Andrews, 1995, p. 167). The importance of this is recognised in the statutory requirements for Language and Literacy in the Revised Northern Ireland Curriculum, which require that teachers should enable pupils to: 'participate in group and class discussions… know, understand and use the conventions of group discussion… share, respond to and evaluate ideas, arguments and points of view and use evidence or reason to justify opinions, actions or proposals' (CCEA, 2007a, p. 55).

Perhaps the most important contribution of a primary school teacher in relation to controversial issues will be to recognise that it is important to prepare children from a young age to build up the experience and skills they will require in order to talk about and cope with conflicting attitudes and significantly different beliefs, whether or not such issues regularly impinge on the primary classroom itself.

Approaching Controversial Issues in the Classroom

There are perhaps three main ways in which controversial issues may enter any school classroom:

(a) Issues which are included in the various curriculum areas of learning, and which we may therefore expect to arise at some time or other – normally at a point which the teacher has determined and for which she may therefore plan.

In a post-primary school a number of potentially controversial issues are likely to be present in the various programmes of study. Experience in Northern Ireland suggests that these may well include a range of History topics such as the Plantations of Ulster, the conflict of 1688–90, the Penal Laws, the Easter Rising of 1916 and Northern Ireland since partition. In Religious Education controversy may arise through the study of differing Christian traditions in Ireland, differing truth claims between the world's religions, questions of family and sexual ethics or issues such as the evolution/creationist debate. Similarly in literacy/literature classes controversy may centre around discussion on attitudes to war and violence, or moral issues raised by novels or poems.

In the primary school there may appear to be fewer obviously controversial topics in the formal programmes of study, but the new 'area of learning' of Personal Development and Mutual Understanding has placed some of these issues much more overtly within its themes and topics, not least around issues of 'similarities and differences', with references to both sectarianism and racism. Indeed, if teachers are open to children's concerns and questions then such issues will almost inevitably arise, perhaps prompted by novels and poems, especially in Key Stage 2. Some children's writers quite deliberately seek to tackle questions of race, gender, religion, third-world poverty, divisions in Northern Ireland, etc., and a skilled teacher will make the most of such opportunities.

(b) Issues which teachers decide to tackle as part of in-school or inter-school work because they feel that they need to be addressed at some stage.

These may be issues which do not necessarily arise naturally (or at the appropriate time) from the formal curriculum, but which teachers may wish to address in the context of pastoral needs or personal development programmes (such as in a form period in post-primary schools) or general studies courses in the sixth form. In primary schools some teachers at Key Stage 2 level encourage their pupils to comment on and discuss contemporary issues as raised by newspapers or television (for instance by requiring that pupils watch the news and current affairs programmes and report back on them). In relation to cross-community inter-school work such discussions may centre on anticipated or actual issues or incidents relating, for instance, to sectarian or racist language, sectarian symbols, provocative graffiti or recent violent incidents; at other times global issues may come to the fore, perhaps in relation to terrorism or disputed military action. The key principle here is one of being prepared as teachers and of helping to prepare pupils to deal sensitively and constructively with such issues.

(c) Unanticipated issues which arise as part of in-school or inter-school work, although it is more likely to be the *timing* rather than the topic which is unexpected, especially when experienced teachers are involved.

Such occurrences are unpredictable, although they should not be unanticipated. Many of the issues will be as above, but they will be sparked off by a comment or question or perhaps by a sudden incident in class, or the sight of a racist or sectarian slogan, or perhaps by comments on divisive local or national events during Northern Ireland's 'marching season' or following violent incidents. It will be particularly important for teachers engaging in joint work to recognise that pupils from different schools may respond quite differently when such an issue emerges, and no less important for those teachers to have discussed in advance their policies and shared strategies for exploring such issues sensitively and effectively.

Similarly, such situations may arise through high level media coverage of international events such as wars or terrorist activity leading to anxiety and questions in class on the part of children. Teachers in many schools were challenged in this way by the attacks on the United States on 11 September 2001 and the ensuing Afghanistan war, and later in relation to the Iraq conflict. This was sharpened by concerns about relations in schools and local communities between Muslims and others.

Teachers who are open to making the most of such issues in order to enlarge the educational opportunities in their classrooms will be concerned with a number of important pedagogical issues. These include the following:

- building an atmosphere of confidence and trust between all members of the class and with the teacher;
- establishing an appropriate and clearly understood role for the teacher;

- developing a range of strategies to encourage the growth of skills in listening, reasoning, researching evidence, discussing and taking account of the views of others;
- ensuring that a range of views is adequately represented;
- creating an atmosphere of openness in which all concerned are challenged and encouraged to clarify their own points of view;
- ensuring that there are appropriate resources available to support the strategies indicated above.

In the case of issues which form part of the programmes of study themselves (as in (a) above), teachers should have time to think through the issues, find suitable resources and decide on appropriate procedures such as active learning, small group discussion, research, role-play, visits to places, use of visitors, access to documents and so forth.

Issues which the teacher deliberately introduces in anticipation of particular needs (as in (b) above), can also be structured and planned for in a similar way. The teacher has the advantage of being able to choose topics and the timing and to work on relevant skills, plan the gathering of information and discuss strategies with colleagues (including those in other schools).

Although the timing or circumstances in which some controversial issues arise may take teachers by surprise (as in (c) above) most of the recognised strategies can still be employed. Sometimes teachers may judge it wiser to suggest the postponement of discussion until there has been time to reflect. Often, however, such issues are better dealt with when they arise. This is a matter for professional judgement and experience.

(In all of the examples above, the situation in Northern Ireland, whereby the majority of pupils continue to attend largely separate schools according to perceived religious/community identity, may on the one hand reduce to some degree the likelihood of controversy because the communities are separate, but on the other hand increase it because of the lack of opportunity for inter-personal and inter-group discussion on these contentious issues. For some educators this reality strengthens the case for the positive inclusion of such issues within the curriculum.)

Procedures and Classroom Strategies

Many of the skills and techniques employed by teachers to deal with controversial issues will be those they use to deal with many other aspects of the curriculum, drawing on a repertoire of approaches ranging from formal class teaching to research and group-work methods. Often, however, the most appropriate approaches will be found to be those which encourage maximum pupil participation and interaction, and these may relate very closely to those advocated in the materials produced in support of the Revised Northern Ireland Curriculum on 'Active Learning and Teaching Methods for Key Stages 1 and 2' and '… for Key Stage 3' (CCEA/PMB, 2007b), and also as promoted in various guidance materials for Citizenship in the English National Curriculum (see, for example, QCA, 2000, p. 19).

Some of the possible strategies are indicated and summarised below. Several of these have been adapted from a Council of Europe publication by Carmel Gallagher (1996, pp. 41–50), based on her experience of applying active learning techniques to the teaching of History in West Belfast at the height of the Northern Ireland Troubles. Others have been gathered from various sources, mostly relating to practical work carried out by teachers and other facilitators in primary and post-primary schools on a cross-community basis in Northern Ireland.

A Whole-Class Story

In preparation for discussion of contentious issues and to encourage listening and sensitivity to other points of view teachers may wish to use familiar stories, newspaper articles or historical accounts in a way which demonstrates different viewpoints. For example, fairy stories may be told from an unexpected angle, such as Little Red Riding Hood from the perspective of the wolf (Bowers and Wells, 1988, pp. 79–81; Leimdorfer, 1992, pp. 3–6). This may also prove to be a valuable 'distancing' procedure (see below), and it can be particularly helpful in teaching pupils to be aware of bias and prejudice and to recognise propaganda and 'loaded' uses of language. The *Primary Values* resource (Montgomery and Birthistle, 2001), originally developed in support of a values-based approach to literacy (and subsequently ideal for Personal Development and Mutual Understanding) also makes use of story as a basis for such discussion, employing techniques such as the Community of Enquiry (which originated with the 'philosophy for children' movement – see Chapter 4) and Circle Time.

Questioning, Discussion and Skills in Groupwork

This may precede more open discussion on a particular issue, and is a way of preparing pupils to understand some of the factual detail and to be aware of different points of view, possibly including time to research the issues. The teacher's questions should be designed to challenge and expand pupils' awareness, which may be particularly useful when the issue involves knowledge of contentious historical events or technical information. Teachers may need to reorganise a room physically in order to facilitate maximum participation in groupwork. In order to prevent one pupil from dominating a group the composition of groups should be flexible and the roles within the group (leader, scribe, reporter and observer) interchangeable. Self-evaluation processes within the groups will also be important. Teachers will need to ensure that the tasks set are challenging and interactive and that appropriate stimulus materials are provided.

Clarification by Brainstorming, Selecting and Ranking

Brainstorming allows pupils to produce a wide range of ideas on a topic in a very short time, after which they can be organised into some order of importance according to the views of the group as a whole. The process involves listening, interpretation, clarification, justification and compromise, and the ideas thus developed can form the basis for better-informed discussion. This may be particularly valuable as a way of introducing new issues.

Verbal Tennis

In pairs the pupils make as many relevant references as possible to a topic within a period of say one to two minutes, taking turns to make one point at a time without repeating points. This may be used as a warm-up or revision exercise and may be a useful alternative, or follow-up, to brainstorming.

Role-Play

When pupils have built up some knowledge and awareness of the dimensions of a particular issue it should be possible for them to characterise different points of view through role-play. This enables them to step outside their own backgrounds and positions and encourages investigation of attitudes and motives, leading to empathy. Changing round roles within groups further develops a sense of understanding how different people in a dispute may feel or act. Role-play has been judged to be particularly valuable in relation to personal, social and moral issues (Jones and Palmer, 1987).

Standpoint Taking

This approach is a variant on role-play and serves the same purpose. In pairs (perhaps established by the device of moving concentric circles of pupils in opposite directions) pupils take a few minutes to persuade their partner of their point of view before reversing roles and trying again. This helps to build awareness of the points on both sides of an argument but, as with role-play, it requires adequate advance research and briefing.

Debating or Tribunals

This familiar strategy allows pupils to present arguments for or against a particular issue, but it can be much more effective when developed as a team effort, with some responsible for research, others for construction of clear arguments and yet others for presentation. Reversal of positions may also be applied so that pupils may argue on both sides of the discussion. As a co-operative activity it may thereby avoid some of the more obvious defects of 'slanging' and point-scoring. It is important to involve all pupils, whether as participants in the discussion, voters or jury.

Teaching Other Pupils

Pupils may work in pairs or small groups to present some information or a particular point of view to others. They will need to ensure that they understand the material and explore ways of presenting it effectively using a range of media and techniques. This is particularly valuable when the topic in question has many facets which need to be broken down into smaller manageable units.

Line-Ups and Walking Debates

Pupils have an opportunity to respond to statements (starting with relatively uncontentious ones and building from there) by moving their position in a line, one end of which represents 'agree', the other representing 'disagree'. They need not contribute orally, but all participate by position and movement. An alternative format is the 'three corners' strategy, where the corners might represent 'yes / no / not sure' (or 'true / false / uncertain', 'always / sometimes / never', etc.). Members of the group can be invited to express why they have taken their particular position, and it is possible to move position according to their responses to the view of others. This helps to demonstrate the variety and continuum of different opinions which may be held within a group and to help members recognise that people with the same perceived ethnic/cultural/religious identity are by no means 'all the same'!

Using Artefacts

Where contention surrounds issues of cultural identity – as in Northern Ireland – it is often the symbols, emblems and artefacts of those cultures that can evoke strong emotive responses. Some group-work leaders have developed activities focusing on such artefacts – flags, political emblems, religious objects, clothes/costumes, etc. – in order to encourage questions, discussion and accurate understanding of their significance, both to those for whom they are familiar and positive and those for whom they are strange or alien or provocative. While such processes require careful handling and a good deal of well informed background knowledge, they can be very powerful in assisting new insights, empathy and mutual respect. Some community relations education support projects have made effective use of such strategies, and a similar approach was taken by a CCEA support manual for Local and Global Citizenship, by using images of the symbols and artefacts on printed cards (CCEA 2003; Unit 1: Diversity and Inclusion).

Using Puppets

Younger children (and sometimes older ones) can often relate to puppets more effectively and immediately than to adults. Puppets can be used to express opinions and to encourage children to respond with their own, or to represent different ethnic/cultural identities and to encourage the children to engage in questioning, role-play and position-taking.[1]

Some particularly useful resources have been developed in Northern Ireland in support of these activity-based approaches, and while any attempt to list these comprehensively would quickly become dated, it is worth mentioning the 'Joined Up' manual, developed by two very experienced community relations workshop facilitators (Lynagh and Potter, 2005), which offers a

---

1   See, for example, the work of Yvonne Naylor in relation to making and using puppets, in the 'Stepping Out' resource which can be found on the *Puppetwoman* website: <http://www.puppetwoman.org/> (accessed 25 June 2010).

detailed and comprehensive approach to preparation, leadership training and classroom activities and strategies in this important area.

Dealing with Strong Feelings

Sometimes, especially in anticipation of strong feelings and heated arguments, it will be necessary to adopt a very conscious set of specific procedures. Stradling, Noctor and Baines suggest four categories of these:

(a) *Distancing procedures*, whereby teachers temporarily step away from an issue to seek analogies and parallels elsewhere, or to explore details of the background and history of a particular issue. This is particularly useful when discussion becomes heated or polarised (such as, to cite one of the authors' own examples, when discussing Northern Ireland within the Province itself). Distancing alone, however, may well prove unsatisfactory as pupils may fail to see the parallels with local controversial issues.

(b) *Compensatory procedures*, which are useful when attitudes seem based on ignorance, or when there is not a broad range of opinion. The teacher may need to be more directive and offer specific alternative points for consideration, or maybe employ a 'devil's advocate' approach. Use of 'for and against' lists, role reversal techniques, small group discussion or other techniques (as listed above) may be helpful.

(c) *Empathetic procedures*, which may be necessary when the issue under discussion involves active discrimination or an unpopular 'other' or a minority (such as racial issues, or sectarian tensions). These procedures may include some of those listed under 'compensatory', but also techniques such as role-play, simulations and use of literature and drama.

(d) *Exploratory procedures*, whereby more complex issues and processes are developed over a period of time through research projects,
case studies and field work, as well as some of the empathetic and
compensatory procedures indicated above.

(adapted from Stradling et al., 1984, pp. 113–14)

Most of those who facilitate the discussion of controversial issues have
adopted a policy of establishing 'ground rules' or 'contracts' with pupils in
order to have recourse to mutually agreed procedures of behaviour (such
as refraining from personalised abuse or sectarian or racist language) in
anticipation of very sensitive areas of discussion. (This useful approach is
discussed more fully in Chapter 7.)

The work of Goleman and others on emotional development (especially Goleman, 1996; see also Chapter 1) has also highlighted the need to
deal with feelings in relation to controversial issues. The dominance of the
affective in such matters helps to explain why such issues are rarely respon-
sive to logical, rational debate. Goleman has proposed that the emotions
must be educated in relation to self-awareness, emotional management,
motivation, the recognition of emotions in others and handling relationships. If this is correct then any effective strategy for teaching controversial
issues must be set in the context of wider and long-term work in personal
development. It follows that teachers engaging in such work need to be
very aware of their own emotional responses and to develop appropriate
personal and interpersonal skills if they are to help pupils in such a process
(see also Lynagh and Potter, 2005, pp. 92–7).

Strategies for Primary Schools

Most of the suggestions above may naturally appear more relevant to second-level schools. In primary schools, and especially at Key Stage 1, the
principal task will be to lay sound foundations for later years – encouraging
discussion, developing skills in listening, creating a sense of openness to

each other's views, etc.. Nevertheless, some of the strategies above (brainstorming, role-play, etc.) are quite appropriate for older primary pupils, and as children move through Key Stage 2 there will be increased opportunities for more structured work from time to time. For example, some primary school teachers have established in their classroom a 'news corner', to which children and the teacher contribute items from newspapers or TV and radio in which they are interested or about which they are concerned. Once a week, at least, the class listens to these various topics and talks about them together. Many primary teachers now make significant use of Circle Time (see, for instance, Mosley, 1996; see also Chapter 9) to help children to feel confident about raising and sharing issues of various kinds in a group context, although this strategy is by no means limited to primary schools. Circle Time and many of the other activities and strategies outlined above feature significantly in the excellent series of resources for each year of Northern Ireland's primary school curriculum entitled 'Living.Learning.Together' (CCEA, 2007–9).

The strategies proposed above largely relate to classroom situations and to the formal programmes of study. More informal processes, such as those associated with conflict management and prejudice reduction programmes, are often employed, however, as are out-of-school settings such as day conferences or workshops in 'neutral venues' or residential programmes, often with the support of various voluntary agencies. (Some indication of the workshop approach is given in Chapter 7.)

The Role of the Teacher

Without teacher confidence the likelihood is that controversial issues will be studiously avoided. In Northern Ireland few teachers have felt themselves adequately prepared and equipped, personally and professionally, and it has not been customary to discuss local controversial issues outside of personally secure adult situations (if at all). Indeed, the teaching profession could be considered to be particularly disadvantaged in this regard because of the very limited opportunities teachers may have for cross-community encounter and exchange (having largely attended separate schools, trained in separate institutions and then moved back to teach in separate schools), and teacher education has seldom focused on such considerations in the past. Teachers have often expressed the concern that if they were to broach controversial topics there would be a serious negative reaction on the part of many parents. Some teachers (perhaps especially some school principals) may well be projecting their own anxieties about such work onto parents. Experience suggests, however, that despite the vocal reaction of a small number, most parents have no objections, so long as teachers are fair and professional, and that pupils often welcome and enjoy such opportunities.

The task of building teacher confidence in relation to tackling controversial issues will not be achieved easily. Some teachers will have given little thought as to whether or not it is part of their professional responsibility. This raises questions for those devising pre-service and in-service teacher education programmes. Enabling teachers to become aware of appropriate strategies and of case-studies of good practice will obviously be important. But perhaps even more significant will be the creation of opportunities for teachers to discuss such issues themselves as a way of relating personal to professional development. This is why in-service teacher education courses in EMU, Citizenship and PDMU have often been designed in such a way as to create space for teachers to talk and explore hitherto undiscussed issues, especially with colleagues whose cultural, religious and political background is different from their own.

Apart from difficulty with the issues themselves, teachers are also often concerned about the role they ought to play in these kinds of discussion with pupils. While most teachers would totally reject any suggestion that they should be free to propagate their own personal views in the classroom, the question remains as to what extent it may be appropriate for them to express their own views at some point. They may be anxious as to whether they can permit completely open discussion of sensitive issues, or if they should censor opinions which they regard as unacceptable, especially with younger children.

In the Schools' Council Humanities Curriculum Project in the early 1970s the case was made very strongly by Lawrence Stenhouse and his colleagues that the only appropriate role for a teacher in such discussion was that of the *neutral chairperson*. In promoting this *procedural neutrality*, as it has become known, Stenhouse and his colleagues argued that for a teacher to reveal his or her views to a class would be to encourage undue and unhelpful dependence by the pupils on the authority position of the teacher. Adoption of procedural neutrality, however, would help to persuade observers that a teacher was in no way seeking to peddle her own beliefs, whether overtly or covertly, while permitting a wide range of opinion to be made available to the pupils for discussion and debate (Ruddock, 1986, pp. 8–18).

This view has however been subjected to considerable criticism on both practical and ethical grounds. Some have suggested that it is a weak, relativist approach which may imply that all opinions are equally valid, risking offering legitimacy to extreme racist or sectarian views (Carrington and Troyna, 1988, p. 4). Others have suggested that procedural neutrality limits the range of teaching and learning strategies open to teachers by implying that the only alternative to neutrality is an instructional role (Stradling, 1984, p. 8). Within Northern Ireland the concept of neutrality has its own difficulties, especially as most schools – and therefore those who teach in them – are overtly perceived as 'belonging' to one community or the other. In a society where avoidance has been commonplace, not to challenge sectarianism by means of a misguided 'neutral silence' is simply to allow it to flourish. Thus the weight of opinion has moved away from exclusive use of procedural neutrality, although there is a general recognition that it can be useful on some occasions as one teaching strategy among several possible approaches.

While it may be deemed advisable to reject an absolutist approach to teacher neutrality it is nonetheless important for teachers to establish clear parameters with regard to the expression of their own views. On occasion, a teacher may deem it appropriate to 'declare an interest' and indicate his or her own position at some stage in a discussion – perhaps at the outset, perhaps at the end or perhaps at a mid-stage, especially if asked directly. In such an instance the teacher's use of language, sense of fairness, relationship with the class and readiness to let a range of other views be aired will be crucial. This may be a particularly useful approach in relation to Religious Education teaching, for example, where it is often very apparent to pupils that a teacher has some kind of personal religious commitment.

Some teachers argue for what has been termed the 'advocate' position, whereby there is a presentation of the available views on an issue followed by a reasoned statement of the teacher's own position (as, for instance, in the approach sometimes adopted in a Catholic school in relation to discussion on issues such as abortion or contraception), but this can suffer from being uninvolving and unimaginative as a classroom technique.

The 'devil's advocate' approach, referred to above, can be a much more tactically valuable position, to be adopted when discussion flags or when there is not a broad range of views among the group. It releases the teacher from the role of chairperson, but is likely to avoid any feeling on the part of pupils that the teacher is unfairly promoting any one particular position because it is understood that the teacher may, in fact, take more than one such position in order to develop the discussion.

Gallagher's experience in relation to controversial History topics led her to argue that teachers have a responsibility to provide awareness of a full range of the different perspectives on a particular disputed issue and to be very conscious of their own views in the matter: 'This implies valuing and protecting a divergence of opinion rather than seeking consensus. It also implies that the teacher examines critically his or her own view of the situation and refrains from intentionally, or unintentionally, giving legitimation to one particular view' (Gallagher, 1996, p. 30).

The key factor in being ready to select and apply one or more of this range of positions, along with other available teaching strategies, is the professional judgement of the teacher. This was emphasised in the Crick Report (QCA, 1998), which wisely gave several paragraphs to the discussion of teaching controversial issues. Bernard Crick himself, indeed, had argued earlier that the teacher in such a situation should be 'dispassionate, rational, sensible, in a phrase, professional and responsible' (Crick and Porter, 1978).

Case Studies in Northern Ireland

There have been several curriculum development and research projects in Northern Ireland which have focused on the place of controversial issues, and indeed some of these were very formative in the process of shaping the educational themes of EMU and Cultural Heritage (see Chapters 3 and 4), just as they have more recently been formative in relation to the transition from the EMU model into one based on Personal Development and Citizenship.

One of the most substantial projects developing the use of controversial issues in the Province's classrooms was the influential *Schools' Cultural Studies Project* (1974–84). Working in a number of second level schools, mostly in the Western and North Eastern Education and Library Board areas, the project set out to develop teacher confidence and skills and to provide teaching materials for a five-year cycle at post-primary level. In its later stages it pioneered the concept of inter-school joint work on controversial issues, and developed town and city trails to provide a backdrop to the discussion. It was particularly strong in its advocacy of a range of discussion techniques, and emphasised the need to approach controversial issues gradually (Robinson, 1981). Several of the key staff of this project have continued to work in this general field to the present time.

During the same period, and also based in the (then) New University of Ulster at Coleraine, John Greer and colleagues were developing the *Religion in Ireland Project* (1974–82), which also emphasised the importance of joint work and discussion techniques in order to enter the somewhat taboo field (especially at that time) of exploration of the Catholic and Protestant Religious traditions. One of the findings of this project was that many teachers lacked a clear sense of how to develop open discussion with pupils. Thus when it was completed (with the publication of pupil materials) the project personnel went on to set up the *Teaching Religion in Northern Ireland Project* (1984–6), which was particularly concerned with developing more satisfactory approaches to classroom discussion on controversial issues in R.E. (Greer et al., 1987). (While the principles advocated by Greer would now seem to be more generally accepted, through perhaps still not widely practised, similar concerns are still expressed in some quarters about the dangers of 'confusing' pupils by engaging in teaching about world religions and their conflicting truth claims.)

Other work at this time was also being carried out in relation to strategies and skills in the teaching of Irish History, especially under the influences of Jack Magee of St Joseph's College and Rex Cathcart at Queen's University, as indicated in Chapter 1 (see Cathcart, 1979). This process came to fruition in the common curriculum programme for History – in which the controversial areas were no longer conveniently omitted – which emerged from the Educational Reform process of the late 1980s and early 1990s.

During the 1990s a project initially designed to develop awareness and discussion in relation to racial issues in primary schools in Britain was introduced into three Education and Library Board areas in Northern Ireland, involving 120 schools, largely from the Primary sector, in sixty cross-community partnerships. *The Heartstone Project* was aimed at Key Stage 2 pupils and used a mixture of legend, traditional fairy tales and real situations to evoke responses on the part of pupils (Heartstone, 1995; Kumar, 1988). The process involved discussion on racism and sectarianism, Circle Time, role-play, drama, dance, field-trips (for example, to churches) and also workshops and regional exhibitions of work. Teachers' evaluations were, on the whole, positive and enthusiastic, but some teachers indicated that they needed more help and confidence with tackling controversial issues. The Project Co-ordinator, however, came increasingly to feel that while story was a powerful medium in this context, a story 'by local authors that directly addressed relationships between Catholics and Protestants' would have been more pertinent and useful for 'heightening awareness of our own prejudices and bias' (O'Kane, 2001). The Project did not continue after funding ran out in 1998, but the use of story as a medium for exploring controversial issues in primary schools was developed further and in a more focused manner in the early 2000s by the *Primary Values* project and resulting materials (Montgomery and Birthistle, 2001; see also above).

A project for the 14–16 age group, *Speak Your Piece*, was established by the University of Ulster in 1994, in association with the Channel 4 Schools Television series, *Off the Walls*. The television programme used documentary material made in Israel and the Palestinian Authority relating to the Middle East conflict, combining this with dramatised snapshots of the Northern Ireland conflict as it affects young people and studio discussions by a group of young people on topics such as identity, religion, culture and politics. Guidance notes and training programmes were provided to enable an extension of the discussion into classrooms and youth groups. The Coleraine-based project team worked with teachers and youth leaders to develop techniques and skills appropriate to the teaching of controversial topics with Key Stage 4 pupils and young people in youth organisations. The basic principles of the project were stated as:

- enabling dialogue which is forthright and inclusive
- providing alternatives to violence and avoidance as ways of responding to conflict
- facilitating participatory decision making which encourages democratic processes.

(McCully, 2001)

Initial documentation for the project recognised that one of the keys to developing work on controversial issues would be in the improvement of teacher confidence (Smith, McCully et al., 1996). A detailed evaluation of this project noted significantly that 'not all teachers and youth workers have the aptitude and ability to explore controversial issues with young people effectively' and indicated particular resistance to such processes on the part of many students in PGCE teacher education programmes. It recognised that at the heart of effective practice 'is the critical importance of a trusting relationship between practitioner and young person which encourages openness to new and often uncomfortable ideas' (McCully, 2001; Section 6).

Elsewhere Alan McCully has presented a profile, based on interviews with teachers and youth workers who participated in the Speak Your Piece project, of effective practitioners in dealing with controversial issues. They are

confident, self-reliant and committed... prepared to take risks... characterised by
flexible and innovative responses to the varied and multiple needs of the young
people they work with. They reflect critically... on their actions and its possible consequences. Their value base is liberal and pluralist yet they understand the values of
the community from which they originate but try hard to empathise with others....
They are conscious that they should model the values and actions they hope for in
young people. (McCully, 2002, p. 18)

The task of producing such practitioners is not, in McCully's view, an easy
one:

The Northern Ireland education system is an academically oriented one and many
teachers would not share the vision of education espoused by the Speak Your Piece
practitioners. ... Work on controversial issues requires confident, skilled risk-takers.
It is difficult to envisage such practitioners being mass-produced to meet young
people's needs. (ibid., p. 19)

Much of the experience gained in this project in particular was channelled
into the development of a specific Northern Ireland model for Citizenship Education. It is probably fair to suggest that the success of such a
programme within schools will hinge on the capacity of teachers to cope
effectively with the teaching of controversial issues.

Of the various NGO and voluntary support bodies that continue to
work in support of schools and other educational institutions on issues of
diversity and mutual understanding, several focus particularly on strategies
and skills in tackling controversial issues, whether with individual schools
and colleges or in inter-school cross-community contexts. Organisations
such as Community Relations in Schools (CRIS), the Corrymeela Schools
Programme, Northern Ireland Children's Enterprise (NICE), the Spirit of
Enniskillen Trust (particularly in their 'Together' and 'Future Voices' Programmes) and the inter-church Youth-Link:NI have all developed effective
models of working with various ages groups, and their approaches are well
worth exploring further, via their websites and publications.

Some General Principles

Alongside the specific strategies outlined above it is possible to propose a number of general principles, most of which relate to day-to-day classroom practice. They are based on a wide range of collected experiences in tackling such work.

(a) The teacher's fundamental task is to create a positive ethos of 'openness' and mutual respect in which all views will be heard, though they must be expressed fairly and without the intention of giving offence.

(b) Discussion of controversial issues will be unlikely to develop far without a sense of trust and security within the group. Such 'safe space' has to be built over time.

(c) Teachers should be aware of the importance and power of emotion in any discussion of contentious issues, including the teacher's own emotional responses.

(d) The teacher should seek to be an example of a good listener.

(e) It will be important to establish ground rules for discussion, by means of some form of contract or agreement with the class.

(f) Teachers should encourage children and young people to recognise the importance of their developing their own views and opinions.

(g) Respect and understanding should be shown for parental and community views, however difficult these may seem from the teacher's perspective. This should not, however, mean that parents can dictate what a school does or does not discuss.

(h) Children need to be helped to recognise that adults hold a range of divergent views but that it is possible to do so rationally, and that argument does not have to lead to unpleasantness, bad temper or violence.

(i) The teacher's views may sometimes be offered if they are asked for, but always with a reminder that some people have different views. As a general principle, the teacher's own views should normally remain in the background.

(j) It will be important to recognise that in such situations teachers and pupils are learners together.

(k) Teachers should know their subject as well as possible, and be aware of the range of divergent views in case they have to present them (in the absence of a range of views).

(l) Teachers should also know their pupils well and be sensitive to their situations: for example, a recent bereavement in a pupil's family could be a factor in deciding how or if to proceed with a particular discussion.

(m) As a fundamental principle skills should be built up steadily and progressively, on a gradient of difficulty, and teachers should not expect too much too soon.

(n) Wherever possible an agreed school/departmental policy needs to be established in relation to the tackling of controversial issues in order to help ensure continuity and support.

(o) A school is a shared space and cannot be completely neutral. If views are expressed which are intended to be, or perceived as being, deliberately offensive – racist, sectarian, homophobic, for example – they must be challenged. Turning a blind eye to such comments or actions is to give the wrong message – at best to suggest that something is 'not serious' and at worst to suggest compliance. In setting ground rules for discussion of controversial issues teachers must emphasise that remarks designed to offend are unacceptable.

Summary

A case has been made in this chapter for the positive and creative inclusion of controversial topics for all ages, and for the gradual building-up of pupil skills in discussion and research which will enable this to be done effectively. It has also been recognised that success in this work will considerably depend on teacher confidence and on opportunities for appropriate personal and professional development. Case studies have been provided and a range of possible strategies and pedagogical approaches has been outlined, together with a number of general principles drawing on the experience of those already engaged in such work.

References

Andrews, R. (1995) *Teaching and Learning Argument*, London: Cassell Education.

Bowers, S., and Wells, L. (1988) *Ways and Means: An Approach to Problem Solving (Fourth Edition)*, Kingston: Kingston Friends' Workshop Group.

Bridges, D. (1986) 'Dealing with Controversy in the Curriculum: A Philosophical Perspective', in Wellington, J.J. (ed), *Controversial Issues in the Curriculum*, Oxford: Basil Blackwell.

Bruner, J. (1960) *The Process of Education*, New York: Vintage Books.

Cathcart, R. (1979) *Teaching Irish History: Wiles Week Open Lecture 1978*, Belfast: Queen's University Teachers' Centre.

CCEA (1996) *Key Stage 2 Curriculum Working Document*, Belfast: Council for Curriculum, Examinations and Assessment.

CCEA (2003) *Local and Global Citizenship – A Resource for Post-Primary Schools*, Belfast: Council for Curriculum, Examinations and Assessment.

CCEA (2007a) *The Northern Ireland Curriculum – Primary*, Belfast: Council for Curriculum, Examinations and Assessment.

CCEA (2007b) *The Statutory Curriculum at Key Stage 3 – Rationale and Detail*, Belfast: Council for Curriculum, Examinations and Assessment.

CCEA/PMB (2007a) *Northern Ireland Curriculum – Learning for Life and Work for Key Stage 3*, Belfast: Council for Curriculum, Examinations and Assessment, Partnership Management Board.

CCEA/PMB (2007b) *Northern Ireland Curriculum – Active Learning and Teaching Methods for Key Stages 1 and 2 / Key Stage 3*, Belfast: Council for Curriculum, Examinations and Assessment, Partnership Management Board.

Council of Europe (1985) *Appendix to Recommendation (No. R[85]7): Suggestions for Teaching and Learning About Human Rights in Schools*, as adopted by the Committee of Ministers on 14 May 1985 at the 385th Meeting of the Ministers' Deputies, Strasbourg: Council of Europe.

Council of Europe (2008) *White paper on Intercultural Dialogue – 'Living Together as Equals in Dignity'*, Strasbourg: Council of Europe.

DENI (1992) *Educational (Cross-Curricular) Themes: Objectives*, Belfast: Department of Education for Northern Ireland, HMSO.

Donaldson, M. (1978) *Children's Minds*, Glasgow: Fontana/Collins.

Edgar, K. (2000) *Circle Time: The Theory and practice in Northern Ireland*, M.Ed. Dissertation, Queen's University of Belfast.

Gallagher, C. (1983) EMU: 83/9 [private circulation background paper], NICED EMU Steering Committee.

Gallagher, C. (1996) *History Teaching and the Promotion of Democratic Values and Tolerance: A Handbook for Teachers*, Strasbourg: Council of Europe.

Garvin, W. (1994) 'Controversial Issues in Biotechnology Teaching', in *Interdisziplinäre Themenberiche und Projekte im Biologieunterricht*, Institut für die Pädagogik der Naturwissenschaften an der Universität Kiel.

Goleman, D. (1996) *Emotional Intelligence*, London: Bloomsbury Publishing.

Greer, J.E., McElhinney, E.P., and Harris, J.E. (1987) *Classroom Discussion: New Approaches to Teaching in Religious Education*, Coleraine: University of Ulster.

HMSO (1985) Swann Committee Report, *Education for All*, London: HMSO.

HMSO (1987) 'Education (no.2) Act (England and Wales) 1986', in *The Public General Acts and General Synod Measures 1986, Part IV*, London: HMSO.

Heartstone (1995) various preparatory and follow-on materials prepared by the Heartstone Project, Longden Court, Spring Gardens, Buxton, Derbyshire.

Jeffs, T. (1988) 'Preparing Young People for Participatory Democracy', in Carrington, B., and Troyna, B. (eds), *Children and Controversial Issues*, London: Falmer Press.

Johnson, D.W., and Johnson R.T. (1992) *Creative Controversy: Intellectual Challenge in the Classroom*, Edina, MN: Interaction Book Company.

Jones, B. (1986) 'Politics and the Pupil', in *The Times Educational Supplement*, 30 May 1986.

Jones, T., and Palmer, K. (1987) *In Other People's Shoes: The Use of Role-Play in Personal, Social and Moral Education*, Exeter: Pergamon Educational Productions.

Kumar, A. (1988) *The Heartstone Odyssey*, Buxton: Allied Mouse.

Leimdorfer, T. (1992) *Once Upon A Conflict: A Fairytale Manual of Conflict Resolution for All Ages*, London: Religious Society of Friends.

Lynagh, N., and Potter, M. (2005) *Joined Up – Developing Good Relations in the School Community*, Belfast: Corrymeela Community and the Northern Ireland Council for Integrated Education (NICIE).

Lynch, J. (1987) *Prejudice Reduction and the Schools*, London: Cassell.

McCully, A. (2001?) *Speak Your Piece*, Coleraine: UNESCO Centre at the University of Ulster <http://unesco.ulster.ac.uk/> (accessed 15 July 2010).

McCully, A. (2002) *The role of the practitioner in facilitating the handling of controversial issues in contested societies: a Northern Irish experience*, paper presented at the Annual Meeting of the American Educational Research Association, New Orleans, LA, April 2002.

Marks, J. (1984) *'Peace Studies' in our Schools: Propaganda for Defencelessness*, London: Women and Families for Defence.

Montgomery, A., and Birthistle, U. (2001) *Primary Values – A literacy based resource to support the Personal Development programme in primary schools*, Belfast: Council for Curriculum, Examinations and Assessment.

Mosley, J. (1996) *Quality Circle Time in the Primary Classroom*, Wisbech: LDA Educational Publications.

NICC (1990) *Guidance Materials for English*, Belfast: Northern Ireland Curriculum Council.

NICED (1983) *Minutes of the first meeting of the Steering Group on Education for Mutual Understanding: 28/06/83*, Belfast: Northern Ireland Council for Educational Development.

NICIE (2008) *ABC: Promoting an Anti-Bias Approach to Education in Northern Ireland*, Belfast: Northern Ireland Council for Integrated Education.

O'Kane, G. (2001) [unpublished notes and teachers' evaluation reports], Heartstone Northern Ireland Co-ordinator.

Pollard, A.. (1988) 'Controversial Issues and Reflective Teaching', in Carrington, B. and Troyna, B. (eds), *Children and Controversial Issues*, London, Falmer Press.

QCA (1998) *Education for Citizenship and the Teaching of Democracy in Schools: Final Report of the Advisory Group on Citizenship – 22 September 1998*, London: Qualifications and Curriculum Authority.

QCA (2000) *Citizenship at Key Stages 3 and 4 – Initial Guidance for Schools*, London: Qualifications and Curriculum Authority.

Robinson, A. (1981) *The Schools' Cultural Studies Project – A Contribution to Peace in Northern Ireland: Director's Report*, Coleraine: New University of Ulster.

Ruddock, J. (1986) 'A Strategy for Handling Controversial Issues in the Secondary School', in Wellington, J.J., *Controversial Issues in the Curriculum*, Oxford: Basil Blackwell.

Short, G. (1988) 'Children's Grasp of Controversial Issues', in Carrington, B., and Troyna, B. (eds), *Children and Controversial Issues*, London: Falmer Press.

Smith, A., McCully, A., O'Doherty, M., and Smyth, P. (1996) *Speak Your Piece – Exploring Controversial Issues*, Coleraine: University of Ulster School of Education.

Stenhouse, L. (1970) *The Humanities Curriculum Project: An Introduction*, London: Heinemann.

Stradling, R. (1984) 'Controversial Issues in the Classroom', in Stradling, R., Noctor, M., and Baines, B., *Teaching Controversial Issues*, London: Edward Arnold.

Stradling, R., Noctor, M., and Baines, B. (1984) *Teaching Controversial Issues*, London: Edward Arnold.

Wellington, J.J. (1986) *Controversial Issues in the Curriculum*, Oxford: Basil Blackwell.

Wilkinson, P. (1982) [article], *Times Educational Supplement*, 15 January.

NORMAN RICHARDSON

11 Snapshots of Effective Practice[1]

Introduction

It has been suggested elsewhere in this book that *at its best* the good practice that has emerged in the development of education for diversity and mutual understanding has helped to promote positive inter-group relationships, greater inclusiveness and openness to others in Northern Ireland's schools and that it has contributed to good quality educational practice in general. Following some initial observations to set the context, this chapter will offer a number of examples of such practice.

The Background

Various models have influenced the approach to education for diversity and mutual understanding in Northern Ireland over the years. A concern to improve community relations has led many to emphasise the importance of contact between pupils and teachers from the separate school systems. Others have emphasised the importance of learning specific skills in exploring and discussing controversial issues, especially in relation to the contentious curriculum areas such as History and Religious Education, while yet others have concentrated on techniques of managing conflict

---

1   This chapter is a much developed version of a paper originally given by the author at the 1997 *Pluralism in Education Conference* in Co. Cavan, Republic of Ireland.

or challenging prejudice. Influences from outside Northern Ireland have been significant, and there has been substantial interchange with educators from Britain, North America and Europe, involving the adaptation and application of various models of multicultural education, peace education, intercultural education and human rights education over the past three decades and more. The relationship between such work and more broadly based international understanding and global education programmes has also been recognised.

In Northern Ireland from the early 1990s the Educational Theme of Education for Mutual Understanding was often presented as fundamentally process-based and concerned with relationships education at a range of levels. The partner-theme of Cultural Heritage, on the other hand, was perceived as requiring a more cognitive approach in order to explore what might be termed 'cultural roots and cultural wings' (for culture is what helps to define and shape a community and at the same time is continuing to redefine and reshape it). In the perception of most of those working in this field, however, these educational themes were inextricably linked in process and content and were ultimately regarded as two complementary aspects of the same idea.

Despite a considerable public perception that such work remains mainly concerned with cross-community contact between schools and pupils, it has often been affirmed, in official reports and other writing, that the most positive and creative approaches to education for diversity and mutual understanding are evident when they are regarded as whole-school concerns with implications for all aspects of the life of a school. From this perspective it has been suggested (in Chapter 1) that there are several dimensions of their sound holistic development, namely:

Within the formal Areas of Learning in the Curriculum
    where some areas clearly bear very direct relationship to issues of diversity and mutual understanding, while others may have only occasional or more limited relevance;

By means of the teaching and learning styles employed by all teachers
whereby discussion, groupwork, empowerment, mutual respect, democratic processes, etc., can help to create an appropriate environment
for learning and for personal and social development;

Through the pastoral or caring structures of the school
through which the school community can develop positive and creative approaches to the management of social behaviour (discipline), to
pupils' emotional development and to providing a caring environment
in relation to the needs of the whole school community (i.e. pupils
and all levels of staff);

In the contact-based community relations programmes which are available to schools
which remain important for a majority of children in Northern Ireland whose schooling is still within a context of separate educational
provision on the basis of 'perceived community background' – i.e.
schools that cater primarily for Catholics or Protestants;

In the ethos of the whole school
which is the sum of the parts of all the aspects of life in the school and
the key to providing children with a holistic experience of learning
for life in a diverse society.

Loosely following this pattern, this chapter will offer some insights, samples
and snapshots of effective practice in education for diversity and mutual
understanding in order to indicate how, at best, such work has been implemented in schools. All the examples cited are real and many of them are
based on the experiences of teachers who have been active in the field and
who have shared them with the present writer. While there is considerable
value in the presentation of in-depth case studies, not least as a means of
encouraging and inspiring future work, it has been preferred here to provide
a broad over-view without identifying individual schools or teachers.

Diversity and Mutual Understanding in the Curriculum Areas of Learning

History

One of the most sensitive areas of learning and teaching in a divided society like Northern Ireland has been how schools have dealt with the uncertain waters of Irish History. In the past the teaching of History was all too often a marker of conflicting tribal perceptions, but during the turbulent 1970s and 1980s a great deal of determination and imagination on the part of some History teachers and others culminated in the establishment of a common programme for History in the Northern Ireland Curriculum (DENI/HMSO, 1989; 1996; CCEA, 2007a, 2007b).[2] This has imbued History teaching with many opportunities for opening up new insights and developing skills in critical thinking and empathetic understanding.

Some schools have chosen to make the History syllabus the focus of joint work, and this has been particularly effective at Key Stage 3 (ages 11–14). Normally working as two schools from the same area, they have shared staff planning, materials, field trips and residentials. In this way the work done separately in class is complemented by joint work and trust is gradually built up as a basis for the discussion of more divisive issues. For example, joint visits to the Belgian site of the 1916 Battle of the Somme, and locally to the Somme Heritage Centre near Newtownards, have helped pupils towards a sensitive understanding of different Catholic/Protestant perceptions of the First World War period.

Teaching about the Irish Famine of the 1840s, once widely perceived as the preserve of the nationalist/Catholic community and sometimes as a propaganda stick with which to beat the British and unionists, now features in the curriculum of all kinds of schools. Primary school children at Key Stage 2 (ages 9–11) have normally approached it through a study of the Victorian period and issues of emigration, enriched by the use of

---

2   History at the Primary Key Stages in the Revised Northern Ireland Curriculum now
     appears as one of three contributory areas in 'The World Around Us'.

well written novels such as 'Under the Hawthorn Tree' by Marita Conlon-McKenna (1990) and often supported by a visit to the Ulster American Folk Park near Omagh. Older (post-primary) pupils may make a more systematic study of the impact of the Famine on both communities in all parts of Ireland, particularly in relation to nineteenth century emigration (again with the support of programmes such as Emigration Studies at the Ulster American Folk Park). Joint study with other post-primary schools can help to provide insights into how such emotive historical events as this may be perceived differently by each community.

Two grammar schools, working on an ongoing cross-community basis, focused their study of the Second World War on learning about *non-British/non-Irish* experiences of that period. Supported by a formal link established through the European Union's Comenius programme the pupils explored French and German perspectives of the war, making full use of email and other contact with schools in those countries. Such work provides insights into issues which may often be obscured because of the dominance of Irish conflicts.

Teaching about the Holocaust and genocide has attracted a considerable literature in recent years, reflecting contemporary as well as historical concerns. A Council of Europe Project on this topic suggested that among its aims was the need to 'stress the importance of understanding the viewpoint of the "other"', and cited 'the alarming rise of anti-Semitism in certain parts of Europe' as one of its key motives (Lecomte, 2001, p. 7). It is not surprising that Northern Ireland's sectarian conflicts are sometimes seen in similar terms to the issues associated with the Holocaust and more recent acts of genocide, including 'ethnic cleansing' in the Balkans, notwithstanding the differences in scale. Some History educators have recognised the value of resources such as the excellent American-based *Facing History and Ourselves*, which has developed an extensive programme of educational services and resources, including online professional development seminars.[3] These have now been promoted in Northern Ireland by some of the Education and Library Boards in partnership with various non-statutory agencies and a number of teachers have participated in training.

3   See <http://www.facinghistory.org/> (accessed 25 June 2010).

Religious Education

Another key subject, in the light of the significance of religious dimensions to the conflict in Northern Ireland, has been Religious Education, though while some teachers have been committed to developing its potential for the open-ended and inclusive exploration of culture and values in a divided society and a diverse world others have perceived this as an absolute no-go area. In the view of the present writer this is deeply regrettable as it implies that some issues are better avoided and, worse still, that better relationships can be achieved through steering clear of controversy. Chief among those who have demonstrated that the converse is true was the late Dr. John Greer of the University of Ulster. His pioneering research and development work over more than two decades provided many teachers with opportunities to explore new ground in R.E. (Greer and McElhinney, 1984; see also Chapter 3). Particular examples of these approaches to R.E. are the following.

The development of inter-church studies through field trips and classroom work has become a feature of R.E. programmes in some schools at Key Stages 2, 3 and 4 (though not an official part of the R.E. Core Syllabus[4]), and also at sixth form level, and a section of the Northern Ireland GCSE examination in Religious Studies also requires young people to study more than one Christian denomination.[5] Encouraged by materials developed by Greer and McElhinney (1985), Lambkin (1992) and organisations such as the Churches' Peace Education Programme (CPEP, 1985/1992) and the Christian Education Movement (Archbold, 1994) teachers and children have learned to make use of a range of local churches and their

4   Ironically the study of diverse church traditions at primary school level is now promoted and supported through Personal Development and Mutual Understanding and the 'Living.Learning.Together' materials (CCEA, 2007–9).

5   Research (Nelson, 2002) suggested, however, that some schools did their best to avoid the harder edges of such study. For example it was possible to meet the requirements of the exam by studying two different Protestant denominations rather than, as intended, a Protestant denomination and the Catholic Church in Ireland. This 'loophole' was, however, closed by means of a change in the requirements of the Revised RE Core Syllabus from 2007.

clergy or other members as educational resources. One school arranged for its Primary 7 class (10–11 year olds) to visit each church in the local town, to record the information in a computer database and then to make a public display of their work in the local library for parents and others. Such trails are also sometimes carried out as a part of joint school activities, with children exploring churches in 'mixed pairs'. In 2009 the Northern Ireland Council for Curriculum, Examinations and Assessment (CCEA) filmed two primary schools taking part in cross-community visits to Catholic and Protestant churches and placed the film on its support website for PDMU.[6]

Broader dimensions of R.E. have been developed in relation to the study of world faiths (Ryan, 1988; 1996; Nelson and Richardson, 2006 and 2007), sometimes in relation to visits to Jewish, Muslim and Hindu places of worship (which in Northern Ireland is possible in the Greater Belfast area though less easy beyond it) and sometimes through the use of story (Richardson, 2005). This is important if children are to begin to understand the links between ethnic and religious diversity and how these can feed into issues of racism and sectarianism. However, the initial statutory Core Syllabus for Religious Education (DENI/HMSO, 1993), prepared by the four largest Christian Churches in Northern Ireland, made no provision whatsoever for the study of world religions, despite complaints from many quarters, not least members of minority faith communities. The Churches' Revised Core Syllabus (Department of Education, 2007) gives only a limited and grudging place to such study at Key Stage 3, still excluding such topics from primary schools.[7] Some schools, nevertheless, have seen beyond this narrow approach and have ensured that world religions are covered within their curriculum. One primary school teacher, who was responsible for Information Technology

6   <http://www.nicurriculum.org.uk/key_stages_1_and_2/areas_of_learning/pdmu/ living_learning_together/visiting_churches.asp> (accessed 15 July 2010).

7   The RE Core Syllabus is produced by representatives of the four largest Christian denominations without any reference to other faith communities and describes itself as 'essentially Christian'. For further discussion of this issue see Richardson (2007). Ironically the study of other faiths and cultures *is* encouraged in the NI Revised Curriculum primary school programmes for PDMU and The World Around Us (History, Geography, Science)!

work with nine to ten year olds, decided to focus on the different religions of the world, and children used a range of IT skills to record, access and present information on aspects of various faiths. The resulting materials made up a highly attractive display which was available to the whole school. Other colleagues, on seeing the results, gained confidence and started to develop their own work on world religions, including a staff development day on the issue. It is perhaps not surprising that some of the pioneering work in introducing world religions has been in the integrated schools sector, though not uniformly. One integrated primary school, for example, has developed a programme for all year groups that ensures that some aspect of religious diversity is taught, including world religions, linking aspects of R.E. and Personal Development and Mutual Understanding (PDMU) in what it has called 'Integrated Studies'. A small-scale research programme in the 1990s, however, disappointingly revealed that some controlled school teachers felt that a limited study of world faiths would be more acceptable than teaching about Catholic and Protestant churches (Curran, 1995)!

Literature

Literacy and Literature also provide excellent opportunities to explore these concerns. Story, whether oral or formal (such as in novels), is one of the most valuable tools of the teacher who wishes to create a more inclusive and plural educational environment, because it is rich in potential for delving into unfamiliar cultural situations and for raising a wide range of issues, whatever the age group. Similar opportunities abound in relation to poetry and drama, and informal role play is one of the most effective means of exploring feelings and encouraging empathy. One controlled grammar school developed a series of lessons exploring the poetry of war and peace, and extended the programme to include visits from representatives of peace groups. Later they repeated the series in partnership with staff and students from a nearby Catholic grammar school.

This is not the place for a thorough investigation of the role of every curriculum area in relation to diversity education, but some other subjects deserve brief mention:

Physical Education (P.E.)

In P.E. the opportunities for developing skills in co-operation (rather than an over-emphasis on competitive activities) and problem-solving are considerable. Situations with a potential for negating self-esteem (such as in the picking of teams or the creation of a 'failure culture' for those not deemed to be sufficiently 'sporty') can be radically changed by teachers who are aware of the importance of developing positive self-image and interdependence. Opportunities also exist for the development of broader cultural awareness through the inclusion of dance in the primary PE Curriculum. One teacher taking part in an action research project explored this in depth and developed an impressive series of lessons for a class of nine to ten year olds in which the emphasis was on discussion aimed towards creative participation in a range of dance routines from different cultural backgrounds. Similarly some integrated schools ensure that pupils learn to play games from both the British and the Gaelic traditions.

The World Around Us / Environment and Society

Within The World Around Us (incorporating primary History, Geography and Science) and the post-primary curriculum area of Environment and Society (which includes Geography and History) some classes have made good use of the exploration of local and wider place names. With the aid of well produced local materials (for example Bardon, 1990) children have discovered the origins of present-day names in Irish, Scandinavian and from Plantation sources, which enables a valuable route towards the discovery of the diverse origins of the peoples of this island. This was a particular challenge to a controlled (*de facto* Protestant) primary school in North Belfast where any straightforward consideration of the Irish language would have presented serious problems of parental opposition, but in the context of place names the process was positive and successful.

Science

A post-primary Science teacher, concerned about the danger of negative attitudes towards Islamic culture following the attacks on America of 11 September 2001, spent some time indicating the important influences of Arab and Islamic culture on European thought, indicating how many important findings in the areas of maths and science from the ancient world would have been lost had they not been preserved and developed by Arabic and other Muslim scholars.

Creative Subjects

Many inter-school activities have also been built around Art, Drama and Music, although perhaps fewer opportunities so far have been taken within the actual curriculum of these subjects for exploring issues of diversity, despite the tremendous potential for it. (Some teachers have articulated their preference for 'informal mixing' in such activities to allow pupils to discover their similarities – though others may perceive this to reflect Northern Ireland's 'avoidance culture'.) A publication for teachers of Key Stage 2 (Richardson, 2001) attempted to rectify this by providing ideas and topics for 'creative approaches to the exploration of diversity', including activities based on use of colours, imaginative role-play, using sound-pictures to represent ideas, songs from different cultures, story- and poetry-writing and whole-class/large-group drama scripts.

In 2008 an initiative called *Belfast Voices* was established in order to develop cross-cultural theatre techniques for student teachers and others to promote dialogue and to combat racism and sectarianism. This project, led by an internationally experienced theatre practitioner, has worked with the Irish Congress of Trades Unions, some of the teaching unions, teacher education institutions and many community groups including Ardoyne Women's Group and those representing Irish travellers, asylum seekers and other ethnic minorities. Funding was acquired from The Equality Commission, Belfast City Council and the Community Relations Council.

Cross-Curricularity

Although cross-curricular activities can be problematical, especially at post-primary level, there has been some effective work in diversity and mutual understanding carried out in this way. The renewed emphasis on *interconnected learning* in the Revised Northern Ireland Curriculum has given an impetus to such initiatives.

Taking some initial ideas from PDMU, along with a broad inclusive approach to R.E., one P6 teacher took the theme of *Celebrations and Religious Festivals* and developed a unit of work incorporating many other curriculum areas of learning, particularly The World Around Us[8] (Geography, History, Science and Technology), the Arts (Music, Drama, Art) and PE, with elements of ICT, Mathematics, Communication skills and Thinking Skills and Personal Capabilities. It could indeed be argued that there has been considerable long-term good practice in this area through the sometimes neglected areas of schools broadcasting. A programme produced by BBC Northern Ireland for lower primary pupils (aged 5–7), for example, *One Potato, Two Potato*, regularly featured themes and topics highlighting cultural diversity, co-operative relationships and similar topics, using story, music, drama and many local references.

European, International and Global

The European and International dimensions in education may be perceived as a valuable adjunct to local dimensions of diversity education. These have been cultivated through the work of specialist staff in the Education and Library Boards and also through agencies such as the British Council and the Council for Education in World Citizenship (CEWC) and various world development organisations. European Union programmes such as

---

8 This topic has now appeared as 'Celebrations and Good Times!' as one part of a set of Thematic Units designed to support The World Around Us and other areas of learning for Years 3 and 4 (CCEA, 2009).

Comenius and *Erasmus* (and, for language-learners, *Lingua*) have been invaluable tools in providing opportunities for broadening pupils', teachers' and student teachers' horizons and the voluntary organisations in particular have been able to demonstrate that international understanding is about much more than language learning. Take-up of these programmes in Northern Ireland has been generally very good, in all educational sectors.

Some primary teachers have tried to ensure that the global dimensions of diversity and mutual understanding are not neglected. One teacher kept a world news corner in his P7 classroom, with newspaper cuttings and other items contributed by the pupils, and once a week at least the children discussed issues from the wider world. Others have made full use of the artwork of flags in relation to studies of European countries, and this has enabled discussion of more sensitive Irish flags-and-symbols-related issues to take place in a broader and thereby more secure context.

Diversity and Mutual Understanding in Teaching and Learning Styles

Some teachers have recognised that it is in the processes of creating a positive classroom environment – whatever subject they may be teaching – that the greatest opportunities arise for establishing an inclusive ethos.

Groupwork Skills

If young people are to have sufficient confidence during their adolescent years to approach controversial issues with sensitivity and effectiveness, skills in discussion and groupwork must be developed from a much earlier stage in their education. This, indeed, is fundamental within the literacy programme in the Northern Ireland Curriculum where, for example, the statutory requirements at Key Stage 2 indicate that teachers should 'enable pupils to... share, respond to and evaluate ideas, arguments and points of view and use evidence or reason to justify opinions, actions or proposals' (CCEA, 2007). Richard Andrews has made a strong case that 'Teaching and Learning Argument' (Andrews, 1995) must begin in early childhood. This has been particularly reflected in the 'Philosophy for Children' movement of Matthew Lipman (2003) and others, which has convincingly promoted the view that children can discuss concepts which may formerly have been regarded as conceptually too difficult for their age group. Lipman's advocacy of a 'Community of Enquiry' approach has been particularly influential and was taken up by the 'Primary Values' resource (Montgomery and Birthistle, 2002) which was designed to support values education and personal development through literacy in Northern Ireland's primary schools.

Circle Time

One of the most effective and popular techniques for encouraging a participative and open classroom has been Circle Time (as discussed in detail in Chapter 9; see also Mosely, 1996; 1998; Mosely and Tew, 1999). There are many instances where children (and, indeed, teachers) have expressed appreciation for the improvement in individual and group self-esteem through this approach, and, in some situations it has been found to be a central component of school transformation (Mosely, 1993). Although often seen primarily as a primary school strategy, the enthusiasm of one particular primary school teacher at an in-service course encouraged a number of post-primary teachers to try Circle Time in relation to Personal and Social Education (PSE), and one also employed it effectively in tackling low-achievement in a History class. A post-primary school principal with a background in drama teaching personally employed a circle time approach with all Year 8 pupils shortly after they enter the school as part of her PSHE programme. Teachers skilled in the technique have found it to be particularly valuable as a means of exploring contentious and emotive issues.

Learning to Co-operate

In encouraging collaborative approaches to learning teachers are helping to lay the foundations for collaborative relationships in the future. One Foundation Stage (Early Years) teacher has described how she seeks to ensure that there are never enough crayons to go round in her classroom, even though she has an adequate supply, in order to help the children to recognise the need to negotiate and share.

Language for Inclusion

The language used by teachers can be a subtle but most important message in relation to inclusiveness. The term *inclusive language* speaks for itself, but the concept can be used beyond the important area of gender relationships. In a society so often dominated by avoidance, in which many people suggest that they are uncomfortable speaking about cultural differences for fear of 'offending someone', it can be very important for children to hear teachers speaking naturally and openly about ethnic, religious, cultural and other forms of diversity, using direct and straightforward language. This was brought home very forcibly when a Catholic teacher at an in-service course expressed (and demonstrated) considerable unease about using the term 'Protestant'. It became clear that she was aware that there were lots of different types of Protestants but thought that they might be offended if they weren't called by their precise name, so, she admitted, she avoided ever using the term. With the help of her Protestant and Catholic colleagues on the course she became much more comfortable in contributing to open and frank discussion over a period of weeks. Sometimes it may be most important for teachers to make opportunities for demonstrating this level of openness. Schools in which this principle has been taken seriously have made considerable progress in terms of relationships with partner schools. A controlled school in a 'flashpoint area' of Belfast over a number of years took its pupils to the confirmation of their Catholic school partner class in the local Roman Catholic church. This could only be achieved by having built up enough trust to speak openly with each other over time.

Diversity and Mutual Understanding in the Pastoral Dimension

In the creation of positive and inclusive relationships the informal and caring aspects of school life are very significant. It is here, perhaps more than anywhere else, that mutual understanding and respect may be seen to be 'caught not taught'.

Positive Behaviour

A holistic approach to pastoral concerns is likely to call into question the appropriateness of terminology. One primary teacher taking part in an in-service course based an action research project around considering the implications of Education for Mutual Understanding for her school's discipline policy. Before long, however, she had concluded that it should be perceived as a 'positive behaviour' policy, emphasising the creative potential and encouraging a 'win-win' approach to dealing with relationships in the school. Another school, engaged in a similar process, issued its 'discipline policy' under the title of *The Happy School* (as recorded in Chapter 6). This particular school, along with others, found the introduction of peer mediation training and practice to be very beneficial with regard to positive behaviour (Tyrrell, 2002; see also Chapter 7).

Including Minorities

Since the early 2000s schools in Northern Ireland have experienced a significant increase in the presence of children from different ethnic, cultural and religious backgrounds. A culturally inclusive ethos is a crucial factor in helping children from any kind of minority, local or international, to feel at home and to be able to learn. Official support for such work was only very slowly set in place[9], however, and many teachers had found it necessary to develop their own awareness and initiatives. One secondary teacher described how she worked hard to include a Chinese girl with little English, using a whole-class collaborative approach in her PE lessons. A Key Stage 1 teacher with a disruptive pupil from a Travelling background used Circle Time to help the children express their feelings, and found that this led to some new friendships with the previously shunned Traveller child.

Messages on Walls

Teachers in many schools have become increasingly conscious of the importance of displays and teaching materials, in their classroom and in public areas of the school, to reflect cultural diversity, including the use of appropriate pictures and welcoming signs in different languages. One school in Belfast, for example, decided to display in its entrance area a photograph of every pupil together with an indication of their cultural or national background.

Involving Parents

The inclusion of parents, especially in relation to inter-school cross-community work, has also been important far beyond the presence of 'additional supervision'. This is particularly important to offset the charge which is sometimes made that any good work done in the school may well be undermined at home. Teachers committed to an ethos of mutual respect and understanding with pupils recognise the importance of a caring relationship with parents too. In a number of primary schools parents are invited to participate in activities which might be perceived to be more sensitive,

9   An *Inclusion and Diversity Service* was established jointly by the Northern Ireland Education and Library Boards in 2007 and a government policy document on 'newcomer pupils' was issued in 2009 (Department of Education, 2009) but both of these focus primarily on language needs.

such as visiting different churches. Two Nursery Schools in a particularly troubled area of north-west Belfast worked with an educational NGO to extend their work with children to the parents. A three-year strategy was developed to encourage the parents to share in joint activities with the children and to develop their own activities in which they would build trust and gradually develop a capacity to have 'harder conversations' about their similarities and differences. By the end of the three years the NGO reported that teachers 'were amazed how much the parents wanted to engage... Stories were shared and an overwhelming sense of commonality of problems was realised'. The project continued and impacted widely on both schools.

Diversity and Mutual Understanding in Cross-Community Contact

Government funding has been available since 1987 for schools and youth organisations wishing to take part in planned and structured inter-school activities, and significant numbers of schools have taken advantage of the voluntary *Schools Community Relations Programme* scheme. However, because of the over-readiness of too many people, inside or outside the education system, to identify Education for Mutual Understanding *solely* with contact there has inevitably been an element of frustration and cynicism when examples of poorly conceived and badly carried out contact programmes have come to light. Yet as one former primary school vice-principal has written: '... contact has indeed enhanced our understanding of EMU and is a valuable means of making the themes relevant in both a relationship and a curricular sense. The skills involved in EMU are implicit in such contact and schools and teachers should see contact programmes as part of a holistic, long-term, whole-school approach to the issues of mutual understanding and cultural heritage' (Edgar, 1997).

As a result of positive experience as well as negative, and of recommendations made by practitioners, academics and those with statutory responsibility for administering contact schemes, renewed emphasis has been placed on the fundamental importance of curriculum work as the basis for school contact programmes (rather than a series of one-off 'outings' or 'trips'). At the same time, however, contact is primarily about inter-personal and inter-group *relationships* and the *processes* by which they may develop. If a programme is solely product-based (seeing the scheme primarily as an opportunity to fund 'going places', for instance) then the relationships will at best be superficial and at worst harmful and counter-productive.

Several of the examples cited already in this chapter indicate this approach to good practice in relation to contact, and these need to be kept in mind when the poorer examples are inevitably publicised. Some further examples of good practice follow.

Residentials

Residential experience has been recognised as a particularly valuable form of contact, as it permits extended contact time with opportunities for both formal curriculum-based study and informal social contact bound together in a single experience. Some of the support agencies that provide residential facilities have developed helpful models for schools to use on residentials. The Corrymeela Community Schools Programme, for instance, offers teachers and pupils the opportunity to explore issues relating to similarities and differences, and this is enhanced by the involvement in the programme of Corrymeela's regular and volunteer staff, several of whom are from a range of different national, linguistic and cultural backgrounds.

Travelling Together

One primary school head teacher became concerned that pupils from different schools travelling to joint activities were allowed to sit anywhere they liked on the bus, with the result that children from one school sat separately, usually at the back if they were on the bus first and made no proper contact with children from the linked school. He now organises the seating so that the children are sitting next to each other during the journey, and also asks his teachers to sit with their colleagues from the other school in order to model good practice.

Extending Contact

Two high schools working together in the West of Northern Ireland successfully accessed additional funding from a voluntary organisation in order to develop their Schools' Community Relations Programme activities. Two teachers were released part-time to co-ordinate the work and to establish a core group of staff from both schools. Joint training days on themes such as conflict were held. Attempts have been made to extend this model to other schools, though with variable success.

Co-operation for Professional Development

Three primary schools in a County Antrim town – two Catholic and one 'controlled' – had worked together through the Schools Community Relations Programme for many years and decided to extend and share their experience. After considerable discussion and staff development they accessed funding to enable them to issue a joint Educating for Diversity project pack and website (2008) entitled 'Our Differences Fit'. The materials offer processes for staff development and teaching ideas for each of the primary year groups, focused particularly on the PDMU strand of 'Mutual Understanding in the Local and Wider Community'. Quite apart from the practical ideas from which other teachers and schools can learn, this project indicates what, at best, can be achieved through long-term, purposeful, collaborative inter-school activity.[10]

---

10   As this book was about to go to press the Department of Education announced its intention to discontinue the Schools Community Relations Programme funding, to the intense disappointment of many teachers and other educators. It seems clear

As funding opportunities for inter-school activities may become more limited in the future, teachers who wish to continue to provide purposeful cross-community contact activities for their pupils in the future will have to be innovative and creative. Greater focus on schemes for integrating schools or on school collaborations will indeed be necessary if the concept of education for a shared society is to mean anything in practice. The time for superficial or token contact between schools is long past!

Diversity and Mutual Understanding in Whole-School Ethos

It has been recognised increasingly that the most effective way to include and develop diversity and mutual understanding is by means of a whole-school approach which recognises the impact of a positive ethos on all involved in the school community, including teachers and other staff members.

Teacher self-esteem is central to a positive ethos. One senior teacher who was also responsible for co-ordinating EMU in her school concentrated her efforts on building mutuality and confidence among colleagues as the best route towards promoting a positive ethos with pupils. She arranged a series of whole-staff activities, including social meetings and outings as well as professional development opportunities, in order to encourage a participative approach towards a shared vision of the school's role. This was in the belief that children respond more positively when they experience positive relationships between teachers.

In another school teachers take part in induction and *staff development* programmes, especially at the start of the school year, utilising many of the interactive group and circle techniques which will later be developed with the children. The principal reported how some teachers found this hard going at first but later saw the benefits for the ethos of the staffroom and the classroom (Murray, 1996; see also Chapter 6).

---

nevertheless that many schools will continue to find ways of sustaining contact with their partner schools.

Perhaps more than anywhere else it is in this dimension of school life where it becomes most evident that mutual understanding is not something which some teachers 'do' or offer to children at certain times, but rather that it is a quality feature of school life in which *all* participate.

Conclusions

This range of snapshots offered above may help to paint a picture of some effective work in relation to diversity and mutual understanding in schools. Continuous discussion with teachers and student teachers suggests that there are still many inherent difficulties in establishing such work more firmly in the everyday practice of schools, but that there are also strengths and opportunities within the present situation.

If a school wishes to take seriously the issues of diversity and mutual understanding it is clear that teacher confidence and self-esteem are important keys to unlocking new potential within a holistic view of education. The mainstreaming of these issues in the Northern Ireland Curriculum has certainly helped, but such work requires long-term commitment, competent leadership (at school level and within the education system in general), adequate support in terms of funding and resourcing and, above all, proper provision of initial and in-service training. The sharing of case-studies, experiences, approaches and models between schools and between countries will be very helpful in these processes, but sound and consistent career-long teacher education, aimed at an integrated approach to personal and professional development, is essential.

Mutual understanding and respect for diversity, under whatever name or form, cannot be just be dropped into a particular educational slot and somehow activated like a new computer software programme. Rather it must be grown, nurtured and developed as a living organism which must become part of the whole life of the school if it is to have any long-term potential. Many teachers and schools, in Northern Ireland as elsewhere, have demonstrated what is possible in this regard, and we owe it to their hard work to ensure that their experience is valued and taken into the system as a whole.

References

Andrews, R. (1995) *Teaching and Learning Argument*, London: Cassell Education.

Archbold, P. (1994?) *A Look at the Main Churches in Northern Ireland*, Lisburn: Christian Education Movement (Northern Ireland).

Bardon, J. (1990) *Investigating Place Names in Ulster: A Teacher's Guide*, Belfast: Northern Ireland Centre for Learning Resources.

CCEA (2007a) *History – Key Stage 3 Non-Statutory Guidance*, Belfast: NI Council for Curriculum, Examinations and Assessment.

CCEA (2007b) *The Northern Ireland Curriculum – Primary*, Belfast: NI Council for Curriculum, Examinations and Assessment.

CCEA (2007–2009) *Living.Learning.Together* (Support materials for Personal Development and Mutual Understanding, for P1 to P7), Belfast: NI Council for Curriculum, Examinations and Assessment.

CCEA (2009) *Celebrations and Good Times!* Thematic Unit for Years 3 and 4, Belfast: NI Council for Curriculum, Examinations and Assessment.

CPEP (1985/1992) *Looking at Churches and Worship in Ireland*, Belfast: Churches' Peace Education Programme (revised version 1992).

Conlon-McKenna, M. (1990) *Under the Hawthorn Tree*, Dublin: O'Brien Press.

Curran, C. (1995) [unpublished survey on teachers' attitudes to cross-community Religious Education], Belfast: Columbanus Community.

DENI (1990; 1996) *History: Programmes of Study and Attainment Targets*, Bangor: Department of Education for Northern Ireland.

DENI (1992) *Educational (Cross-Curricular) Themes: Objectives*, Bangor: Department of Education for Northern Ireland.

DENI/HMSO (1992) *Core Syllabus for Religious Education*, Bangor: Department of Education for Northern Ireland.

DENI/HMSO (1996) *Programmes of Study and Attainment Targets*, Bangor: Department of Education for Northern Ireland.

Department of Education (2007) *Revised Core Syllabus for Religious Education*, Bangor: Department of Education for Northern Ireland <http://www.deni.gov.uk/re_core_syllabus_pdf.pdf> (accessed 25 June 2010).

Department of Education (2009) *Every School A Good School – Supporting Newcomer Pupils*, Bangor: Department of Education for Northern Ireland.

Edgar, K. (1997) *Cross-Community Contact in Practice* [unpublished paper given for the South Eastern Education and Library Board at their launch of the Schools' Community Relations Programme].

Educating for Diversity (2008) *Educating for Diversity – Our Differences Fit*, Lisburn: St. Aloysius Primary School, Harmony Hill Primary School, St Joseph's Primary School, International Fund for Ireland <http://www.educatingfordiversity.com/> (accessed 25 June 2010).

Greer, J., and McElhinney, E. (1984) 'The Project on 'Religion in Ireland': An Experiment in Reconstruction', in *Lumen Vitae*, XXXIX(3).

Greer, J., and McElhinney, E. (1985) *Irish Christianity*, Dublin: Gill and Macmillan.

HMSO (1989) *The Education Reform (Northern Ireland) Order 1989*, Belfast: Her Majesty's Stationery Office.

Lambkin, B. (1992) *Opposite Religions?* Belfast: Northern Ireland Centre for Learning Resources.

Lecomte, J.-M. (2001) *Teaching about the Holocaust in the 21st Century*, Strasbourg: Council of Europe Publishing.

Lipman, M. (2003) *Thinking in Education* (2nd edn), Cambridge: Cambridge University Press.

Montgomery, A. and Birthistle, U. (2002) *Primary Values: a literacy based resource to support the Personal Development Programme in primary schools*, Belfast: Northern Ireland Council for the Curriculum, Examinations and Assessment.

Mosely, J. (1993) *Turn Your School Around*, Wisbech: LDA.

Mosely, J. (1996) *Quality Circle Time in the Primary Classroom*, Wisbech: LDA.

Mosely, J. (1998) *More Quality Circle Time*, Wisbech: LDA.

Mosley, J., and Tew, M. (1999) *Quality Circle Time in the Secondary School – A Handbook of Good Practice*, London: David Fulton Publishers.

Murray, A. (1996) 'EMU in Practice', in *Developments in Integrated Education*, Belfast: NI Council for Integrated Education.

Nelson, J. (2002) *The R.E. Class as an Interface between Christian Traditions*, paper given at the CULRE/NATFHE Conference on The Interface of Religion and Education, September.

Nelson, J., and Richardson, N. (2006, 2007) *Local People, Global Faiths* (Books 1 and 2), Newtownards: Colourpoint Education.

Richardson, N. (2001) *Making Rainbows – Creative Approaches to Exploring Diversity*, Belfast: Enelar Publications.

Richardson, N. (2005) *People Who Need People* (updated edn), Belfast: Churches' Peace Education Programme.

Richardson, N. (2007) *Sharing Religious Education: a brief introduction to the possibility of an inclusive approach to R.E. in Northern Ireland*, Belfast: Stranmillis University College Research Resources for Religious Education (RRRE) <http://www.stran.ac.uk/media/media,119910,en.pdf> (accessed 25 June 2010).

Ryan, M. (1988) *Small World: A Handbook on Introducing World Religions in the Primary School*, Belfast: Stranmillis College Learning Resources Unit.

Ryan, M. (1996) *Another Ireland: An Introduction to Ireland's Ethnic-Religious Minority Communities*, Belfast: Stranmillis College Learning Resources Unit.

Smith, A., McCully, A. et al. (1997) *Speak Your Piece: Exploring Controversial Issues*, Coleraine: University of Ulster, Speak Your Piece Project.

Smith A., and Robinson, A. (1996) *Education for Mutual Understanding: The Initial Statutory Years*, Coleraine: Centre for the Study of Conflict, University of Ulster.

Tyrrell, J. (2002) *Peer Mediation: A Process for Primary Schools*, London: Souvenir Press.

PART 3

Moving Forward

MICHAEL ARLOW

12 Diversity, Mutual Understanding and Citizenship

Introduction

This book tells part of the story of how the Northern Ireland education system has responded to violent conflict and the complex realities from which it emerged. This chapter is written a little more than decade after the initiation of the Social, Civic and Political Education Project (SCPE), an initiative which gave shape to *Local and Global Citizenship* (LGC), a new element within the Revised Northern Ireland Curriculum. It describes the development, characteristics and implementation of LGC and seeks to identify challenges to the effectiveness of the initiative.

Of course, 'education on its own cannot be expected to manage or resolve identity-based violent conflicts' (Bush and Saltarelli, 2000) but it does make a difference, for better and for worse. A decade after the Agreement debates continue about what sort of relationships should characterise the shared future of communities here. There are those who wish to forget that there ever was a conflict, or if there was, to believe that it was nothing to do with them. Conversation about sectarianism and conflict may be considered distasteful or even harmful. Others seem determined to ensure that the violent conflict does not go away. Gallagher's (2004) warning that 'an enduring feature of ethnic conflict lies in the speed with which fury can sometimes be raised' cannot yet safely be ignored.

Education has a role in developing the capacity of young people to contribute to a sustainable democratic society in Northern Ireland. Local and Global Citizenship has secured a space in the curriculum, for many if not all young people, where the future can be debated; where identities can be explored; where they can become accustomed to dialogue and to the language of democracy, human rights and social justice and where they can find ways to participate in shaping their communities.

I have not attempted to draw precise linkages between Education for Mutual Understanding and the development of, or provision for, Local and Global Citizenship (LGC). Linkages do exist in terms of policy development, methodology and personnel. The values represented by EMU have secured a more central place in the Revised Curriculum and are shared by all subjects including LGC. Aspects of effective practice in citizenship still reflect effective practice in EMU. However, if there are strong resonances, there are also clear distinctions and some of these will be considered below. While 'Diversity and Mutual Understanding' remains an important theme, LGC has a wider agenda and places significantly more emphasis on social justice, human rights and political education than was the case with EMU policy and practice.

*

SCPE emerged at a time of extraordinary change in the social and political landscape of Northern Ireland. Devolution and the institutions that it brought into being opened up unprecedented opportunities for the development of local approaches to key social and political issues. Changing times and new circumstances posed a challenge to build on our own local experience and expertise and to respond in new ways with renewed vigour. The challenge, particularly for those dealing with the legacies of the conflict, was well stated in the 1998 Belfast Agreement:

> The tragedies of the past have left a deep and profoundly regrettable legacy of suffering. We must never forget those who have died or been injured, and their families. But we can best honour them through a fresh start, in which we firmly dedicate ourselves to the achievement of reconciliation, tolerance, and mutual trust, and to the protection and vindication of the human rights of all. (Northern Ireland Office, 1998)

An ambitious agenda for change emerged and included the Culture of Tolerance Reports, reviews of Post-Primary Education, the Northern Ireland Curriculum, Public Administration, and the Community Relations Programme. It seemed that everything was under review and that there were few fixed points in the Northern Ireland Education System.

In this context of change, it was hardly surprising that serious thought was given to the way in which the curriculum prepares our young people for participation in the social, civic and political dimensions of local and global society. Over the last ten years, considerable resources and energy have been committed to the development and implementation of more appropriate and robust provision.

Dramatic change has continued to be a defining feature of the educational landscape. The 'Eleven Plus' is gone, if only in name. By 2010 the functions of education bodies including the Education and Library Boards, the Council for the Curriculum Examinations and Assessment, will be assumed by the new Education and Skills Authority and the implementation of the Curriculum Review will be complete. Reviews of North South co-operation on educational exchange and of Department of Education Community Relations policy are ongoing.

Citizenship Education

During the 1990s and the early years of this century Citizenship Education became an increasingly high priority in many countries around the world. In the Republic of Ireland, Civic, Social and Political Education was made a mandatory part of Junior Cycle in 1996. Until September 2002 the United Kingdom was almost unique among European and Pacific-rim countries in having no statutory provision for citizenship education in the curriculum.

In the late 1990s a number of research reports indicated that young people in Northern Ireland wanted areas related to citizenship to be addressed more effectively through the curriculum. The Youthquest 2000 Survey (Smyth et al., 1997) found that only one third of young people surveyed had opportunities to discuss such issues as sectarianism in school. In other research during the previous year, eighty per cent of young people surveyed expressed a desire to learn about politics at school (Fearon et al. 1997). 'Inside the Gates: Schools and the Troubles', a report on research conducted by Save the Children, recommended that the curriculum should respond to young peoples' 'expressed desire to address controversial issues related to this society, the recent history of Northern Ireland and contemporary events as they happen' (Leitch and Kilpatrick 1999).

Shortly after the Agreement, the Council for the Curriculum, Examinations and Assessment (CCEA) hosted the 'Society 21' conference where it was strongly argued that the existing curriculum did not provide 'sufficient opportunity for educating young people about democracy and constructive civic and political participation' (CCEA, 1999). Reflecting a desire 'to contribute towards the maintenance of peace' it was proposed that recommendations for a citizenship curriculum should be developed, building on the work of EMU and the experience of our neighbours.

Social, Civic and Political Education Project

Arising from ongoing work at the University of Ulster, in September 1998 the SCPE Project was established in the University's School of Education supported by CCEA and the Citizenship Foundation. The project aimed to produce the following:

- A curriculum proposal for Key Stage 3 (KS3);
- A group of trained, committed and knowledgeable teachers;
- A citizenship programme operating in twenty-plus post primary schools;
- Guidance material;
- A directory of relevant resources;
- Experience to inform the curriculum review.

The approach to curriculum development taken by the SCPE Project was a deliberate attempt to move away from a bureaucratic, 'top down' model, to a more practitioner led, 'bottom up' approach involving teachers and other stakeholders in the education system and beyond. The selection of this curriculum development model strongly influenced both the conceptual framework and the characteristics of what is now known as LGC.

The project worked with twenty-five schools over a four-year period. Each school nominated a teacher with responsibility for SCPE and a Senior Management Team link to advise on whole-school and management issues. Training and consultation days were used to develop the curriculum framework, to train the teachers, to plan and reflect on piloting and to review the needs of the group. Three separate evaluations of the project were conducted, two internally and one by the University of Leicester (Watling, 2001). These evaluations were significant, not only in shaping the programme but also in building broader support in the education system.

The Department of Education secured Ministerial approval for an expansion of the pilot in September 2001 along with a major in-service training programme led by CCEA in collaboration with the Education and Library Boards (ELBs). The project was absorbed into the CCEA Curriculum Review Process in January 2002 and the area adopted the name Local and Global Citizenship.

In the course of 2002, each of the five ELBs nominated an officer with responsibility for citizenship. In two cases the existing EMU officer was nominated, in the remainder, new appointments were made. The Department of Education provided additional funding to support all five posts, roughly equivalent to half of each salary. CCEA worked closely with up to three officers from each ELB to prepare for the in-service training programme which began in November 2002.

The Department of Education wrote to all post-primary schools in May 2002, inviting them to join the pilot in one of four phased expansions beginning in 2002–3. Each school was offered in-service training for up to five teachers. Each teacher was to receive seven days of training, including one residential, over a three-year period. Schools were to introduce LGC only after one year of training had been completed.

The Curriculum Review

A comprehensive review of the Northern Ireland Curriculum had been launched by CCEA in 1999 in order to 'meet the changing needs of pupils, society, the economy and the environment' (CCEA, 2000). The first phase focused on aims and values of the curriculum and proposed the introduction of three new elements: Personal, Social and Health Education, Education for Employability and Citizenship. The values of EMU and Cultural Heritage were presented as being placed at the heart of the curriculum and supplemented by Citizenship. The Environment and Society Area of Study seemed to be the most likely home for Citizenship alongside History and Geography.

It was proposed that the primary curriculum would include 'Living in the Local and Wider Community' (later renamed: Mutual Understanding in the Local and Wider Community) as a strand of Personal Development. Key Stage 4 (KS4) was to focus on key skills and the CCEA Modular GCSE, Social and Environmental Studies was to be reviewed in an attempt to bring it into line with the proposed Citizenship Programme and to include the strands of Employability, and Personal Development. It evolved to become the GCSE in Learning for Life and Work and gave shape to a new learning area. Regrettably, early possibilities of the development of a full Citizenship GCSE dissipated.

It rapidly became clear that there were problems with Key Stage 3 (KS3). Even without the three additional areas, it was recognised as being fragmented and overcrowded. In the context of the review, it 'sat uncomfortably' (CCEA, 2003a) between the integrated curriculum areas at the primary level and the focus on key skills and core strands at KS4. To encourage balanced delivery it was proposed that each subject would be allocated a percentage of curriculum time: 5 per cent in the case of Citizenship (CCEA, 2000). The proposal received very little support in consultation and all attempts to specify time allocations were abandoned.

In a new, more radical discussion paper, CCEA proposed that KS3 would be specified as curriculum areas rather than subjects; statutory requirements would be limited to minimum entitlements for every pupil; and a significant number of pupils would complete KS3 in two rather than three years. In consultation, there was support for a more minimal and flexible curriculum, but feedback on other proposals was largely negative or inconclusive.

The third and final phase of the review was focused on resolving the issues at KS3. As part of the solution, the KS4 model was adopted, Citizenship was moved from within Environment and Society and, following GCSE provision, was placed within a new Learning Area: Learning for Life and Work, along with Education for Employability and Personal Development (CCEA, 2003c).

CCEA sent advice to the Minister of Education in December 2003 proposing a three-year KS3 emphasising connected learning, comprised of seven Learning Areas and Religious Education. The advice was broadly accepted; the Revised Curriculum and a three-year phased implementation process ending in 2009–10 were made statutory in the Education (Curriculum Minimum Content) Order (Northern Ireland) 2007.

Mutual Understanding in the Local and Wider Community

At Key Stages 1 and 2, eight subjects were combined into six Learning Areas and Religious Education in an attempt to encourage more connected learning. The Area of Personal Development and Mutual Understanding includes the strand Mutual Understanding in the Local and Wider Community addressing the following themes:

Foundation Stage (Years 1 and 2)
- Relationships with Families
- Relationships in School and the Community

Key Stage 1 (Years 3 and 4)
- Relationships with Family and Friends
- Relationships at School
- Relationships in the Community

Key Stage 2 (Years 5, 6 and 7)
- Relationships with Family, Friends and at School
- Relationships in the Community
- Relationships with the Wider World

Piloting began in eleven schools during 2002 supported by a number of key resources including, *Primary Values* (Montgomery and Birthistle, 2002), and packs produced by Amnesty International and the Churches' Peace Education Programme. The process of implementation was supported by sample teaching plans and teaching and assessment materials.

Local and Global Citizenship at Key Stages 3 and 4

The Education Order (HMSO, 2007) requires that schools provide learning opportunities at Key Stages 3 and 4 in relation to seven Learning Areas, Learning for Life and Work and Religious Education. At KS3 Learning for Life and Work is to be delivered 'through cross-curricular, thematic, and/or specifically time-tabled provision and extra curricular activities' (CCEA, 2007).

The characteristics of LGC at Key Stage 3 informed the developments at Key Stage 4 and will be discussed below. The KS4 proposals were amended to comply with a Ministerial request that 'the very particular needs of young people living in Northern Ireland's difficult and divided circumstances are explicitly and realistically addressed' (CCEA, 2003b) and the Order requires that pupils should be able to:

- respond to the specific challenges and opportunities which diversity and inclusion present in Northern Ireland and the wider world;
- identify and exercise their rights and social responsibilities in relation to local, national and global issues;
- develop their understanding of the role of society and government in safeguarding individual and collective rights in order to promote equality and ensure that everyone is treated fairly;

- develop their understanding of how to participate in a range of democratic processes;
- develop awareness of key democratic institutions and their role in promoting inclusion, justice and democracy;
- develop an awareness of the role of non-governmental organisations.

In addition to the curriculum requirements there is a GCSE option of Learning for Life and Work that was intended to meet the curriculum requirements for each of the three strands. A pilot of the GCSE course involving approximately fifty schools began in September 2003. Anecdotal evidence suggested that many teachers found difficulty with the Citizenship element, principally it seems, because few of them had an opportunity to participate in the LGC training programme operated by the ELBs. Since September 2004 the Learning for Life and Work GCSE has been available to all schools and a revised specification is available for first assessment in summer 2010. Some stakeholders have expressed serious concerns about the consistency of the citizenship element with the philosophy, approach and content of KS3 provision.

Local and Global Citizenship

During the initial SCPE pilot, the particular context of Northern Ireland and experience from elsewhere shaped the development of a number of understandings about the nature of citizenship education. From these understandings defining characteristics emerged including a conceptual framework, a values base and specific teaching and learning approaches. Subsequently, some elements were embedded in the LGC specification, some were promoted in guidance, and training or resource materials while others were abandoned. This section explores some of those understandings and the characteristics that emerged from them.

'Citizenship' is itself a contested term and the particular circumstances of Northern Ireland add their own nuances (see McCully, 2008; McEvoy, 2007; Smith, 2003). For example, the conflicting and diverse expressions of national identity in Northern Ireland (see for example, Smyth et al.,

2000 and the Northern Ireland Young Life and Times Survey, 1998–2007) render untenable any citizenship programme based on a patriotic model or to promote one national identity or one political viewpoint over another (see Smith, 2003).

Any attempt to lend support to a 'middle ground' or any other shade of political opinion, was recognised as being as undesirable as it was impractical (for a useful discussion of related issues see McEvoy et al., 2006). It was also felt that approaches relying on the promotion of political correctness or that attempted to lead pupils to a predetermined outcome would result in avoidance of important issues and superficial or false consensus. The approach chosen was one that promoted frank and open exchange of views in a safe context, characterised by critical reflection and action.

The focus was placed firmly on teaching young people *how* to think and *how* to do: not *what* to think or *what* to do. That being the case, it ought to be possible for an individual to participate fully an LGC course but retain their original viewpoint, even if that viewpoint is, for example, sectarian or racist. The emphasis is less on promoting individual attitudinal change than on developing an understanding of how to participate in a diverse society: more, for example, on countering sectarian behaviour than on countering sectarian attitudes. Uncomfortable though this approach may, at times, be, it allows for the authentic consideration of serious issues and presents opportunities for new ways of thinking, of doing and of being a citizen to emerge.

The Belfast Agreement was signed more than ten years ago and while young people at KS3 today have little or no memory of a world before it, they still live with the legacy of conflict. Individuals, families and communities bear the scars of violence and for many the real threat of violence has not gone away. Sectarianism remains and our society is still shaped by policies and structures that reinforce sectarian patterns of living. Undoubtedly, LGC has a role to play in dealing with the legacy of the past. If History explores the broad context in which the conflict emerged, LGC makes direct connections between recent history and the contemporary world to explain present realities. The main emphasis of LGC however, is not on the past but on the future, or perhaps more accurately, on the transformation of the present.

In this context, students are encouraged to see the possibilities for change and for a better future. LGC facilitates critical reflection on society as it is, to identify strengths and weaknesses, and then to envisage a community of the future: a society that is more inclusive, more just and more democratic. By developing the skills necessary to engage in democratic processes, to seek practical and realistic ways to influence and contribute to efforts to narrow the gap between the world as it is, and their community of the future, they are challenged to hold governments, communities and each other to account. In doing so they are exposed to alternatives to violence but also to the dangers of avoiding challenging or contentious issues.

The conceptual framework is at the heart of LGC and is the basis of the statutory entitlement. It is comprised of four closely interrelated thematic areas each of which is to be explored in local and global contexts:

- Diversity and Inclusion
- Equality and Social Justice
- Democracy and Active Participation
- Human Rights and Social Responsibility

From the outset, the concepts and language used to describe them were acknowledged to be difficult. In addition, the concepts themselves were conceived of as being as problematic in that they give rise to issues that are open to multiple, conflicting and changing interpretations.

In any topic selected for investigation, each of the thematic areas in the conceptual framework will have a greater or lesser degree of relevance. Focussing on each individual thematic area will offer insights from a distinct perspective. However, there is also a progression in the conceptual framework that leads to a shift in emphasis during the course from Diversity and Inclusion, arguably the most accessible thematic area, through to Democracy and Active Participation.

Human Rights and Social Responsibility was identified as being of particular importance, providing a foundation for the other themes by introducing key human rights language and concepts. Through negotiation of and compliance with a classroom Bill of Rights, and topic-based investigation of human rights instruments, the intention was to enable young people to clarify, evaluate and critique their own views and actions, and those of others. However, it has been argued that the curriculum text does not sufficiently recognise of the role of human rights as internationally accepted standards by which governments may be held to account (McEvoy, 2007).

Diversity and Inclusion explores the development and expression of individual and group identity; how conflict arises and may be managed; and how community relations and reconciliation may be promoted. Young people are encouraged to reflect on their own emotional reactions to expressions of diversity and to consider strategies for dealing with difference through management of emotional responses and sensitivity to the emotions of others. As with each of the themes, the perspective provided by Diversity and Inclusion is limited and needs to be complemented and challenged by perspectives offered by each of the other thematic areas. For example, promoting 'community relations' or reconciliation without reference to perspectives offered by each of the other themes has the potential to be counterproductive and dominated by partisan political agendas. Similarly, addressing individual prejudice is of limited value unless wider systemic issues are also addressed.

As the concepts of diversity and inclusion are explored, the challenge emerges of how to ensure that a diverse society can also be an equitable and just society. The thematic area of Equality and Social Justice considers society's need for rules and laws to safeguard individual and collective rights, and to ensure that everyone is treated equally and fairly. It explores how inequalities may arise as well as the experience of inequality or discrimination on the basis of group identity. The work of international organisations, governments and NGOs to promote equality and social justice is considered.

The final perspective or thematic area is Democracy and Active Participation. Here the focus is on ways to participate in, and to influence democratic processes in school and in wider society. Basic characteristics of democracy are explored along with some key democratic institutions and their potential role in promoting inclusion, justice and democracy. The need for rules and laws, methods of enforcement and consequences of law breaking are investigated. Finally, young people are asked to, 'Investigate an issue from a range of viewpoints and suggest action that might be taken to improve or resolve the situation' (CCEA, 2007).

During the pilot phase, proposals had been developed for an action project with the potential to be used as assessment, similar to that in CSPE. However, as the curriculum review progressed it became clear that the action project model did not fit well with emerging thinking on assessment structures and was replaced in LGC proposals by a more limited, less ambitious and less useful exercise.

Guidance materials and supporting resources strongly encourage the use of enquiry based active and participatory approaches to teaching and learning. These are not simply preferred pedagogical approaches, nor are they unique to LGC. They are defining characteristics of LGC emerging from the nature and content of the conceptual framework or from piloting.

In view of the problematic and contested nature of the thematic areas and topics to be explored, traditional didactic approaches to teaching and learning are difficult to sustain. For example, LGC aims to develop the capacity of young people for active and participatory citizenship. Few would argue with the proposition that this capacity is best developed through active and participatory teaching and learning approaches. Effective learning about democracy includes the experience of participating in democratic processes. The teacher becomes a facilitator of enquiry and is no longer simply an expert imparting a predefined body of knowledge. Teachers are encouraged to foster a classroom climate characterised by trust, respect and openness where young people are supported in expressing, and questioning, genuinely held opinions. In doing so they create a more democratic learning space where there are opportunities for teachers to share with pupils' choices about, and responsibility for learning. The classroom has the potential to become a community of enquiry in which contemporary, relevant issues and students' personal views on them are discussed, clarified and challenged.

LGC represents a deliberate and determined attempt to move away from the long and noble tradition of content-based civics programmes, which have succeeded only in convincing earlier generations of students, and their teachers, that learning about the social, civic and political dimensions of life is dull, remote and disempowering.

Evaluating LGC Implementation

The Education and Training Inspectorate survey of LGC provision (ETI/ DE, 2006) was generally positive noting good progress in most schools and drawing attention to high levels of engagement and participation in the best lessons. Only a small number of schools were described as neglecting or dealing inadequately with issues related to Northern Ireland, and of using overly didactic approaches.

The University of Ulster UNESCO Centre evaluated the development and introduction of Local and Global Citizenship between 2002 and 2007 and the final report (2008) observed that 'The development and implementation of Local and Global Citizenship in Northern Ireland is a good example of carefully crafted, conceptually sound, evidence-based curriculum development and the effective management of change'.

The evaluation found that LGC has had significant positive impacts on pupils. Their interest in local and international politics increased, as did their expectations of democracy in schools. Perceptions of community relations were more positive. Interestingly, identity continued to be defined by religious and political factors and trust in political institutions declined. The report found that 'Explicit teaching and learning about citizenship can impact significantly on pupils' confidence, attitudes and behaviours in relation to citizenship issues'.

In schools, the use of active teaching and learning strategies has increased with positive results although active participation through civic or political engagement is more limited. Links between citizenship issues, school and pupils' lives were often not exploited. Even where school councils existed pupils often regarded them with a degree of scepticism.

Teachers reported high levels of satisfaction with inservice training although more emphasis on whole-school approaches and theoretical aspects of citizenship would have been valued. Perhaps as a consequence, significant variations in teachers' interpretation of the aims of citizenship were reported. Differing approaches to citizenship education were also found in teacher training institutions.

The report concluded that LGC 'if implemented with commitment in schools and supported... by statutory and other support agencies...

could make a tangible contribution to creating greater tolerance, equality and stability in Northern Ireland's Society... It deserves to be robustly supported and sustained.'

While both reports were broadly positive, they also highlight issues that have the potential to impact negatively on effective delivery of LGC over the long term. Based on the evidence currently available, McEvoy (2007) has warned that 'It would be reasonable to suggest that some schools may struggle to find adequate time for effective delivery; timetabling constraints may result in untrained teachers delivering the subject; pupils may receive minimum exposure to the subject particularly if it is delivered in a cross-curricular manner'.

Challenges identified, and recommendations generated in these two reports provide the basis for an agenda for development, which will be discussed below.

Issues and Challenges

Over the last ten years the development and implementation of Local and Global Citizenship has been supported by significant, and in some respects unprecedented resources. However, up scaling from pilot to mainstream is a notoriously difficult and complex challenge to manage successfully. As the Curriculum Review progressed the enormous possibilities for experimentation open to a small-scale pilot were, inevitably, eroded as broader curriculum policy issues increasingly shaped the LGC curriculum text and context. In what, at times, was a very fluid and rapidly changing situation, part of the challenge was to ensure that essential learning from piloting, from EMU and from the implementation of citizenship elsewhere, survived in a useful and sustainable form in the emergent curriculum. Nevertheless, it is arguable that the potential impact and effectiveness of LGC was diminished in the process. It is clear that there are significant issues and challenges arising from the Revised Curriculum, from the implementation process or from changing circumstances.

While the development of LGC at KS4 was informed by developments at KS3, it did not have the benefit of the same extensive piloting and planning. When LGC at KS4 was placed within Learning for Life and Work GCSE, it seemed that there was at least a possibility of a full GCSE in Citizenship. However, this was not to be, and ultimately Learning for Life and Work emerged as new Learning Area within which LGC was placed (rather than Environment and Society) at both Key Stages. I believe that the decision to relocate citizenship has harmed citizenship provision in a number of respects and 'may have damaged the credibility of citizenship education' (McCully, 2009).

The current provision at GCSE continues to generate concern. The Learning for Life and Work GCSE was open to all schools before all had completed the citizenship training programme and McCully (2008) cites anecdotal evidence of 'some teachers feeling conscripted and ill-prepared'. More recently, some of those most closely associated with citizenship have pointed to a lack of clear progression and consistency of values and approach between the KS3 programme and even the most recent iteration of the GCSE Syllabus. Consequently, there is anecdotal evidence of teachers with a commitment to citizenship avoiding, and being advised to avoid current GCSE provision.

It is likely that the relocation of citizenship to Learning for Life and Work together with the failure to offer a full GCSE in Local and Global Citizenship, has inhibited the ability of the education system to respond as had been hoped and makes the development of specialist citizenship teachers unlikely. There is already a worrying and growing tendency for schools to advertise Learning for Life and Work teaching posts and it is possible that in future, pre-service and inservice training and support for citizenship will be replaced by Learning for Life and Work provision. It is difficult to imagine a primary degree or teaching course that would adequately prepare individuals to teach the disparate areas of LGC, Personal Development and Education for Employability. The result would be to undermine the status and distinctiveness of citizenship and devalue the investments of time and resources already made.

As Gallagher has observed, 'No matter how good the programmes we devise, it is all about how it is delivered... it's about the curriculum and a whole lot more' (in Jeffers and O'Connor, 2008). Part of that 'whole lot more' was to develop a critical mass of individuals and organisations interested in and committed to citizenship education. This was particularly important in view of difficulty of embedding a new curricular area. A variety of stakeholders within and beyond the education system were encouraged to become involved in advocacy for and debates about citizenship, in shaping the curriculum and in resource development.

The need to develop a critical mass of citizenship teachers within schools was recognised and the Department of Education agreed to fund in-service training for up to five teachers from each school. It was anticipated that citizenship PGCE courses would emerge and the qualification would ultimately be required for LGC teachers. While Initial Teacher Training provision for LGC continues to evolve, these aspirations have not yet been fulfilled. As the Education and Library Boards transition to the Education and Skills Authority there are likely to be opportunities to consolidate and build on existing effective practice in in-service training. There is also a risk that existing shared understandings and commitments will be lost and the gains made over recent years will be dissipated.

As reform and structural change continue in the education system, it becomes increasingly important to continue to develop the critical mass of citizenship educators. I believe there is a pressing need for a forum for reflection and debate and to build consensus about the role and purposes of citizenship education. Advocacy is required to secure progress to date and to further the development of citizenship. The aims and approaches of citizenship education are sometimes not as well understood as they need to be in schools, in teacher education or at policy and political levels. Effective advocacy and shared understandings open up possibilities for significant benefits in a number of areas.

The UNESCO Centre evaluation (2008) offers an agenda for ongoing development. For example, closer alignment between citizenship education and the Department of Education's community relations policy and funding has the potential to offer more structured, reflective and better funded experiences to young people and schools. Support for education for democracy and whole-school involvement in citizenship education would be enhanced by the introduction of a statutory requirement for schools to operate effective school councils. In schools there is a need for discrete timetabled citizenship classes supplemented by cross-curricular links as well as community links and extra-curricular activities.

The evaluation report also points to a need for renewed dialogue with stakeholders to develop a 'shared understanding of the meaning of citizenship education within contemporary society'. Much energy has been focussed on introducing specific language and approaches to citizenship education in Northern Ireland. Contexts in schools and wider society have changed in the last decade. The expertise and confidence of teachers have grown. The issues confronting our society have evolved and changed as we have lived with the Agreement and the consequences that have flowed from it. There is a growing need to interrogate afresh the concepts that underpin LGC. Teachers and young people will increasingly need to move beyond current understandings of the conceptual framework if they are to develop or maintain the critical edge that those involved in the creation of LGC aspired to. Part of that task is an educational one but citizenship education also needs to be understood and shaped by wider society in order to be relevant, challenging and effective.

*

Recently, Andy Pollak has commented that 'Several decades of community relations and, multiculturalism and education for mutual understanding have not merely failed – for the most part they haven't even been properly tried' (in Jeffers and O'Connor, 2008).

There is still a risk that in many places, the same can be said of Local and Global Citizenship. There are significant challenges if we are to ensure that it is 'properly tried' and embedded in schools and education support services. I agree with McCully's (2008) positivity about what has been achieved, as well as his concern for the future of Local and Global Citizenship:

> I am hopeful that the formal education sector has moulded an initiative of potential to address Northern Ireland's considerable social and political divisions. On the other hand I am under no illusions as to the capability of the education sector to subvert its intentions in practice.

References

Bush, K., and Saltarelli, D. (2000) *The Two Faces of Education in Ethnic Conflict*, Florence: UNICEF.

CCEA (1999) *Developing the Northern Ireland Curriculum to Meet the Needs of Young People Society and the Economy in the 21st Century*, Belfast: Council for the Curriculum, Examinations and Assessment.

CCEA (2000) *Northern Ireland Curriculum Review: Phase 1 Consultation*, Belfast: Council for the Curriculum, Examinations and Assessment.

CCEA (2002) *A New Approach to Curriculum and Assessment 11–16*, Belfast: Council for the Curriculum, Examinations and Assessment.

CCEA (2003a) *Advice to the Minister for Education on Statutory Requirements at Key Stage 3*, Belfast: Council for the Curriculum, Examinations and Assessment.

CCEA (2003b) *Advice to the Minister for Education on Statutory Requirements at Key Stage 4*, Belfast: Council for the Curriculum, Examinations and Assessment.

CCEA (2003c) *Pathways – Proposals for Curriculum and Assessment at Key Stage 3*, Belfast: Council for the Curriculum, Examinations and Assessment.

CCEA (2007) *The Statutory Curriculum at Key Stage 3: Rationale and Detail*, Belfast: Council for the Curriculum, Examinations and Assessment.

ETI/DE (2006) *Report on the Introduction of Local and Global Citizenship at Key Stage 3 in a Sample of Post-Primary Schools (Inspected: January/February 2005)*, Crown Copyright 2006, Bangor: Education and Training Inspectorate, Department of Education.

Fearon, K., et al. (1997) *Politics: The Next Generation*, Belfast: Democratic Dialogue.

Gallagher, T. (2004) *Education in Divided Societies*, Basingstoke: Palgrave Macmillan.

Gallagher, T. (2008) 'Good Practice in Citizenship Education', in Jeffers, G., and O'Connor, U. (eds), *Education for Citizenship and Diversity in Irish Contexts*, Dublin: Institute of Public Administration.

HMSO (2007) *Education (Curriculum Minimum Content) Order (Northern Ireland) Statutory Rule 2007 No. 46*, Belfast: Her Majesty's Stationery Office.

Jeffers, G., and O'Connor, U. (eds) (2008) *Education for Citizenship and Diversity in Irish Contexts*, Dublin: Institute of Public Administration.

Leitch, R., and Kilpatrick, R. (1999) *Inside the Gates: Schools and the Troubles: A Research Report into How Schools Support Children in Relation to the Political Conflict in Northern Ireland*, Belfast: Save the Children.

McCully, A. (2008) Reflections on the Local and Global Citizenship Programme in Northern Ireland, in Jeffers, G., and O'Connor, U. (eds), *Education for Citizenship and Diversity in Irish Contexts*, Dublin: Institute of Public Administration.

McEvoy, L., McEvoy, K., and McConnachie, K. (2006) 'Reconciliation as a Dirty Word: Conflict, Community Relations and Education in Northern Ireland', *Journal of International Affairs*, 60(1), 81–106.

McEvoy, L. (2007) 'Beneath the Rhetoric: Policy Approximation and Citizenship Education in Northern Ireland', *Citizenship and Social Justice*, 2(2), 135–58.

Montgomery, A., and Birthistle, U. (2002) *Primary Values*, Belfast: CCEA.

Northern Ireland Office (1998) *The Agreement*, Belfast and Dublin: Governments of The UK and Ireland.

Northern Ireland Social and Political Archive (1998–2007) *Northern Ireland Life and Times Survey* <http://www.ark.ac.uk/nilt> (accessed 10 January 2009).

Smith, A. (2003) Citizenship Education in Northern Ireland: Beyond National Identity? *Cambridge Journal of Education*, 33(1), 15–31.

Smyth, M., et al. (2000) *The Youthquest 2000 Survey*, INCORE, University of Ulster.

UNESCO Centre, University of Ulster (2008) *Evaluation of the Pilot Introduction of Education for Local and Global Citizenship into the Revised Northern Ireland Curriculum*, Coleraine: University of Ulster.

Watling, R. (2001) *Social Civic and Political Education Project: External Evaluation*, University of Leicester: Centre for Citizenship Studies in Education.

NORMAN RICHARDSON

13   Evaluating the Northern Ireland Experience

> Whether people like it or not, there is a growing sense of acceptance that 'learning to live together' is part of the fundamental work to be done by everyone regardless of where they position themselves along the political, religious, educational continuum.
>
> — (Participant in a focus group, 2003)

Over the several decades during which educational interventions focusing on diversity and mutual understanding have been taking place in Northern Ireland, the most regular questions from all quarters – teachers; parents; educationists; the general public – have been: 'Does it work? What, if anything, has it achieved?' If the key values underpinning such work are that respect for diversity and for the dignity and integrity of others are desirable qualities in the process of developing a shared future (what some might term 'social and community cohesion'), it is inevitable that the process will come under scrutiny by those who wish to know if it has been effective. Some brief indication has already been given of research carried out on these activities in Northern Ireland (in Chapter 4), and also of some of the criticisms applied over the years to this dimension of education (in Chapter 5). The purpose of this chapter is to reflect on the processes that have been in development since the 1970s and to consider their impact in order to see what has been learned over this period and how it can inform continuing work in a somewhat changed local and global context. In the light of these assessments of the effectiveness of such work, the chapter will also focus on some of the criteria that schools and others may apply in order to evaluate the impact and progress of their own work in this sphere, whether in Northern Ireland or elsewhere.

Assessing the Educational Initiatives

Various evaluations of projects focusing on diversity, mutual understanding and community relations education in general have appeared over the years, presenting assessments of the strengths and weaknesses of such work. Among the most important of these texts are:

Education for Mutual Understanding: Perceptions and Policy – Smith and Robinson
    (University of Ulster, 1992)
Education for Mutual Understanding: The Initial Statutory Years – Smith and Robinson (University of Ulster, 1996)
Values in Education in Northern Ireland – Montgomery and Smith (CCEA and
    University of Ulster, 1997)
Inside the Gates: Schools and the Troubles – Leitch and Kilpatrick (Save the Children, 1999)
The Real Curriculum at the end of Key Stage 2: N.I. Curriculum Cohort Study – Harland et al. (NFER, 1999)
Report on the Educational Themes (Primary Inspections 1998–99) – Education and
    Training Inspectorate (1999)
Towards a Culture of Tolerance: Education for Diversity (Department of Education
    for Northern Ireland, 1999)
*Report of a Survey of Provision for Education for Mutual Understanding (EMU) in
    Post-Primary Schools (Inspected: 1999/2000)* – Education and Training Inspectorate (2000)
Is the Curriculum Working? The Key Stage 3 Phase of the N.I. Curriculum Cohort Study,
    Harland et al. (NFER, 2002)
A Review of the Schools Community Relations Programme 2002, O'Connor, Hartop
    and McCully (Department of Education, 2002)
*Teachers' and Pupils' Educational Experiences and School-Based Responses to the Conflict
    in Northern Ireland*, Leitch and Kilpatrick (Journal of Social Issues, 2004)
*Evaluation of the Pilot Introduction of Education for Local and Global Citizenship
    into the revised Northern Ireland Curriculum* – University of Ulster UNESCO
    Centre (2009).

Indications of the main findings of this research are given in Chapter 4 and elsewhere in this book. Each evaluation has offered an appraisal of the effectiveness of such work in some or many of its aspects, and has made suggestions for improved practice. Several have highlighted limited training opportunities and teacher reluctance to engage with controversial issues as being among the greatest obstacles to progress, but some of these reports have also noted significant impact on the professional outlook of some teachers as one of the major positive outcomes. There has also been an encouragement in some of them towards a much broader diversity context for such work rather than the perceived narrow focus on relationships between Catholics and Protestants in Northern Ireland. Many observers called for increased support at all levels for programmes of this kind, but some proposed more radical changes, and the impact of such recommendations ultimately led to the move away from the educational themes approach of the 1990s towards more specifically focused and timetabled curriculum areas of learning.

This chapter will summarise the key issues that have emerged from this range of reviews in terms of perceived strengths and weaknesses and as a guide to the self-evaluation process that teachers and schools will need to undertake in relation their own work in this field.

Weaknesses

Confusion with Contact

It is clear that one of the principal difficulties in establishing effective practice in diversity and mutual understanding programmes in schools has been the too-close association with inter-school cross-community contact schemes. This was a particular problem in relation to Education for Mutual Understanding in the 1990s and even since then, and the point has been well noted in previous chapters of this book. The intended breadth and scope of EMU became substantially confused with one particular implementation strategy and it seems quite clear that when many teachers and members of the general public referred to EMU they were thinking almost exclusively of activities pursued by two schools working together. This was certainly the unquestioned assumption behind a provocative newspaper headline in 1995: 'EMU Scheme Has Failed!' (Belfast Telegraph, 03/04/95). It cited examples of inter-school cross-community contact which had been at best token and at worst blatantly abusive of the system which was set up to fund such activities. In this perception the purposes of EMU became reduced to 'EMU trips', and many EMU Co-ordinators in schools were perceived as little more than the arrangers and fund-holders for such activities. What should have been a challenging dimension of a much broader process all too often became an end in itself. If a teacher's aim was to avoid getting into anything too controversial, then an outing with another school could be seen as a relatively 'safe' pursuit, and thus many children had little or no opportunity to engage in real encounter because they were simply follow-ing the same activity in parallel groups, with their separateness relatively intact. With this kind of bad press contact programmes often appeared to be slight, shallow or ineffective, and were sometimes judged a waste of time and money. The fact that there was also some very good practice in cross-community contact, as a dimension of broader work, did not make press headlines!

Limitations of the Contact Hypothesis

While acknowledging that these processes were always intended to involve more than cross-community contact, it is nevertheless important to reflect on a strategy which proposes that increased contact between separated groups will improve community relations. Awareness of the limitations of the contact hypothesis as a basis for community relations work has been widely reported, particularly by Cairns (1985) and Trew (1989; see also Niens and Cairns, 2005). It has been generally concluded that evidence on the impact of contact schemes is very limited, especially where the recog-nised key conditions for such work are ignored. Guidelines gathered from the literature and provided to schools by the Department of Education and the Education and Library Boards over the years always indicated that certain conditions must be employed if contact programmes were to have any chance of making an impact, such as the need for groups to be equal status, for activities to be collaborative and purposefully leading towards shared goals, for continuity and regularity in the process, for curriculum relevance and for the support of school senior management, etc.. There can be little doubt that a more rigorous application of these principles would have led to higher quality contact as a dimension of such work. Additionally, research in the United States (McCarthy, 1991) has been critical of any kinds of multicultural initiatives if they fail to deal with issues of structural inequality and differential power relations in society.

It was to emphasise the fuller purposes of contact that the Cross-Community Contact Scheme, originally introduced in 1987, was re-named *The Schools' Community Relations Programme* by the joint Education and Library Boards in 1997. Undoubtedly some contact work has impacted positively the attitudes and practice within some schools or groups of schools, and some teachers have acknowledged the importance of involvement in such work as a positive influence on their own personal and professional development. Similarly some research has indicated a range of benefits on the part of the awareness of pupils and even parents (Smith and Dunn, 1990). Nevertheless it is hard to escape the conclusion that some of the apparent ineffectiveness of this dimension of education was as a result of superficial or casual use of the contact strategy.

Lack of Leadership

Another widely identified difficulty was the lack of informed and committed leadership in many schools, without which the work of enthusiastic individual teachers could easily be marginalised or even undermined. Some head teachers may have paid lip-service to the ideals associated with such work but have failed to commit time, staffing and money to its effective implementation. In its review of post-primary schools the Inspectorate noted that:

> In a majority of the schools, management arrangements for policy making and planning were judged to be poor or very poor. Without the overt, as well as the implicit support of the principal and the governors, the EMU theme tended to have a low profile among the staff, and co-ordinators expressed their frustration at the lack of support and status given to their work (ETI/DE, 2000; 6.1)

Even up to the present time little priority has been given within the system for ensuring that training courses for head teachers and senior management have included this dimension of education.

Teachers' Uncertainty and Lack of Training

Many teachers seemed unsure about how to carry out work in education for diversity and mutual understanding, especially once they had begun to understand that it was more than just cross-community contact. The emphasis on cross-curricular themes did not always help, and while some teachers felt this to be highly contrived, others were very wary of tackling contentious issues, such as in History or Religious Education. While these limitations seem to have been evident in both primary and secondary schools it is probably true that the difficulties were felt more acutely at the secondary level where subject departments and timetables are more rigid. The primary class teacher has more opportunities to contribute to pupils' holistic development, as has been very evident in some schools, whereas the secondary teacher may be much more restricted unless he or she is consciously working within a well defined school policy.

These apparent deficiencies in the awareness and skills of teachers and management suggest that the key factor towards change will be in the provision of more and better training. Many reports have highlighted this problem (for instance, Smith and Robinson, 1996; DENI, 1999; Potter, 2002), but the reality is that until recently there have been very limited opportunities made or taken within the system for training in the various aspects of diversity and mutual understanding. In initial teacher education (ITE) the emphasis in the past was all too often focused on contact between students from different backgrounds, rather than on courses which dealt with personal and professional development, and many members of the teaching staff in ITE had likewise received no relevant training. Very good work was done in designing and leading in-service courses by a handful of staff in the Curriculum, Advisory and Support Services of the Education and Library Boards, but provision was limited and patchy and in some areas there were far fewer such courses than in others. Some relevant award-bearing academic courses, at diploma or Master's level, were offered for serving teachers at various times since the early 1990s, but these remained limited in number and in take-up. The proliferation of other priorities for schools made it difficult even for those teachers who wanted to extend their awareness and skills in this field to take up places on the courses that were available.

Limitations of the 'Cross-curricular Theme' Model

In their influential report, Smith and Robinson (1996) indicated in particular that much of the work in EMU revealed a lack of progression and coherence, suggesting that this militated against a more holistic approach to the work in many schools. They identified that a major difficulty for many teachers was the nature of the 'cross-curricular (educational) theme', which seemed to lack focus or substance and therefore often became 'elusive' or obscure, especially for pupils. Undoubtedly any aspect of the curriculum which is supposed to be everybody's responsibility, as with the educational themes, runs the danger of becoming *everybody else's* responsibility.

Good Practice Overshadowed

Although there have been many instances of good practice in EMU and related work which could be offered to offset the negative experience, it is not difficult to see how poor practice can easily overshadow and discredit the good and thereby dominate both public and professional perceptions.

Strengths

If it is important to learn the lessons from the weaknesses of this model as outlined above, it will be no less important to do so from its strengths, in order to continue to develop and extend these important concepts within a revised curriculum context and to ensure that they are implemented more effectively.

An International Model

Despite a wide range of terms, emphases and contexts, the ingredients of education for diversity and mutual understanding in Northern Ireland seem fundamentally similar to equivalent programmes in other parts of the world. Not only are the emphases very much the same, but the difficulties of implementing such work also bear striking resemblance. Northern Ireland has undoubtedly had much to learn from the experience of others over recent decades, but it has sometimes been evident that in both vision and the scope of our work we have also been able to encourage and assist others in making sense of their own struggles. Recognition of the importance of dealing with issues of diversity and conflict through education is widespread and has become even more significant in the post-9/11 world. Various approaches to this are evident in literature from organisations such as the United Nations and the Council of Europe[1] and these local and global links have been noted by the present writer elsewhere (Richardson, 1997; 2002; 2008).

---

1   See the Council of Europe Publications website section on intercultural and human rights education: http://book.coe.int/EN/.

A Balanced Model

Despite the criticism that the initial versions of community relations education or EMU did not deal adequately with the sharper issues of differences
– sectarianism, violence, justice, human rights and democracy – a glance
at some of the curriculum development projects and materials which were
produced over the years reveals that a sharper edge was always present.[2]
As with similar work in other places, the various programmes in Northern
Ireland indicated some consensus around a balanced approach with a basis
in self-esteem and positive personal relationships, expanding into issues of
wider relationships, the management of conflict, prejudice and discrimination, cultural and religious diversity, and broader global issues. The sharper
edge was undoubtedly significantly blunted by a lack of teacher awareness
of this broad approach, while others perhaps applied it selectively and in
some cases over-cautiously, or simply lacked the necessary skills and confidence. The emergence of Local and Global Citizenship and PDMU in
the Revised Northern Ireland Curriculum certainly represents this broadly
based and balanced approach although it seems clear that without significant investment in ongoing support and training there is a danger that the
same limitations may continue to be experienced.

A Challenging Model

Despite the difficulties arising from many teachers' sense of inadequacy in
dealing with contentious local issues there is evidence that work in this area
has promoted more rigorous critical thinking and a readiness on the part of
teachers and learners to challenge their own assumptions and attitudes. In
the Inter-School Links project of the late 1980s Smith and Dunn reported

---

2	For example, the *Schools Cultural Studies Project* in the late 1970s and early 1980s
	(SCSP, 1978); the *Irish Christianity* materials produced by John Greer and colleagues
	(Greer and McElhinney, 1985); the publications of the *Churches' Peace Education
	Programme* from the late 1970s onwards (for example, Rogers, 1991); the *Opposite
	Religions?* series, by Brian Lambkin (1992), etc. Many of these are indicated in
	Chapters 3 and 4.

that a jointly planned and carefully monitored cross-community history project with post-primary pupils 'generated a certain amount of uncertainty in pupils' minds which may have been crucial in encouraging them to develop an "understanding" of the complexity of inter-group relations in Northern Ireland... [which] seems to be a step in the learning process, on the road toward critical thinking' (Smith and Dunn, 1990, p. 36).

Other research (Leitch and Kilpatrick, 1999; Harland et al., 1999) has suggested that where pupils feel respected, secure and listened to by their teachers there can be a similar willingness on the part of pupils to examine assumptions and look afresh at controversial issues. At the same time it has to be acknowledged that such accounts are relatively rare, suggesting that there is still only a relatively small number of schools where such an approach has been in place.

A Transformative Model

Measurement of attitudinal change is extremely difficult, although it is understandable that this should be a focus in relation to work that focuses on developing respect and mutual understanding in a conflict or post-conflict situation. It is, however, no less important to consider how such work has affected teachers and schools. The evidence, both written and anecdotal, suggests that those who have become significantly engaged in these processes have found it to be challenging and transformative. According to some researchers, it has extended the vision and widened the world of many teachers, and promoted reflective and innovative practice (Smith and Robinson, 1996; CCEA, 1999). This is very important, for without schools and teachers that have come to value an ethos of diversity and mutual respect there is little likelihood that pupils will learn to take a similar view. The school must be able to model the qualities which it seeks to set at the heart of its community, and there is evidence that this work has been one of those processes which has enabled schools to get a clearer sense of fundamental values (Montgomery and Smith, 1997) and to renew their vision. This was well illustrated by the remarks of a post-primary school principal who had spent some time as a field officer developing EMU:

I found it an absolutely marvellous help and found as well the sort of open mind it gives you to be receptive to all sorts of signals and concerns and issues... it has given me a much more 'wide-angled lens' view of everything that goes on in the school... From a management point of view I certainly found it exceptionally valuable. (from a focus group discussion, 2003)

Education with a Human Face

Whatever the disadvantages of the 'cross-curricular theme' permeation approach, one of its less observed but significant features was to liberate education from the rather utilitarian and mechanistic aura which came with the introduction of a prescribed National Curriculum in England, Wales and Northern Ireland. At its best the 'educational themes' model promoted a whole-school approach including, but also going well beyond, the formal curriculum programmes, and this emphasis will be no less important within the Revised Curriculum framework. Respect for diversity and the development of mutual understanding should be understood fundamentally as being about the climate of a school – a humanising influence, highlighting the importance of relationships at all levels within the school and opening doors to wider relationships beyond. In an education system still too easily dominated by examination results and league tables, there is a need for leavening influences which focus on visions, values and attitudes; on qualities which cannot be revealed by crude statistical comparisons.

Personal Story

A significant point from the perspective of the present author, not often noted in the research and formal evaluations, is the number of people who have indicated that their strong commitment to education for diversity and mutual understanding is based on their own 'personal story'. For some it was the experience of a 'mixed' background – coming from a cross-community family or growing up in a mixed community – which had contributed to an openness of outlook; for others it was a profound experience – a close personal encounter with someone from 'the other community', or a travel opportunity, or even a negative experience of sectarianism; for some it had been an opportunity to live or study away from Northern Ireland; for yet others it was a personal challenge which had grown out of a professional development course. This strengthens the case for believing that an experiential approach must be at the heart of work of this kind, at school level and in teacher education.

Limited but Real Progress

Notwithstanding the limitations and difficulties there is clear evidence that quantitatively and, more importantly, qualitatively, there has been progress over the years of the development of various processes around education for intercultural understanding in Northern Ireland. This is perhaps particularly evident to those who have worked in the field over a long period of time. Since the relative barrenness of the 1970s there have certainly been sea-changes of attitudes at many levels in the system and now it is normative to find official statements about the purposes of education and the role of teachers and schools highlighting the importance of 'developing opportunities for shared and inter-cultural education at all levels' and preparing pupils 'for life in a diverse and inter-cultural society and world' (OFMDFM, 2005, 2.4). Given the political climate of Northern Ireland over so much of that time we should not be too surprised that the progress has not been quicker, and we would be unwise to look for sudden and rapid progress in the future even if the political situation continues to improve. It is too easy just to bemoan the failures or to be frustrated by the schools that still do not seem to have engaged with these issues at any significant level. The progress that has been made has provided a basis for learning from previous mistakes and misjudgements in order to build new strategies. Local and Global Citizenship, PDMU and government policy statements about the role of education in building a shared future did not just appear out of thin air. Fears have been expressed from time to time that such work might be abandoned because of critical reviews or changed priorities, but despite uncertainties in relation to support and funding the principles and ideals associated with education for diversity and mutual understanding do seem to be more effectively embedded in the system at the time of writing than they did a decade and more ago.

Indicators of Effective Practice

No single set of monitoring standards has been agreed or applied in respect of the various aspects of education for diversity and mutual understanding, although a report on the contact-based Schools' Community Relations Programme argued that monitoring should be more rigorously employed on the basis of 'exemplar indicators which define aims and outline relevant measures of progression' (O'Connor et al., 2002). In the absence of such agreed standards it has been left to various individuals and institutions to define their own indicators. The Education and Training Inspectorate (ETI) of the Department of Education issued guidelines on two occasions during the 1990s on their approach to *Evaluating Schools* (DENI, 1992; 1998) in which the area of positive school ethos was highlighted:

> The ethos, or distinctive character and atmosphere of a school, reflects the extent to which the school... promotes the all round development of its pupils within a caring community. (DENI, 1998, p. 4)

In this document the indicators of effective ethos included good relationships between teachers and pupils; the promotion of confidence and self-esteem; mutual valuing and respect and appreciation of the views of others. Much more specifically, however, the ETI later indicated that in an inspection of post-primary schools (2000) they would be considering the degree to which Education for Mutual Understanding was evident in four main areas:

- the culture of the school – ethos;
- methods, processes and outcomes – quality teaching and learning;

- the curriculum – including the timetabled curriculum and other experiences which enhance the curriculum, such as meeting with young people from different backgrounds;
- management; roles and responsibilities – referred to as 'scaffolding'.

In a survey of the introduction of Local and Global Citizenship in a small sample of post-primary schools by the ETI (2006) it was these same four areas that were used as the basis for 'questions and prompts', including a specific reference to inter-school community relations contact, suggesting a deliberate sense of continuity with the previous EMU model.

Based on the various reviews and assessments indicated above, an expanded set of guidelines is offered here in order to provide schools and other educational institutions with a self-evaluation tool.[3] It is suggested that effective work to develop an inclusive, intercultural ethos and practice should involve consideration of the following issues:

Relationships

Is there evidence of a whole-school ethos of mutual respect based on self-esteem and positive, inclusive relationships throughout the school community (teachers, parents, pupils, ancillary staff, etc.)? Are differences openly valued and respected?

Management

Do the principal and senior management team give positive leadership in this area of the school's life and learning? Do they encourage staff openness to discussion on issues around diversity and related concerns? Is there easy and regular contact/communication with senior management on

---

3   This is adapted from a document circulated to a number of schools by the present author during the period 1999–2001 (Richardson, 1999).

these issues? Is there an established and regular process to enable shared monitoring/reviewing/evaluating of progress? Is there a sense of shared responsibility for these issues among the teaching staff as a whole?

Behaviour

Is there a positive behaviour policy that encourages good relationships between pupils and between all members of the school community? Does this include strategies for handling conflict creatively and for counteracting prejudice, including racism and sectarianism?

Approaches to Teaching and Learning

Is there an emphasis on the importance of good skills in listening and communication, including the encouragement and improvement of skills in participative group work, discussion and the sharing of ideas? Do teachers recognise the central importance of encouraging self-esteem and positive attitudes in their teaching and in their pastoral relationships with pupils? Is there a commitment to reflective practice on the part of the teaching staff?

Curriculum/Programmes of Study

Do teachers demonstrate a broad awareness of the relevance of diversity, mutual understanding and related themes throughout the curriculum, rather than just 'pigeon-holing' these issues in certain key subjects? Do teachers have confidence in their capacity to deal with controversial issues in class? Do they have an awareness of appropriate resources? Is there a sense of *coherence* and *progression* across the school in relation to issues of diversity and mutual understanding?

Staff Development

Is there a well informed co-ordinator with responsibility for giving leader-ship in these areas, supported by senior management? Are there opportuni-ties for personal and professional development for all teachers, including the possibility of attending relevant courses? Are ancillary staff ever included in these processes, particularly in relation to the development of positive behaviour and conflict management?

Relationships with the Community

Does the school work to establish good communication with the local community and across communities, including with any ethnic or cul-tural minorities that may be present in the local area? Is there an ongoing programme of cross-community contact involving pupils and teachers in meaningful joint work and social relationships? Are the inter-school cross-community pupil relationships sustained outside the school? Are teachers attempting to extend and deepen their relationships, professionally and personally, with colleagues from linked schools?

Reviewing the Revised Model

Many of those who contributed to the more recent development of Per-sonal Development and Mutual Understanding (PDMU) and Local and Global Citizenship (LGC) were well aware of the strengths and weak-nesses of previous approaches and had themselves been involved in the development and monitoring of earlier work of this kind. They were also significantly aware of the points at which it was important to try to ensure some continuity with the previous models.

At the time of writing the Revised Northern Ireland Curriculum is still in its infancy and so the possibility of evaluation lies somewhere in the future. The exception to this, however, is in the development of the Northern Ireland model of Citizenship Education which was under way in the form of a pilot programme between 2002 and 2007, before the Revised Curriculum was finally set in place. An evaluation by the University of Ulster UNESCO Centre (commissioned by CCEA, the Northern Ireland Curriculum body) took place over much of the pilot programme period, involving a large number of pupils, teachers and schools. Its key findings indicate a positive approach by many teachers and pupils and a readiness to engage with the issues and active learning methodologies associated with LGC, including an apparent new openness to local community relations issues and a keen interest in focusing on 'newer' issues such as racism and other themes within the global reach of the subject. Concerns about confidence in teaching controversial issues were expressed by teachers, however, and both teachers and pupils continued to seem more comfortable with tackling global issues rather than local ones. Teacher education, at all stages, was also a key issue, particularly in relation to ensuring continuity from initial training through continuing professional development. The report also encourages schools to view Citizenship not just as a subject but as a whole-school concern relevant to ethos and to the needs of pupils, teachers and the wider community. Although Citizenship Education is clearly understood as being about more than just community relations, the report nevertheless recognises the importance of 'the potential contribution of this intervention to the major challenge of achieving sustained peace and stability in Northern Ireland' (UNESCO Centre, 2009, pp. 116–17), and elsewhere it concludes that:

> The indications are that, over time, if implemented with commitment in schools and supported and sustained by statutory and other support agencies, this intervention could make a tangible contribution to creating greater tolerance, equality and stability in Northern Ireland's society. As an intervention which aligns political, social and educational agendas it deserves to be robustly supported and sustained. (op.cit., p. 20)

Moving Forward

Taking account of the various evaluations above some issues are clearly
recurrent and persistent. Training for the Revised Curriculum already
suggests that the opportunities and problems will be very similar to those
experienced in the development of EMU. Although the concept of the
educational theme has now been abandoned one of its undoubted strengths
was in encouraging whole-school ownership of some issues. If there is a
case for well-trained specialist teachers of PDMU and LGC, there is still
surely a case for whole-school support in relation to issues of diversity,
democratic values, community relationships, sectarian or racist behaviour
and related matters. This point has been made in the UNESCO Centre
evaluation of the Citizenship Pilot Programme, cited above, emphasising
that citizenship education has implications for: 'school culture, relationships and democracy, as well as whole-school teaching, learning and assessment' (UNESCO Centre, 2009, p. 16). It would indeed be a backward
step if many teachers were to feel relieved of these holistic responsibilities
because all such responsibility had now been passed on to a designated
specialist or co-ordinator.

Training in subject knowledge, appropriate pedagogy and especially
in dealing with controversial issues all remain high priorities. Teachers
need to feel that they are building on the experience built up in the past
and that there is a good level of continuity in the system. There is a need
to *affirm* the existing hard work of teachers and others in this area; the
values inherent in previous models and the developmental thinking which
has continued to take place over the past four decades must not be lost or
appear to be marginalised.

Whatever shape it may take in the future there can be little doubt that
we need some form of intercultural education in our education system, no
less than in other parts of the world. Experience in Northern Ireland since
the early 1970s indicates that good quality education must address the
realities of life in a diverse society, including its conflicts and divisions, and
help children and young people to deepen their awareness of those realities
while offering skills and strategies for coping with them. It is in this sense

that we may judge that education for diversity and mutual understanding has developed steadily over time, learning from previous work, and that it still has something significant and essential to offer within education and to the wider community in Northern Ireland and elsewhere.

References

Belfast Telegraph (1995) *EMU Scheme Has Failed, Says Council*, David Watson, 3 April 1995.

Cairns, E. (1987) *Caught in Crossfire: Children and the Northern Ireland Conflict*, Belfast and New York: Appletree Press and Syracuse University Press.

CCEA (1997) *Mutual Understanding and Cultural Heritage: Cross Curricular Guidance Materials*, Belfast: Council for the Curriculum, Examinations and Assessment.

CCEA (1999) *Developing the Northern Ireland Curriculum (Advice to the NI Minister of Education on curriculum review)*, Belfast: Council for the Curriculum, Examinations and Assessment.

DENI (1992) *Evaluating Schools 1992*, Bangor: DENI Inspectorate, Department of Education for Northern Ireland.

DENI (1998) *School Improvement – Evaluating Schools*, Bangor: Education and Training Inspectorate, Department of Education for Northern Ireland.

DENI (1999) *Towards a Culture of Tolerance: Education for Diversity (Report of a Working Group on the Strategic Promotion of Education for Mutual Understanding)*, Bangor: Department of Education for Northern Ireland.

ETI/DE (1999) *Report on the Educational Themes: Primary Inspections 1998–99*, Crown Copyright 1999, Bangor: Education and Training Inspectorate, Department of Education.

ETI/DE (2000) *Report of a Survey of Provision for Education for Mutual Understanding (EMU) in Post-Primary Schools (Inspected: 1999/2000)*, Crown Copyright 2000, Bangor: Education and Training Inspectorate, Department of Education.

ETI/DE (2006) *Report on the Introduction of Local and Global Citizenship at Key Stage 3 in a Sample of Post-Primary Schools (Inspected: January/February 2005)*, Crown Copyright 2006, Bangor: Education and Training Inspectorate, Department of Education.

Greer, J. and McElhinney, E. (1985) *Irish Christianity: Five Units for Secondary Pupils / Irish Christianity: A Guide for Teachers*, Dublin: Gill and Macmillan.

HMSO (1989) *The Education Reform (Northern Ireland) Order 1989* (Article 8), Belfast: Her Majesty's Stationery Office.

Lambkin, B. (1992) *Opposite Religions? Protestants and Roman Catholics in Ireland since the Reformation* (3 Pupils' books and accompanying teachers' guides), Belfast: Northern Ireland Centre for Learning Resources.

Leitch, R., and Kilpatrick, R. (1999) *Inside the Gates: Schools and the Troubles*, Belfast: Save the Children Fund.

Leitch, R., and Kilpatrick, R. (2004) 'Teachers' and Pupils' Educational Experiences and School-Based Responses to the Conflict in Northern Ireland', in *Journal of Social Issues* 60(3), 563–86.

McCarthy, C. (1991) 'Multicultural Approaches to Racial Inequality in the United States', *Oxford Review of Education*, 17(3).

Montgomery, A. and Smith, A. (1997) *Values Education in Northern Ireland*, Coleraine: School of Education, University of Ulster; Belfast: Council for Curriculum, Examinations and Assessment.

NFER (1999) *The Real Curriculum at the end of Key Stage 2 – N.I. Curriculum Cohort Study*, Slough: National Foundation for Educational Research (on behalf of the NI Council for Curriculum, Examinations and Assessment).

NFER (2002) *Is the Curriculum Working? The Key Stage 3 Phase of the N.I. Curriculum Cohort Study*, Slough, National Foundation for Educational Research (on behalf of the NI Council for Curriculum, Examinations and Assessment).

Niens, U. and Cairns, E. (2005) 'Conflict, Contact and Education in Northern Ireland', in *Theory into Practice*, 44(4), 337–44.

O'Connor, U., Hartop, B. and McCully, A. (2002) *A Review of the Schools Community Relations Programme 2002*, Bangor: Department of Education.

Potter, M. (2002) *The Corrymeela Teacher Education Project: Work with Beginning Teachers 2001–2002* [privately circulated report], Belfast: Corrymeela Community.

Richardson, N. (1992) *Roots, if not Wings! Where did EMU come from?* Coleraine: Centre for the Study of Conflict at the University of Ulster.

Richardson, N. (1997) *Education For Dealing With Conflict: Towards A Whole-School Approach – Lessons from the Northern Ireland Experience*, unpublished paper given at the 1997 conference of the European Network for Conflict Resolution in Education – ENCORE, in Miercurea-Ciuc, Romania.

Richardson, N. (1999) *Evaluating Mutual Understanding – Indicators of good practice in relation to EMU/CH* [privately circulated Inservice handout], Belfast: Stranmillis University College.

Richardson, N. (2002) *Schools as Bridges: Education for Living with Diversity*, unpublished paper given at the Ninth Annual Conference on Education, Spirituality and the Whole Child – Education for Peace, University of Surrey at Roehampton.

Richardson, N. (2008) 'Education for Religious Tolerance: the Impossible Dream?' in Patalon, M. (ed.), *Tolerance and Education – Studia Kulturowa 2/2008*: 39–53, Pedagogical Institute, University of Gdansk <http://studia.kulturowe.ug.gda.pl/sk-2.pdf> (accessed 25 June 2010).

Rogers, P. (ed.) (1991) *Power to Hurt: Exploring Violence*, Belfast and Dublin: Churches' Peace Education Programme.

SCSP (1978) 'Objectives of the SCSP', in *Network No.6*, March 1978, Coleraine: Schools Cultural Studies Project.

Smith, A., and Dunn, S. (1990) *Extending Inter-School Links*, Coleraine: University of Ulster Centre for the Study of Conflict.

Smith, A., and Robinson, A. (1992) *Education for Mutual Understanding: Perceptions and Policy*, Coleraine, University of Ulster Centre for the Study of Conflict.

Smith, A., and Robinson, A. (1996) *Education for Mutual Understanding: The Initial Statutory Years*, Coleraine, University of Ulster Centre for the Study of Conflict.

Trew, K. (1989) 'Evaluating the impact of contact schemes for Catholic and Protestant children from Northern Ireland' in Harbison, J. (ed.), *Growing Up in Northern Ireland*, Belfast: Stranmillis College Learning Resources.

UNESCO Centre (2009) *Evaluation of the Pilot Introduction of Education for Local and Global Citizenship Into the Revised Northern Ireland Curriculum*, Coleraine: University of Ulster School of Education.

TONY GALLAGHER

Final Thoughts

Almost from the moment the Northern Ireland conflict burst into violence over three decades ago, people looked to the schools system to somehow or other solve the problem. Over those years a variety of strategies was pursued, including initiatives in key curricular areas, the development of entirely new curricular programmes, contact programmes, integrated schools and the development of collaborative networks of schools. In this volume we are concerned primarily with curricular interventions within schools, particularly those with a specific focus on issues of division and understanding. In part, one reason for doing this is that the received wisdom about this work is that it failed to make any significant impact. For this reason a good place to begin this short reflection is to ask whether this was because the burden of expectation that was placed on the schools was too high, or the conditions within which the interventions were attempted were insufficiently supportive, or the judgement of received wisdom is, in fact, incorrect.

A useful starting point is provided by Richardson's analysis of the evidence of impact in which he highlights, on the negative side, evidence that teachers were reluctant to get directly involved in difficult issues, they were provided with insufficient training and they received insufficient support from school leaders. All of these represent significant constraints on the capacity of teachers and schools to engage with a controversial intervention, but all also represent constraints which are fundamentally interlinked. Such became clear in an intervention designed to promote a more positive approach to diversity in pre-school settings (Connolly et al., 2006). This early years education intervention focused on ethnicity, disability and sectarianism and provided pre-school teachers with training dealing with each theme. Unusually, however, the project also used randomised control trials to evaluate the effectiveness of the intervention. The first studies of impact indicated a positive impact on approaches to diversity based on race or disability, but limited effect on the issue of sectarianism. On further exploration it emerged that, despite the training, the pre-school teachers were reluctant to address an issue that was normally a taboo topic in Northern Ireland and so had held back. Fortuitously, since this weakness in the intervention has been identified through rigorous evaluation methods, this meant that the level of training on this specific issue could be significantly cranked up directly to address this sense of reluctance. The experience highlights also the importance of training and high quality evaluation of impact. As a related aside, it is quite striking, given the amount of resources that have been expended on this area, just how little solid evidence is available on which to assess impact and effectiveness. The importance of training emerges also in Arlow's account of the development of the citizenship education initiative.

The issue of leadership is important also, but not just in the way described by Richardson: support from school leaders is important (or perhaps the corollary is even more true, that is, that school leaders who are dismissive or oppose work of this kind are almost certainly going to ensure that little of it is carried out in their schools, whereas school leaders who are indifferent may be happy to let enthusiastic teachers get on with it), but support from the wider education system is also very important and, throughout most of the period, has been largely absent. This is not to say that work on the promotion of reconciliation is not identified as a priority for the education system in Northern Ireland: in various ways this has almost always been identified as a priority, but the reality is that it has been one amongst a number of priorities and it has never been a high enough priority that schools felt free to engage with reconciliation work at a cost to other priorities, particularly those related to standards and performance. Further, apart from occasional reviews by the Education and Training Inspectorate, there has been relatively little regular oversight of schools' work in this area.

Both factors, that is, limited evaluation and limited priority, come together in the strategy based on providing opportunities for contact between Protestants and Catholics. Richardson identifies as a weakness of work on mutual understanding that it became too closely linked to contact initiatives, and that these were based on a weak version of the contact hypothesis. There is little doubt that this is true. What is also true, however, is that despite the fact that for many years the Department of Education spent the largest proportion of the community relations budget, and the largest element of the Department's spending was on contact programmes, there was only ever limited evidence-based evaluation of the effectiveness of contact. Indeed, for many years it seemed that the only indicator that mattered was the proportion of schools that were involved in contact initiatives, or, in other words, an activity indicator rather than an impact indicator. It is hardly surprising then that most work on contact programmes showed little evidence of development, or engagement with controversial issues, or that the general level of understanding of or discussion on the contact hypothesis remained extraordinarily shallow. Fortunately this has changed in recent years (Hewstone et al., 2008), but we are left wondering how different things might have been had this work been given a serious level of priority, had there been more use of rigorous evaluation of effectiveness, and, in consequence there had been more critical engagement with the theory and practice of contact.

Thus far we have tended to focus on the negative, but there is also a positive side which is ably represented in these chapters, but which has perhaps never before been given sufficient attention. In part this is because of a long standing tradition in Ireland of 'begrudgery', which is probably best thought of as a reverse 'Panglossian' orientation to the world in which all things that happen are likely to be for the worst, there is little worth celebrating, and anything good that does occur will probably not last. The main body of the chapters in this volume bring together the accumulated wisdom and experience of people who have been working on the difficulty of addressing issues related to diversity in a society which, for much of the period in which they were working, was literally tearing itself apart. The lessons that emerge from these chapters represent an extraordinary record of achievement on the pedagogy of inclusion and engagement with diversity. A key contribution of this volume may be in bringing this body of work together.

The practice that is covered throughout the chapters of this volume relates to inclusive strategies for the development of school policy, conflict resolution and peer mediation techniques, the use of circle time as a means of promoting inclusive dialogue and strategies for addressing controversial issues. Throughout all the accounts we see again and again the importance of a whole-school focus in this work: attempts to teach a positive approach to diversity and reconciliation cannot be compartmentalised into a discrete slot as if it is purely a technical exercise, but rather it has to be embedded with an ethos of practice that infuses the entire institution. This is hardly surprising, since the notion of reconciliation is predicated on a particular form of relationships, but the rhetoric around this practice will be meaningless if it is not matched by consistent patterns of relationships with the school. Such relationships are necessary if we are to create the type of safe space that will encourage engagement with difference.

Virtually all the examples we have seen have a strong focus on pedagogy, more particularly an inclusive pedagogy that seeks to find ways to involve and value all members of a class. Indeed, it may be that the development of such innovative pedagogy is the real success of work in this area, albeit that, as Richardson notes, it is often overshadowed by the weight of examples of poor practice. There may also be important lessons for our understanding of Northern Ireland itself. The problems many of the people represented in this volume set out to address are difficult, but they are worth engaging with. It is not always possible to see simple causal connections between actions and outcomes, and the rewards for being involved in this work are often intrinsic, rather than obvious. Furthermore, they are addressing dynamic problems which change and evolve over time: our understanding of the issues changes over time, the nature of the problem changes over time, and, potentially, the effectivity of specific solutions may vary over time.

What also may vary over time is the way we judge teachers and schools in their contributions: whereas society will turn to teachers and schools in moments of crisis and demand action, it is much less common that praise will be heaped on their heads if they succeed: there are always fewer acknowledging responsibility than those seeking credit. Indeed, there is an all too regular pattern that governments cannot be persuaded that a situation is serious until there is a crisis, and cannot be persuaded that the problem still remains once the immediate crisis is over. A simple illustration demonstrates the dilemma: over the summer months of 2009, during which the two main parties in the Northern Ireland Executive yet again failed to find any basis for a new agreed community relations policy, a quick survey of local newspapers I carried out using the internet identified over fifty articles dealing with sectarian attacks on Churches, Orange Halls, GAA Clubs, schools or homes. What was more striking, however, was the limited evident response of anger to such promiscuous sectarianism. The major problem of political violence has largely ended, but the issue of sectarianism clearly remains to be addressed. And nor is it sufficient to write off a generation of engagement in schools on these issues simply because there were many examples of weak or poor practice: as we see repeatedly throughout this volume, the clearly evident problems in practice were not due to a paucity of good information, advice or expertise, and nor was it due to the lack of an inclusive pedagogy. The tools existed, or were being developed, but perhaps only the will to prioritise the work and promote the use of the tools effectively was lacking.

The collapse of the former Soviet Union and its satellites in East and Central Europe at the beginning of the closing decade of the twentieth century opened up a pandora's box of ethnic tensions and conflicts, some of which have continued to rage ever since. Within a decade the 9/11 attacks on the Twin Towers in New York and the subsequent invasions of Afghanistan and Iraq heightened tensions between the West and the Muslim world, a tension that was doubly significant since Muslims form a significant religious minority within Europe. In response to both developments the Council of Europe established a project to explore interculturalism, resulting in the publication of a White Paper on intercultural dialogue in 2007. Among their main recommendations were the promotion of models of participation and democratic citizenship, the prioritisation of the acquisition of intercultural competences and the need to create open spaces for genuine dialogue. But their prescription also importantly recommended a move away from the fetishisation of difference that has occurred in some forms of multiculturalism which appear to have done little more than 'slice-and-dice' society into independent silos in which there is an ever decreasing space for the development of a language of a common good. Schools can play a key role in developing these intercultural skills and dispositions, and in creating the civil spaces within which such dispositions can be lived in practice. The evidence contained in these chapters represents the work and accumulated wisdom of extraordinary people who have made extraordinary achievements over many years. Their example shows just how much has been achieved through work in education and the legacy that is available to be taken forward. But a lesson also is that the priority remains and the work is not yet done.

Refences

Connolly, P., Fitzpatrick, S., Gallagher, T., and Harris, P. (2006) 'Addressing diversity and inclusion in the early years in conflict-affected societies: A case study of the Media Initiative for Children – Northern Ireland', in *International Journal of Early Years Education*, 14(3), 263–78.

Hewstone, M. et al. (2008) *Can contact make a difference? – Evidence from mixed and segregated areas of Belfast*, Belfast: OFMDFM.

Notes on Contributors

The Editors

TONY GALLAGHER (co-editor) is a Professor of Education and Pro-Vice-Chancellor at Queen's University Belfast; between 2005 and 2010 he was Head of the School of Education. His main research interest lies in the role of education in divided societies and while the main focus of his work has been Northern Ireland, he has also worked in Israel/Palestine and Southeast Europe. He is currently leading a number of research and development projects on collaborative networks among schools.

NORMAN RICHARDSON (co-editor) was formerly a teacher in primary and post-primary schools and now lectures in teacher education programmes at Stranmillis University College, Belfast. His main areas of teaching and research are in religious and cultural diversity, inclusive Religious Education and intercultural education. He has also worked as an ecumenical peace education officer for the Irish Council of Churches and is actively involved in inter-religious programmes.

Foreword

BARRY VAN DRIEL is the Secretary General of the International Association for Intercultural Education and the International Director for Teacher Training and Curriculum Development at the Anne Frank House. He is also a senior education consultant to the Organisation for Security and Cooperation in Europe (OSCE) and UNESCO.

Other Contributors

MICHAEL ARLOW (Chapter 12) was a teacher for ten years before working with the Social, Civic and Political Education Project as Research and Development Officer and, later, Director. He was Principal Officer for Citizenship Education at the NI Council for Curriculum, Examinations and Assessment during the early stages of the implementation of Local and Global Citizenship. Subsequently, he taught at Queen's University Belfast and Florida Gulf Coast University. He is currently an education consultant based near Belfast.

KATHRYN EDGAR (Chapter 9) taught for more than twenty years in primary schools in Co. Down, Northern Ireland. After some years as a school vice-principal she moved to the Behaviour Support Team and then the Primary Team in the South Eastern Education and Library Board. Since 2005 she has worked with the NI Council for Curriculum, Examinations and Assessment in relation to the primary curriculum area of Personal Development and Mutual Understanding and particularly in co-developing the *Living.Learning.Together* resource.

ANNE MURRAY (Chapter 6) has been Principal of Oakgrove Integrated Primary and Nursery School in Derry/Londonderry since its opening in 1991. She is an Associate of the Regional Training Unit and has been involved in school leadership training for the past twelve years. She was Vice Chair of Northern Ireland's Council for Curriculum, Examinations and Assessment (CCEA) for nine years and was involved in shaping the revised NI Curriculum. She is a strong believer in child-centred education and the pupil voice – Oakgrove operates child-led Peer Mediation and was the first school in Northern Ireland to become a UNICEF Rights Respecting School.

MARY POTTER (Chapter 8) has worked with the Corrymeela Community in the areas of Youth and Schools and Teacher Education. She currently works as a consultant in the area of Good Relations within the formal education and youth/community work sectors and has written materials for Personal Development and Mutual Understanding (PDMU) in the Northern Ireland Revised Curriculum. She is also the co-author of *Joined Up: Developing Good Relations in the School Community*.

JERRY TYRRELL (Chapter 7) was born in London and moved to Northern Ireland under the auspices of the Fellowship of Reconciliation. In 1988 he became the Project Director of the Quaker Peace Education Project (QPEP), based in Derry/Londonderry, an action research project of the University of Ulster's Centre for the Study of Conflict. It was later renamed The EMU-Promoting-School Project (EMUpsp) and focused particularly on 'identifying and developing untried strategies' and establishing school-based peer mediation programmes. He died in December 2001, aged 51, shortly before the completion of his book on peer mediation for primary schools.

SEAMUS FARRELL, who completed and edited Jerry Tyrrell's chapter, was Research Coordinator with QPEP and EMUpsp and now works as a free-lance facilitator for a range of community and community relations education programmes.

Index

RETHINKING EDUCATION

Rethinking education has never been more important. While there are many examples of good, innovative practice in teaching and learning at all levels, the conventional education mindset has proved largely resistant to pedagogic or systemic change, remaining preoccupied with the delivery of standardised packages in a standardised fashion, relatively unresponsive to the diversity of learners' experiences and inclinations as well as to the personal perspectives of individual teachers. The challenge of our times in relation to education is to help transform that mindset.

This series takes up this challenge. It re-examines perennial major issues in education and opens up new ones. It includes, but is not confined to, pedagogies for transforming the learning experience, any-time-any-place learning, new collaborative technologies, fresh understandings of the roles of teachers, schools and other educational institutions, providing for different learning styles and for students with special needs, and adapting to changing needs in a changing environment.

This peer-reviewed series publishes monographs, doctoral dissertations, conference proceedings, edited books, and interdisciplinary studies. It welcomes writings from a variety of perspectives and a wide range of disciplines. Proposals should be sent to any or all of the series editors: Dr Marie Martin, mmartin@martech.org.uk; Dr Gerry Gaden, gerry.gaden@ucd.ie; and Dr Judith Harford, judith.harford@ucd.ie.